COLLINS GUIDE TO BIRD WATCHING

COLLINS GUIDE TO

BIRD WATCHING

BY

R. S. R. FITTER

WITH 49 LINE DRAWINGS BY
R. A. RICHARDSON
AND 112 PHOTOGRAPHS BY
ERIC HOSKING, JOHN MARKHAM
AND OTHERS

COLLINS
ST JAMES'S PLACE, LONDON

First Edition	1963
Reprinted	1963
Reprinted	1967
Second Edition	1970
Reprinted	1972
Reprinted	1974

SBN 00 212018 6

© *R. S. R. Fitter, 1963*
Printed in Great Britain
Collins Clear-Type Press
London and Glasgow

HOW TO USE THIS BOOK

PART ONE gives advice on how to watch birds (p. 15), what to feed them with (p. 22) and how to give them first aid if they are oiled or injured (p. 30).

PART TWO briefly describes how to identify the commoner British birds (p. 46).

PART THREE tells you where to go to see birds in the British Isles, both by habitat (p. 158) and by locality (p. 167). By using these two sections together the reader should be able to know what birds he is likely to see in any locality in the British Isles.

ACKNOWLEDGMENTS

I am very much indebted to my wife, who has read this book in both manuscript and proof; to R. A. Richardson who has read it in manuscript; to my son Julian for preparing the index; to G. Atkinson-Willes for supplying information; and to the following who have gone to great trouble to check portions of Part Three: E. Balfour, J. V. Bateman, G. Boyle, A. J. Bull, J. W. Campbell, D. H. Coggins, W. M. Condry, H. H. Davis, G. des Forges, J. W. S. Ellis, I. J. Ferguson-Lees, E. Gillham, F. C. Gribble, J. M. Harrop, Canon G. A. K. Hervey, Mrs. G. Hickling, R. A. O. Hickling, J. M. McMeeking, N. C. Moore, C. A. Norris, Sq/Ldr N. W. Orr, G. A. Pyman, Maj. R. F. Ruttledge, Col. H. Morrey Salmon, A. E. Smith, K. G. Spencer, C. F. Tebbutt, L. S. V. Venables, A. E. Vine, Dr. C. W. Walker, Mr. & Mrs. G. Waterston, K. Williamson.

CONTENTS

WATER BIRDS

SURFACE FEEDERS

DIVING BIRDS

PART THREE: WHERE TO LOOK

BIRD HABITATS

LAND HABITATS

WATERSIDE HABITATS

TOPOGRAPHICAL GUIDE

ENGLAND

WALES

SCOTLAND

IRELAND

THE LESSER ISLES

PLATES

PART ONE: HOW TO WATCH BIRDS

Birds are much the most popular form of wildlife in Britain to-day. This is partly because they are so attractive, and partly because they are the most conspicuous larger wild creatures in our not always very wild countryside. It is easy to go for a long walk in the country without seeing any wild mammals, reptiles or amphibians, except for a few rabbits and grey squirrels and an odd frog or toad, but on the same walk you would undoubtedly see or hear at least a score of different kinds of wild birds and in many places thirty or forty.

Nowadays more and more people find their mental refreshment, and manage to maintain a balanced mind in an ever more nerve-racking world, by visiting the country at week-ends or on holidays. So it is not surprising that more people than ever before are coming to enjoy our wild birds and to realise that they are an important part of our natural heritage. Moreover, birds can be enjoyed in town parks and gardens almost as much as in the countryside, and even if you are flat-bound in a city you can often tempt a few birds to your window-sill or watch them in the trees outside. When I lived for five years in a flat overlooking Highgate Cemetery in North London, I saw fifty-five different kinds of birds from my windows, including such apparently unlikely ones as the heron, lapwing, mallard and tufted duck.

Bird watching has the advantage of being a pastime which can cost you either next to nothing or quite a lot of money, according to whether your means and inclination lie towards sitting in your garden and taking quiet walks in the park or the country, or to expensive optical equipment and trips to Iceland or southern Europe. And in between there are plenty of opportunities for young people to have cheap and adventurous holidays in the wilder and pleasanter parts of the British Isles. For at bottom the bird watcher needs no other qualifications than an observant mind and a capacity to enjoy simple things. The birds are there to be watched everywhere from Trafalgar Square to Conachair, the great cliff on far-flung St. Kilda.

GETTING TO KNOW THE BIRDS

Some people enjoy watching birds feeding on the lawn or at a bird table, but shrink from trying to identify more than half a dozen very familiar kinds because they fear it will be too difficult. But in fact it is no harder to learn to distinguish different kinds of birds than it is to identify wines or motor cars or to tell the symphonies of Brahms from those of Beethoven. The main requirement is a good view of the bird, and this can be achieved both by using binoculars and other optical equipment and by attracting the birds nearer to you by providing them with nestboxes or with food at bird tables and elsewhere. Some bird reserves have specially constructed wooden hides for visitors to watch from.

When you first start watching birds, you must not, of course, expect at once to be able to identify every bird you see. Even experts often fail to get a good enough view of a bird to be able to name it with certainty, and beginners need a better view than experts. You can certainly distrust the "expert" who always confidently puts a name to every bird he sees, however brief the view. This is not to say, of course, that some bird watchers cannot identify birds correctly with far briefer views and fewer clues than others. Such distinctive features as the gannet's plunge, the kestrel's hovering and the chaffinch's white shoulder patch enable experienced bird watchers to identify them at great distances.

On the other hand, it is easy to be misled by a first brief impression, as the following cautionary tale shows. I was sitting at breakfast in a room in Kent, when I saw through the top of the window and against the light a much foreshortened view of a bird flying away from me. At first I took it for a jackdaw, but then its rather jerky flight became apparent and "jay" flashed through my mind. Finally, as the bird flew on and the foreshortening effect wore off, it became painfully apparent that it was in fact a magpie. Normally, of course, one look at its very long tail is enough to identify a magpie at once, not to mention its black and white plumage, which on this occasion was obscured against the light.

As I wrote in *The Pocket Guide to British Birds*, there is no primrose path to proficiency in bird watching, no short cut that does not involve the expenditure of much—extremely pleasurable—time and patience. Nobody expects to become a good cricketer or golfer without much practice, and the same applies to bird watching. The beginner soon finds that the more birds he watches, the easier it becomes to identify them, because he comes to know what to look for. It is vital to know which parts of a bird to concentrate on in the few seconds before it flits restlessly out of sight or flies swiftly out of range. With gulls, for instance, the colour of the bill and feet and the pattern of black and white on the wing-tips are important, while with pigeons and doves you need to verify the presence or absence of black or white marks on various parts of the neck, wings and tail.

There are one or two very elementary rules about bird watching, such as keeping still and walking silently, which hardly need to be mentioned. If you walk around with a gun and make loud bangs at intervals, you cannot expect to see many birds. Should you spot some birds at a distance which you want to investigate more closely, walk slowly and steadily, disguising if possible the actual movement of your legs by such cover as bushes or low stone walls. Many birds will stay still while you are approaching them, but fly away as soon as you stop, so stop behind cover if you can. Most experienced bird watchers pick up as many birds by sound as by sight, so if you have a companion it is best to reduce talk to a minimum when you are actually in the field, or you will hear nothing. One, the number recommended by Bernard Shaw for committees, also has its advantages on bird-watching expeditions, though the social pleasures of bird watching are not negligible, and for a beginner the company of a more experienced friend is an invaluable aid.

One of the first things the beginner notices as he becomes more aware of the birds around him is how they change with the nature of the country. The garden birds, tits, blackbirds, thrushes and so on, are found in woodland also, but in the woods they are joined by others, such as woodpeckers, warblers and pheasants, which are less often seen in gardens. Open farmland, both grass and arable, has its special birds, such as skylarks and partridges, while many warblers prefer the hedgerows or bushy commons. Moorland again has its own bird community, including meadow pipits, wheatears and red grouse, while the approach to water always brings in fresh birds. In marshes or by the edge of fresh water, for instance, you find reed buntings and sedge warblers, and on the open water moorhens, coots, grebes, ducks and swans. The wading birds prefer mainly muddy places, some liking fresh water, others salt, and many being equally at home on both. The salt water again brings an entirely different set of birds, gulls, auks, sea ducks and the like. Some of these, like the terns, nest on low sand dunes; others, such as razorbills and guillemots, breed only on high cliffs. A fuller analysis of the habitat preferences of the commoner British birds will be found in Part Three (p. 158).

BOOKS AND GRAMOPHONE RECORDS

Since few people can arrange always to be accompanied by a more experienced bird watcher, an identification book with good colour plates should have a high priority among the equipment of a bird-watching beginner. There are too many such books to be listed here, but perhaps I may be allowed to mention the two I have written myself, both illustrated by R. A. Richardson, Warden of Cley Bird Observatory: *The Pocket Guide to British Birds* (Collins, 25s.), with 64 colour plates and 48 plates in black and white, covering all important plumages of the commoner and some less common British birds; and a paper-back, *Fontana Bird Guide* (Collins, 2s. 6d.) with illustrations in black and white only. The present book has been specially written as a complementary volume to *The Pocket Guide*, which illustrates in colour all the British birds that the beginner is likely to see, including all those mentioned on pp. 47-157 of this book.

When you graduate to bird watching on the Continent, you will also find *A Field Guide to the Birds of Britain and Europe*, by Roger Peterson, Guy Mountfort and P. A. D. Hollom (Collins, 25s.), useful. This also is fully illustrated in colour, by the premier American bird artist, Roger Peterson. Other good identification books for British birds are Bruce Campbell's *Birds in Colour*, Edmund Sandars's *A Bird Book for the Pocket* (colour) and James Fisher's *Bird Recognition* (no colour; three out of four volumes published so far).

For many years the more advanced British bird watchers have been using Witherby's *Handbook of British Birds*, in five volumes, as their indispensable reference book, but this was completed in 1941 and is now getting increasingly out of date, though the field descriptions of birds by the late Bernard Tucker can still not be bettered. It is being steadily replaced as the British bird-watcher's bible by Dr. David Bannerman's *The Birds of the British Isles*, of which ten out of a projected dozen volumes had appeared by the beginning of 1962. *The Handbook* itself has been potted by P. A. D. Hollom into the one-volume *Popular Handbook of British Birds*, and this has recently been supplemented by the same author's *Popular Handbook of Rarer British Birds*, which includes all the rarities omitted from the other volume. Another first-class general introduction to British birds is T. A. Coward's *The Birds of the British Isles and their Eggs* in three volumes, first published forty years ago but recently revised by the late A. W. Boyd.

The bird watcher interested in field ornithology as a scientific sport is well served by a number of excellent short handbooks. E. M. Nicholson's *The Art of Bird Watching* (1931) and James Fisher's *Watching Birds* (1940) were the books which launched the present wave of popular bird watching, and since the war we have had Stuart Smith's *How to Study Birds* (1945), Bruce Campbell's *Bird Watching for Beginners* (1952) and W. D. Campbell's *Bird Watching as a Hobby* (1959). There is also a good general introduction to the techniques of bird study in *The Ornithologists' Guide*, edited by Major-General H. P. W. Hutson for the British Ornithologists' Union (1956), and this can usefully be supplemented by *The Bird Watcher's Reference Book*, by Michael Lister (1956).

Books about other aspects of British birds are legion. David Lack's *The Life of the Robin* (1943) remains the best book about a single bird published in recent years, while Edward A. Armstrong's *The Wren* and James Fisher's *The Fulmar* are the most comprehensive of the eight bird monographs so far published in the New Naturalist series; the others have dealt with the redstart, yellow wagtail, greenshank, herring gull, hawfinch and house sparrow. (This last, by J. D. Summers-Smith, is among the best). The books by P. E. Brown and Gwen Davies on the reed warbler, by David Lack on the swift, by R. M. Lockley on shearwaters and puffins, by David Snow on the blackbird and by K. G. Spencer on the lapwing are all also excellent. In the more discursive genre which has somewhat gone out of fashion in recent years, Edward A. Armstrong's *Birds of the Grey Wind*, about his native Ulster, is outstanding, while Richard Perry's writings on birds in Shetland, the Cairngorms, Holy Island and elsewhere are unjustifiably neglected.

There is no really first-class popular magazine devoted to birds, though *Country-Side*, journal of the British Naturalists' Association, is an excellent small popular general natural history magazine. *British Birds* is addressed especially to the keen ornithologist and bird watcher who is interested in migration and bird distribution and likes to keep up to date with developments in bird biology and behaviour. The British Trust for Ornithology has two journals, the general *Bird Study* and the specialised *Bird Migration*, which are aimed at much the same sector of bird watchers as *British Birds*. Both the journals of the Royal Society for the Protection of Birds, *Bird Notes* and *The Junior Bird Recorder*, have a more popular appeal.

The importance of bird songs and calls as aids to identification makes *Witherby's Sound-Guide to British Birds*, by Myles North and Eric Simms, an immensely valuable tool to expert and beginner alike. This collection of a baker's dozen of records of the songs and calls of 195 British breeding or regular migrant birds is far and away the best that has ever been made of the voices of British birds. Six excellent records of Western European bird songs can also be had from the R.S.P.B.

MAKING NOTES

Since you may now and then be confronted with a bird which you cannot identify from your books, it is a good idea to get into the habit of making the sort of notes that will enable more experienced friends to identify it for you. It is fatal to rely on memory alone, and "a little yellow and brown bird with some white on it somewhere" is not very helpful. If, however, you can say that it was the size of a sparrow, had a thick seed-eating bill, yellow on the head and underparts, chestnut on the upperparts and white in the tail, then it will not take your friend long to diagnose a cock yellow-hammer.

Make your notes on the spot if you can, preferably before you consult any book, and try to get down as many details as possible under the following headings, using Fig. 1 as a guide for the names of the various parts of a bird.

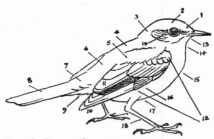

Fig. 1 Parts of a typical bird

1	Forehead	11	Secondaries
2	Crown	12	Wing-coverts
3	Nape	13	Chin
4	Mantle	14	Throat
5	Scapulars	15	Breast
6	Rump	16	Flanks
7	Upper tail-coverts	17	Belly
8	Tail	18	Tarsus
9	Under tail-coverts	19	Ear-coverts
10	Primaries		

1. Size, compared with some fairly common bird, and general shape.
2. General colour above and below.
3. Any conspicuous marks or patches, their colour and approximate position on the bird.
4. Size and shape of bill, legs, wings, tail and neck.
5. Colour of bill, legs, feet and eyes.
6. Actions and character of gait or flight, e.g. whether hops or runs, flight direct or bounding.
7. Any call notes or song.
8. Comparisons with any other birds that come to mind, e.g., "flies like a jay," "reminds me of a large swift."

You will not, of course, get down anything like full details under all these headings, but manage as much as you can in the time available. After the bird has gone and you have looked it up in your books, you may want to pursue the identification further, or enter it in your notebooks—and every bird watcher should keep at least a diary of some sort. Then the following data should be added:

9. Date, time, place, weather.
10. Habitat and general surroundings.
11. Angle of vision and conditions of light; distance of bird from observer, and whether binoculars used or not.
12. Whether bird was at rest, swimming or in flight. If you suspect you have seen something as rare as a hoopoe or a golden oriole, it is highly desirable to find another witness with some degree of expertise in bird identification. Nowadays records of rare birds are apt to be looked at askance unless they were seen by more than one person, preferably including somebody who has seen the species before.

Many bird watchers find great pleasure in compiling lists of birds they have seen, either each year or in their garden or home district or county. This practice is looked down on by superior scientific persons, but it is an excellent way of building up interest in the early stages of a bird watching career, and more than one eminent ornithologist still keeps it up. Excellent printed lists for this purpose can be had from the British Trust for Ornithology, a comprehensive one covering western Europe and a shorter one giving the birds most likely to be seen on an ordinary country walk in Britain.

BINOCULARS

Though there is much pleasure in watching birds in a garden or elsewhere with the naked eye, even greater enjoyment can be derived with the aid of modern optical equipment, especially binoculars. Most people use the words field glasses and binoculars interchangeably, but in fact field glasses are an old-fashioned type of non-prismatic instrument that is now quite out of date. The whole subject of the choice, use and care of binoculars is of the utmost importance for successful bird watching, and beginners are well advised to consult the British Trust for Ornithology's excellent field guide, *Binoculars and Telescopes for Field Work*, by J. R. Hebditch, to which the following paragraphs owe much.

The main qualities to be sought in a good pair of binoculars are magnification, wide field of view, good light and a clear image. It is also desirable that they should not be too heavy, though the weight of a heavy pair can be relieved by the simple method devised by Bert Axell, the Warden of Minsmere Bird Reserve, and illustrated in Plate 1. The best makes of glass are all marked with two figures, separated by $\times$, e.g. 8×40. The first figure measures the magnification, and the second the width of the object lenses in millimetres. Since the main aim of using binoculars is to make the bird appear larger, it might be thought that magnification was all-important and the higher the better. But in fact once you get above about $9 \times$, you start sacrificing other desirable qualities. A magnification of $6 \times$ is just adequate but little used nowadays, $7 \times$ and $8 \times$ are the standards used by most bird watchers, and $9 \times$, as Mr. Hebditch points out, is becoming increasingly popular. From $10 \times$ upwards the involuntary shake of the hands holding the binoculars also becomes magnified and may nullify the effect of magnifying the bird. Another disadvantage of higher magnifications is that they both necessitate frequent refocusing and decrease the field of view. A wide field of view is highly desirable for scanning; once the bird has been located, a more powerful glass with a narrow field of view is more useful, until the bird flies off again. However, glasses between $6 \times$ and $9 \times$ usually have a field of view of 130 to 150 yards at 1000 yards' range, which is generally regarded as satisfactory; it is in fact more than is provided by the Royal Navy's standard glass, a 7×50, which has a field of 121 yards at 1000 yards' range.

For winter bird watching especially, the most important quality of a glass is its light-gathering power, measured by the diameter of its exit pupil. This figure is obtained by dividing the magnification into the width of the object lens, so that an 8×40 gives 5, and a 7×50 gives 7; it is this high light-gathering power which makes the 7×50 such a good night glass and obviously appeals to the Navy and to many experienced bird watchers as well. Any figure over about 4 is all right, because if the maximum image brightness is to be obtained the exit pupil of the glass should not be smaller than the exit pupil of the viewer's eye. The diameter of the human eye pupil varies according to age: about 7 mm. in children up to 12, falling to 6 mm. in the teens, 5 mm. in the 20's and eventually down to 2-3 mm. To add to the complication, pupils contract on bright days and expand at night. The best night glasses are therefore binoculars with exit pupils of 7 mm. or so, like the 7×50.

The clarity of the image, so important to the bird watcher, depends primarily on the quality of the workmanship on the instrument. So it is wise to stick to binoculars made by old established and well-known firms, such as Ross, Zeiss and Barr & Stroud. A good second-hand pair from one of these is little more expensive than and infinitely to be preferred to the cheap new glasses of foreign make for which many inexperienced young bird watchers fall.

For all normal bird-watching purposes centre-focusing is much better than individual eyepiece focusing, for it can be altered quickly with one finger. Bird watchers who, like myself, wear spectacles out of doors, should do one of three things: have spectacles with hooks over the ears that can quickly be pushed up; have very shallow eyecups to their binoculars; or get a pair of binoculars with one of the special fitments that enable spectacle-wearers to lift them straight to their spectacled eyes. Personally, I am all in favour of the last solution; I find my Spectaross 8 × 40's highly satisfactory; they both enable me to get on to a bird as quickly as if I had no spectacles, and prevent the intrusion of light and reduction of field of view that shallow eyecups entail.

When using binoculars, it is always wise to start by hanging the lanyard round your neck, or if you are going to climb over rough ground, across your shoulder. A dropped or bumped glass means an expensive repair. Focusing is simple enough and should soon become automatic. Start by bending the two limbs of the binoculars so that your eyes fit easily into the two eyepieces, and keep them like that, for even the split second spent in this adjustment may make all the difference in spotting your bird. If your pair is centre-focusing, first close the eye opposite the adjustable eyepiece and focus with the centre wheel for your other eye. Then repeat the process with the first eye, focusing with the adjustable eyepiece until the image is perfectly clear. The adjustable eyepiece should not need to be moved again, all focusing being done with the centre wheel.

When not in use, binoculars should always be kept in their case and not allowed to knock about the house. Clean the lenses with some soft material, such as chamois leather, to avoid scratching them. If the image appears fuzzy and the glass in apparent need of repair, avoid at all costs the temptation to "do it yourself." The repair of prismatic binoculars is a highly skilled job, to be undertaken by craftsmen only. Finally, binoculars are so vulnerable to petty theft that an insurance policy (very cheap) is a prudent precaution.

Though binoculars are the best instruments for all ordinary bird watching, when it comes to distant ducks or waders at rest on estuaries or large reservoirs, a telescope, with its much higher magnification and smaller field of view, is useful. In ordinary countryside, however, or for birds in flight, it is pretty useless.

FEEDING THE BIRDS

The best way of attracting birds to your garden all the year round is to provide them with as much natural food as possible. Dig over a few square feet of soil each day, so that they can find worms and other soil animals. Plant plenty of sunflowers and other seed-bearing plants, and don't cut down their dead stems in the flower borders too soon. Leave a few seeding thistles and groundsels wherever you can, for the goldfinches especially. Weeds of all kinds are to be encouraged in a bird watcher's garden; birds seem to prefer their seeds to those of most garden plants. Plant as many berry-bearing shrubs as you can, such as cotoneaster, pyracantha, rowan, hawthorn, stranvaesia, cherry, viburnum, berberis and holly. Thrushes especially will come to your garden in hard weather to feed on these berries, and you may even get a waxwing, for when these uncommon winter visitors do visit our shores they are more often than not seen feeding on berry-bearing shrubs in suburban gardens.

In hard weather, however, and even in most ordinary winters, many of these natural or semi-natural sources of food will give out, and if you want to keep the birds in your garden, you will have to feed them. During prolonged frost you may even save their lives in this way. If you are very busy you may find the ready-made commercial all-purpose foods such as Swoop a help—it certainly does attract the birds—but there are plenty of everyday foods that will serve your purpose just as well.

Tits, for instance, like cheese and fats, such as old cooking fat or cooked bacon and ham rinds, as well as old bones and all kinds of nuts, cob-nuts, monkey-nuts and coconut. Blackbirds, thrushes and starlings love rotten apples, but it is no good offering birds apple peelings or banana skins. Pied woodpeckers are increasingly visiting bird tables, where they like to find uncracked nuts to take away and split at leisure. Finches and sparrows will eat grain or bird seed, but be careful where you scatter this, or you may find some queer weeds coming up in your flower-beds later on. Foods that appeal to a wide variety of birds include shredded suet, wholemeal bread, oatmeal, coarse oats and small lumps of cheese.

If you are prepared to go to the lengths of cooking food especially for your birds, your menus can include boiled rice mixed with melted fat, a compote of pressure-cooked bones and fish scraps, and potatoes boiled or baked in their jackets and chopped up (they needn't be the best quality potatoes!). Further recipes are to mix the chopped potato with coarse oats or oatmeal and fat; and to make a "birds' pudding" by mixing crumbs of stale bread or cake with fat and a few currants. One way of offering these seemingly unappetising concoctions to those who will appreciate them is to wedge portions into small cavities in tree trunks or branches, as illustrated in Plate 2. Incidentally, raw bones, meat and fat should be cooked before you hang them up, especially in the country. Otherwise the birds may carry lumps away and disseminate among your neighbours' livestock the viruses of such deadly diseases as fowl pest and swine fever.

Mealworms, which you can buy at most pet shops, are ambrosia to insect-eating birds. Armed with these, you will have no difficulty at all in taming your garden robins to come and feed from your hand—one at a time, of course, and in different parts of the garden, or you will have the most fearful battles about your head. Mealworms are not true worms, but the grubs of a beetle, and once you have a stock it is easy enough to breed more. Punch a few holes in the lid of a large tin, line the bottom with some sawdust or old rags, and put the mealworms in with some bran or slices of wholemeal bread to feed on. If you allow some of the grubs to change into cream-coloured pupæ, and later into beetles, you will ensure a future supply of mealworms.

Here are a few bird-feeding don'ts. Avoid dried shredded coconut at all costs, because birds cannot digest it and may die after eating it; an ordinary fresh coconut cut in half is quite all right, however, except in the nesting season, because it must not be fed to young birds. When you feed bread to the birds, it is better to use wholemeal rather than the modern mass-produced white bread. Finally, don't put out more bread or other food on the ground than your garden birds can cope with in a day; if much is left by sundown, you will attract rats and mice.

Fig. 2 Fat-basket for tits

Birds are not orderly guests; the biggest served first and the devil take the hindmost are the only rules at their dinner table. So it is important to provide separate dining facilities for the larger and smaller ones, and especially to try and keep away the greedy sparrows and starlings. Tits normally feed while hanging upside down on swaying branches, so you can help them and usually keep away the sparrows by hanging up their food. You can do this either directly, as with half-coconuts or bones, or nuts threaded on a string or wire (Plate 3), or in some receptacle, such as a little wire basket (Fig. 2), a "tit bell," "tit cone," or "tit cylinder" (Plate 2), or on a tray suspended from a branch. Wire baskets can be easily made by clasping together two six-inch squares of chicken-type wire. These devices can, of course, also be used on window-sills, or on trees opposite first-floor windows, by those who have no gardens. Some tiresome sparrows learn to feed from these supposedly sparrow-proof gadgets by hovering in front of them; when this happens there is not much you can do, except perhaps suspend the feeding altogether for a few days and hope that the sparrow or sparrows which have learned this trick will clear off somewhere else. Some people advocate putting out plenty of food for the sparrows on the lawn, but this remedy may prove worse than the disease. Another point to remember is not to hang the food where a strong wind can blow it against a wall or post; birds can be stunned or even killed in this way.

Tits will also come, with other birds, to a bird table mounted on a pole[1] (Plate 3). These are easily home-made; the top should be about 18 in.

[1] The Royal Society for the Protection of Birds offers a fine selection of garden bird equipment of all kinds, including nut cylinders, scrap baskets, seed hoppers, tit cones, bird tables both hanging and pole-supported, and nest boxes for tits and robins. Particulars from the Society's headquarters, The Lodge, Sandy, Beds.

by 2 ft. and the pole a smooth metal one, to stop cats, rats, mice and grey squirrels from climbing up. Mice can also be warded off a wooden pole by a "mouse guard," like the devices that prevent rats from climbing down ships' hawsers (Fig. 3). It is also a good idea to provide a bird table with some sort of roof, to prevent the food getting wet and soggy in the rain. Bird tables should be sited not too far from bushes or other cover, so that if cats, sparrowhawks or other unwelcome guests gate-crash the meal, the birds can quickly dive to safety. Cats, of course, should be strongly discouraged in gardens where birds are fed regularly, and so should unruly dogs that bark at birds. It is downright cruel to lure birds to a garden that is infested with cats, as if a satanic hotel-keeper were to invite guests to a hotel with a man-eating tiger in the garden. Even if the cats are certified "non-burderers," their presence will make the birds very nervous. However, the cats of the house can be trained to avoid the bird feeding area of the garden, and a dog is a useful warden against strays.

Fig. 3 Bird table with mouse guard

Not all birds like to fly up to bird tables to feed, so scatter some on the ground for the blackbirds, thrushes and hedge sparrows. Black-headed gulls will also come to feed on the ground in quite small suburban gardens, especially in hard weather. They are, of course, well known for their habit of visiting windows high up in London office blocks when food is on offer.

DRINKING AND BATHING

Many people forget that there is no water in their gardens and attract birds to feed there without providing any. Standing water is sufficiently rare in most built-up districts to make the provision of a bird bath, or even a small vessel with drinking water only, one of the most efficient means of attracting birds to a garden. The late Bernard Riviere of Woodbastwick, Norfolk, once wrote that he had thirty-two different species of bird bathing or drinking at his garden pool, including two kinds of woodpecker. A small garden pond (Plate 4) with a shallow edge is the best for both bathing and drinking, but shallow bowls or dishes are better than nothing. The water should not be more than two inches deep. If you are making or buying a bird bath, try and get one with a shelving bottom as in Fig. 4; the pedestal is optional.

In really cold weather you will either have to break the ice each morning, when you will find that the birds go straight in, despite the cold, or take some preventive action. This can consist either in pouring in a kettle of boiling water in the morning, or in putting a lighted candle or night-light under an inverted flower-pot or old tin beneath the water bowl. You will sometimes hear people advocating the addition of a few drops of glycerine to the water overnight. This certainly stops the water from freezing over, but the birds hate it in the morning, as the glycerine sticks to their beaks.

NESTBOXES

At least thirty different kinds of wild bird have been induced to lay their eggs in nestboxes or other artificial nest sites in woods and gardens in the

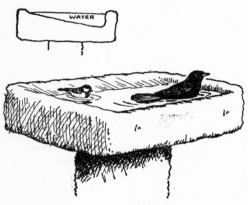

Fig. 4 Bird bath

British Isles in recent years. Those that are most easily tempted away from natural nest sites are the four common hole-nesting tits (great, blue, coal, marsh), the robin, pied and spotted fly-catchers, house and tree sparrows, common redstart, pied wagtail, starling, taw-ny owl and mallard. This is therefore a most effective way of attracting birds to parks and gardens, and is the subject of another of the British Trust for Ornithology's invaluable field guides, *Nestboxes*, by Edwin Cohen.

There are two main types of nestbox in use: a cylindrical or rectangular box with a small entrance hole, used by tits, redstarts, tree sparrows and pied flycatchers (Fig. 5); and a ledge or tray, with or without a roof to protect it, used by robins, spotted flycatchers and pied wagtails (Fig. 6). Larger versions of the tit-type box are favoured by starlings, and larger ones still by hole-nesting ducks, such as goosanders and goldeneyes (Fig. 8). In Sweden goldeneyes use these boxes regularly, and experiments have recently been made with them to try to tempt the goldeneyes which stay late into the spring on some Scottish lochs. Owls prefer an elongated chimney or barrel (Fig. 7). In Holland flask-shaped baskets made from osiers or straw are very successfully used to attract nesting mallard, and it is surprising that more use has not been made of these in Britain. Fig. 9 illustrates an artificial nest site adapted to the special requirements of the treecreeper, which likes to slip through a crack into a narrow space, as in its favourite natural sites behind loose pieces of bark or ivy stems against a tree. Plate 4 shows a common "natural artificial" site, often used by robins as well as spotted flycatchers, but in fact robin-type nestboxes are more effective than old kettles scattered about the garden. Swallows will often nest on ledges specially put up for them under the rafters of barns or outhouses, and artificial nests can also be made for house martins. Care should be taken to site both of these where mud or droppings falling from the nest are not likely to incommode people entering doors or looking out of windows.

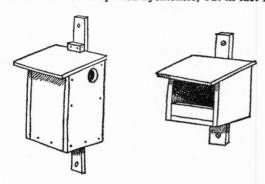

Fig. 5 Nestbox for tits (minimum size 5″ × 5″ × 9″)

Right: Fig. 6 Nestbox for robins, flycatchers, and wagtails (minimum size 5″ × 5″ × 6″)

Precise details of the type of nestbox favoured by all these birds, and a number of others, such as swifts, barn owls and kestrels, and how to make them, can be found in the B.T.O. field guide. Simple examples of both the tit-type and the robin-type box may be had from the Royal Society for the Protection of Birds (see note on p. 24). For those who fancy themselves as handymen, Figs. 10 and 11 show how to make a tit-type and a robin-type nestbox respectively from a piece of half-inch deal board measuring 1 ft. by 2 ft. Birds do not mind a simple unadorned design, and are certainly not attracted by the fiddly bits of ornament seen on some commercial nestboxes. The lid can be fastened with a small brass hook.

Fig. 7 Nestbox for owls

*Fig. 8 Nestbox for hole-nesting ducks, such as goosander
and goldeneye (minimum size 15″ × 30″ ; hole 6″)*

Right: Fig. 9 Artificial treecreeper nest site

Nestboxes should be put up well before the nesting season, which for this purpose starts about the middle of March, when on fine days tits may often be seen prospecting for nest sites. Make sure that they are firmly affixed to the tree or fence, so that they cannot either fall or blow down, nor vibrate in a high wind; the lid should also be securely fastened. The best aspect for a nestbox is away from both the hottest sun and the prevailing direction of rainstorms; this usually means somewhere in the two northern quadrants. It is also a good idea to ensure that the entrance hole is slightly inclined forward, to keep out both sun and rain. Keep away, too, from the runnel of rainwater that often comes down a tree-trunk and is usually marked by a line of green lichens, for this can make a nestbox damp. At the end of the nesting season it is a good idea to clean the nest-boxes out, for the old nest material harbours parasites.

If your garden is safe from marauders of various kinds, especially cats and small boys, you can indulge in the luxury of fixing your nestboxes low enough to lift the lid off and look inside to see what is going on. But this privilege is one that should be sparingly used, for the sake of the birds. Always remember that by inducing a pair of birds to nest in a nestbox, you have undertaken a special responsibility for the safe rearing of their family. Cats will often wait for young birds to emerge from a nest, and kill them as they flutter to the ground, so if you or one of your neighbours has a known "burderer" cat, think very seriously before you put up any nestboxes; it would be kinder by far to discourage the birds.

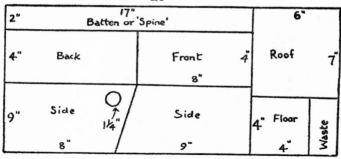

Fig. 10 How to make a nestbox for tits

There is no need to provide nesting material as well as a nestbox, though cotton-wool or any fibres laid out nearby will be used with alacrity. Never put any material in the nestbox; it will just be built over. Birds like to do it themselves.

HANDLING BIRDS

From time to time it is necessary actually to handle a wild bird: when one gets into the house and has to be removed; when one is picked up sick or injured; and, of course, when a bird is ringed under the British Trust for Ornithology's ringing scheme (see p. 36). How a bird should be held in the hand for ringing is shown in Plate 5, but this aspect of handling, which does not affect the majority of bird watchers, is thoroughly covered by the Trust's Field Guide No. 6, *The Bird in the Hand*, by R. K. Cornwallis and A. E. Smith, on the admirable advice in which I have drawn freely in this and the next section.

When you catch or take hold of a bird, it is of the utmost importance to grasp it as a whole, pinning the wings against the side of the body from the start. Never grab at a bird so that you catch hold only of a wing, or part of the tail. The loss of feathers from wing or tail, the likely result of careless grabbing, may be a serious matter to the bird, incapacitating or even grounding it till it next moults. Always hold a bird firmly enough to stop it struggling, and especially flapping its wings, yet not so firmly that you press against its body, for even a slight pressure can kill a small bird. Many of the larger birds, and some small ones such as tits, can peck sharply with their bills, so do not give them the chance; hold them by the neck immediately behind the head. Large birds can also be kept quiet by placing a cloth over their heads, and hawks and owls are more easily handled if their talons are given some harmless object to hold.

Do not hold birds in the hand for longer than is absolutely necessary,

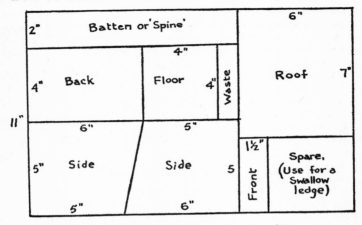

Fig. 11 How to make a nestbox for robins

especially on hot days when your hands may be slightly damp with sweat, for moisture always damages the set of a bird's plumage. It is thus especially important to avoid, if possible, handling birds whose plumage is wet from the rain. Should a bird collapse or faint from exhaustion or shock while in the hand, release it at once. If it does not recover fairly quickly, breathe gently into its open beak or move its wings carefully to give artificial respiration.

Whenever you can, put a captive bird quickly into a temporary cage, either an old canary cage or a large cardboard box fitted with a rough perch. Wild birds, so long as they are not ill or injured, should, of course, be released just as soon as possible after they have been caught, but it is inadvisable to do this after dark or they may fail to find a safe roosting place.

FIRST AID FOR BIRDS

There are many occasions on which one is confronted with a sick or injured bird and wants to be able to do something to help it. People soon learn who are the bird lovers in any district, and tend to bring along to them any injured birds they may find, confident that something will be done to help or heal. The taking of a wild bird to tend it and release it again, like the taking of a bird to ring and release, is specifically allowed by the Protection of Birds Act. A leaflet by F. B. Lake, giving detailed treatments for sick and wounded birds may be had from both the British Trust for Ornithology and the Royal Society for the Protection of Birds; here only brief indications, partly based on it, can be given.

Many casualties, alas, are so far gone that the kindest thing is to kill the bird at once, and this also is permitted under the bird protection laws. A bird that is gasping for breath will probably die quite soon anyway; one with its beak broken across, exposing the bone, or with the "shoulder joint" of its wing broken, will only survive, if at all, as a hopeless cripple. A bird of pigeon size may be killed humanely either by wringing its neck as with poultry or by holding its legs and swinging its head sharply against a hard surface, such as a tree or wall, to smash the skull. To kill smaller birds humanely, either press the thumb hard against the left side of the breast to stop the heart, or press suddenly and very hard with the ball of the thumb against the breast-bone, which immediately makes the bird unconscious. Never on any account attempt to drown a bird.

If you are unfortunately obliged to kill a badly injured or sick bird, or if you find a freshly dead one, your local museum may welcome the opportunity to acquire a specimen for its skin collection. But ask before you send any specimens; if there is no local demand, both the University Museum at Oxford and the Royal Scottish Museum at Edinburgh[1] are glad to receive suitably packed and prepared bodies. Birds believed to have died of disease should be sent to the Veterinary Laboratory, Eskgrove, Lasswade, Midlothian, to help the scientists to learn more about the causes of birds' deaths. The Royal Society for the Protection of Birds (The Lodge, Sandy, Beds.) is always glad to hear of instances of large numbers of birds being found dead, but do not send bodies unless asked.

Correct packing and preparation of dead bird specimens, to whatever destination, is important. In cold weather, wrap the bird in tissue paper and post it as soon as possible with a note of the place, date and circumstances of death. If the weather is at all warm or delay in the post is likely, it is advisable to slow up the process of decomposition by injecting it with a formaldehyde solution of 10 parts glycerine to 90 parts of 10 per cent formaldehyde, obtainable from most chemists. Use a hypodermic syringe to inject it into the abdominal and thoracic cavities and through the eye into the brain; a swab soaked in the solution should also be placed in the throat. It is always advisable to plug the specimen's bill, nostrils and cloaca with cotton-wool. Specimens in which decomposition has already begun, of course, not be sent.

We can now return to the less grim subject of minor injuries that can be coped with by anybody who is reasonably skilled at first aid and has the time and patience to dance attendance on the bird for some days afterwards. Some birds may be picked up exhausted after migrating against strong winds or when half-starved during severe weather. These should need only food, drink and rest before being released the following morning. Gunshot flesh wounds, broken legs and broken wrist and finger bones of the wing can be dealt with by the application of normal first-aid techniques, though broken bones need to be fairly fresh to respond well to splinting. F. B. Lake draws attention to subluxation of the carpal joint, a common

[1] Material should be addressed to the Keeper, Department of Natural History, Royal Scottish Museum, Edinburgh, 1.

injury often mistaken for a broken wing. In this the tip of the wing bearing the flight feathers is twisted outwards and prevents the bird from flying. He recommends cutting all the flight feathers off short with a pair of scissors, which means that the bird will not recover its power of flight till the next moult, during which time it will, of course, have to be looked after.

Oiled birds (Fig. 12) present many acute problems to the would-be good Samaritan. If they are heavily oiled, they are hopeless cases from the start,

Fig. 12 An oiled razorbill

and any bird that has been starving for a long time in a cold sea will pretty certainly die of pneumonia fairly soon. The best chance of saving a life is to tackle a fairly lightly oiled bird caught soon after it first struggles ashore, but of course these are the very birds still lively enough to flap back into the sea as you approach. Mrs. Katherine Tottenham, author of the book *Bird Doctor*, recommends starting by wrapping the patient in cotton-wool from bill to tail, leaving only the eyes and nostrils clear. Then she puts it into a wicker cat basket, which is closed and stood by the kitchen boiler. Within this "cocoon" warmth is soon generated, the damp feathers dry, and some of the more liquid oil is absorbed in the cotton-wool. After a couple of hours the bird begins to perk up, and can then be unwrapped and fed. It is important to feed it first, before the lengthy process of cleansing begins. It is virtually impossible to clean the feathers without destroying what remains of their insulating properties, and it is because they lose this insulation and become waterlogged that so many oiled birds die of cold, wet and pneumonia. Fuller's-earth may be used as a preliminary decontaminant and then, as recommended by the R.S.P.C.A. in their pamphlet *Oil Pollution of Sea and River Birds*, detergents at the rate of ¾ oz. to a gallon of water heated to 80° F., followed by a thorough rinsing. Some of the worst soiled plumage may be cut away. In any case you will now have completely unfitted your patient to return to the sea; if put in water it will become waterlogged and sink. This means again that

1. A method of relieving the weight of a heavy pair of binoculars

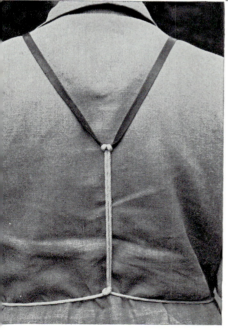

2. FOOD FOR TITS: *left*, wedged into a cavity in a branch (here attracting a Blue and a Great Tit); *below*, suspended in a "tit cylinder"

3. *Above*, a bird-table mounted on a pole. *Right*, nuts threaded on a string for tits

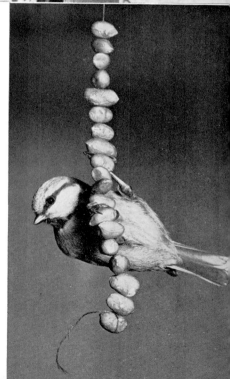

4. GARDEN ATTRACTIONS: *above*, Blue Tits bathing and drinking at a small pond; *left*, Spotted Flycatcher nesting in an old kettle

5. Holding a Pied Flycatcher for ringing

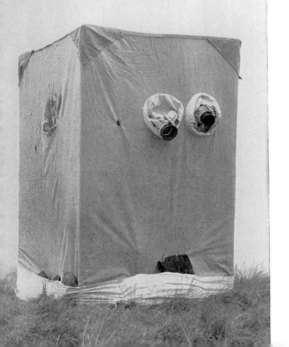

6 & 7. HIDES: *above*, erected on poles in a reed-bed; *left*, for photographing, with cameras in position; *above right*, beside a Little Owl's nest in the thatch of a haystack; *below right*, camouflaged, for watching Nightjars

8. DEVICES FOR STUDYING BEHAVIOUR: *above*, a Ringed Plover displaying to its own reflection in a mirror; *below*, a Willow Warbler attacking a Cuckoo's head mounted on a stick

you will have to keep it till the next moult, so that helping to save the lives of seabirds is not a task to be lightly undertaken. Never use petrol, turpentine or similar substances to try and clean oil off birds' plumage, but vegetable oils such as olive and eucalyptus are permissible.

Another type of bird waif all too often brought to known bird lovers by well-meaning neighbours and small boys is the fledgling supposed to have been abandoned by its parents. Much the best thing to do in this event is to insist on the immediate return of the "orphan" to where it was found, when nine times out of ten its parents will continue to care for it. Parent birds do not abandon their offspring, and only exceptionally are both killed, so that fledglings found alone should be lifted to a place of safety nearby and left to call attention to themselves by their shrill cries of hunger. Only if it has been watched for some time and you are sure that it has really lost its parents, should you accept the arduous task of rearing a young bird. Len Howard, well known as the author of *Birds as Individuals*, stigmatises as "baby snatching" the habit of carrying off any young bird found by the roadside, by people who are trying to be kind but actually being cruel.

If you have landed yourself with a bird to look after, by taking on an injured or oiled bird or an apparently deserted fledgling, you will find yourself in need of some advice on how to rear and look after it. For the foster mother of a fledgling, I would recommend an excellent article on hand-rearing birds by Maxwell Knight in a recent issue of *Bird Notes*, the RSPB's quarterly journal. For rearing the fledglings of most small song birds he advises ten meals a day, composed of the "soft-bill food" sold by pet shops mixed with a little egg yolk, "filling in the gaps between with small pieces of chopped up earthworm or mealworm plus any small moths and flies that can be caught." Other birds, of course, require different food and treatment; birds of prey in particular need roughage in the shape of soft feathers, fur or even tissue paper so that they may form pellets which are regurgitated through the bill.

Adult song birds can be fed with food roughly along the lines indicated for feeding birds in the garden on p. 23. In an emergency give bird-seed to any wild seed-eating bird and, for the first few feeds only, soaked bread to insect-eaters. Birds of prey again need a special diet, with meat and roughage. Most oiled birds are razorbills (Fig. 12) or guillemots, and these need to be gently tempted with raw fish. Mrs. Tottenham finds that it may take an hour just to persuade the bird to start eating. The actual process of feeding consists in opening the bird's bill between forefinger and thumb, inserting the second finger crosswise as a prop, and pushing sprats or small slivers of herring or other raw fish inside. But don't forget that all seabirds can and do peck, and the larger ones, especially guillemots, can inflict quite nasty wounds if you start prising open their bills before they are properly tamed and used to you. The B.T.O. Field Guide also advises a small dose of castor oil, say a teaspoonful, to help the bird to get rid of the oil it has consumed in the process of trying to preen itself clean.

THE LAW OF BIRD PROTECTION

The Protection of Birds Act, 1954, has reduced the law relating to the protection of wild birds in Great Britain to comparative simplicity. All birds are now protected throughout the year, except for a short black list,[1] which may be killed or taken at any time by authorised persons, and a number of game birds, wildfowl and waders, which may only be taken outside the close season. Some sixty rare species and their eggs are also protected by special penalties of up to £25 per bird or egg. The main defect now remaining in our bird protection legislation is the loophole by which small boys are permitted to continue collecting the eggs of certain common birds, such as blackbirds and thrushes. This retrograde provision obstructs the efforts of teachers and others to persuade children and young people of the importance of helping to preserve our national heritage of wild birds. A large range of song birds, and a few others such as owls and woodpeckers, may not be sold alive in this country unless they are close-ringed and have been bred in captivity. This does not affect bona fide breeders of cage birds, but hits at illegal catching of song birds and the importation of birds caught in the wild from abroad.

The RSPB has issued a leaflet of advice as to what to do if you see an offence against the bird protection laws being committed. Much depends, of course, on the nature of the offence, whether it is cruelty by young hooligans, illicit shooting, or nest robbery by schoolboys or adult klepto-maniacs. You will probably not have time to summon the police or the local R.S.P.C.A. inspector, so do what you can to frustrate the act, take a name and address if you can, or at least a car number. Memorise the appearance of the offender, so that you can identify him again, and make an accurate note as soon as possible of what you have seen, for you may have to give evidence in court. Get the names and addresses of any other witnesses too, and then go to the police with as complete information as you can, after which it is a good idea to notify the RSPB also. Quite a number of successful prosecutions are now being brought against people who shoot birds illegally as a result of good detective work by members of local natural history societies. A watertight case against an egg thief is more difficult, because only a police constable has powers of search, so it is highly desirable to fetch a policeman if you suspect that an egg thief is at work.

BIRD PHOTOGRAPHY AND SOUND RECORDING

More and more bird watchers are taking to photography, which is a specialised and highly technical activity beyond the scope of this book.

[1] Cormorant, carrion and hooded crows, feral pigeon, great and lesser black-backed gulls, herring gull, jackdaw, jay, magpie, rook, shag, house sparrow, starling, stock dove and woodpigeon, and in Scotland only, gossander, red-breasted merganser and rock dove.

The best and most up-to-date book of advice on the techniques of bird photography is *Bird Photography as a Hobby*, by Eric Hosking and Cyril Newberry, from which I give here a few very elementary tips. John Warham's *Technique of Bird Photography* is another good book.

With an ordinary general-purpose camera you cannot hope to photograph small birds, and must confine yourself to large birds at close range, such as ducks, gulls and other water birds on park lakes. For bird photography in general a 35-mm. camera is necessary, and the equipment recommended by Hosking and Newberry as the best for top quality bird studies from a hide at close range is a quarter-plate field camera. To get within photographic range of wild birds, you must usually construct a hide of some kind, or use a telescopic lens or both. Plates 6 and 7 illustrate the ordinary type of hide used by most bird photographers.

Its nest is the easiest place to lure a bird within range of the camera, though sometimes putting down food or water is also effective. The bird photographer who chooses to work on birds at the nest must, of course, take on the responsibility for seeing that no harm comes to the eggs or young. It is the unwritten rule of British bird photographers that the interests of the bird come first. This means that if a hen bird shows signs of nervousness at the nearness of the hide, it must be moved back or even away altogether, while if the nest is so well hidden that extensive "gardening" of the vegetation, exposing the eggs to crows and other predators, is necessary, then another nest must be sought. Much pleasure can be derived from photographing birds at bird tables in gardens or even from the windows of houses, and it is certainly best for beginners to try their hands at this type of photography, which can do no harm to the birds, rather than risk disaster to a nest, even of a common bird, through inexperience. Another risk, this time to the photographer himself, lies in trying to photograph the nests of birds on inland or mountain cliffs without ropes or other equipment, experience in rock climbing, or at least advice from an experienced rock climber.

Many photographers, having mastered the art of still photography, would like to move on to cine photography, where many of the techniques are quite different, though hides are just as necessary. Most people can only afford 8-mm. cine cameras, but the appreciably more expensive 16-mm. ones produce better results and their films can be shown publicly, and even on TV if good enough. Advice on both still and cine photography of wildlife can be had from the Films Officer of the Council for Nature, and on cine also from the Nature Cine Club, a recently formed body which specialises in making films of birds and other wildlife.

Some of the devices used by both still and cine photographers in the study and photography of bird behaviour are illustrated in Plate 8, which shows the use of mirrors to make birds perform aggressive displays against supposed intruders, and the use of stuffed predators for the same purpose. Even a cuckoo's head is enough to arouse the wrath of a willow warbler (see Plate 8).

Sound-recording of bird songs and calls is also becoming increasingly popular, and this technique is so new that little has been written about it yet. The best short account of both the techniques and problems involved is Myles North's in *The Ornithologists' Guide* (see above, p. 15); also the last chapter of Eric Simms's *Voices of the Wild* (1957). In addition to a tape-recorder, which may be portable or run off the mains, you need a microphone and, to obtain the best results, also a parabolic reflector. Lengths of cable are also usually required, to enable the microphone to be taken for some distance from the tape-recorder to the place where the bird is likely to sing. It is important to remember that extraneous sounds, such as aircraft overhead or traffic on main roads and railways, high wind in the trees and even other birds' voices can easily spoil the best recording.

SCIENTIFIC ORNITHOLOGY

With bird photography and sound recording, we are brought from simple enjoyment of birds and the elementary know-how of putting names to them, which are the main scope of this book, to the verge of scientific ornithology, which is the province of the various books mentioned on p. 18. In these you will find information about how to ring birds, how to carry out various kinds of bird census and how to engage in the various other activities that have made bird study one of the major scientific sports of the age. Many of my readers will, I hope, graduate from plain enjoyment of birds to these highly rewarding and scientifically valuable pursuits.

The British Trust for Ornithology is the body mainly concerned with scientific bird study for the amateur, and a summary of its principal permanent inquiries may be useful. Much the most important is the Bird Ringing Scheme, in which some 600 amateur ringers (banders is the transatlantic equivalent) ring upwards of a quarter of a million birds in Britain every year. Immensely valuable information, both about migration and about the longevity of birds, is now being gained from this scheme. The actual process of ringing consists in encircling the legs of birds with small, numbered light metal rings inscribed " Inform British Museum (Natural History), London, S.W.7 " or some abbreviation on the smaller rings. It has been proved that these rings when properly put on—and ringers now have to be properly trained and licensed—do no harm to the bird. Some birds have been recovered ten or more years later still wearing their rings.

Another permanent B.T.O. research scheme is the Nest Records Inquiry, under which many bird watchers fill in a card for each nest they find, showing the size of the clutch, when each egg was laid, when the young hatched and fledged, and other important information to help build up our still scanty stock of facts about the breeding biology of British birds. A third inquiry is the annual Sample Heron Census, by which a regular index of the British heron population has been maintained ever since the original census of 1928. This has shown that the British heron population is a stable one, falling sharply after severe winters, but soon recovering its former level. The Trust runs many other short-term inquiries, such as the recent ones on the breeding populations of the mute swan and the peregrine, the winter distribution of the whooper swan, the habitats of the lapwing and the deaths of birds on roads. All these are maintained and supported by voluntary organisers and amateur participants.

Another long-term inquiry is the Wildfowl Trust's monthly wildfowl count throughout the year, which covers all the major fresh waters in Britain to which ducks resort.

A SHORT HISTORY OF ORGANISED BIRD WATCHING IN BRITAIN

William Turner, Dean of Wells in the sixteenth century, was the first English bird watcher, indeed, apart from the Emperor Frederick II, the first European bird watcher too. As a true scion of the Renaissance, he wrote *A Short and Succinct History of the Principal Birds Noticed by Pliny and Aristotle*, but he was so good a field observer that his evidence can still be used to refute those who have recently suggested that the kites of medieval London were black kites not red ones, for he knew both and only the red kite in England. After him we jump a hundred years to come to Francis Willughby, a Warwickshire country gentleman, who joined with the Cambridge don John Ray to write what, as E. M. Nicholson has recently pointed out, can claim to be the first British bird identification book. A further leap of a century brings us to Gilbert White, another clergyman, and George Montagu, another landowner and a military man. Gilbert White, with his classic *Natural History of Selborne*, which has made this quiet Hampshire parish among the most famous in England, was the first modern field ornithologist. Among his contributions was the separation of the three species of leaf warbler: willow warbler, chiffchaff and wood warbler. George Montagu wrote the *Ornithological Dictionary* (1802), which remained a standard work for the greater part of the century. These five, three clergymen and two landowners, were the early standard-bearers of British bird watching, and set the tone down to the middle of the last century. For its first three hundred years, bird watching in Britain (it would be fairer to say in England, for it was virtually non-existent in Scotland, Ireland and Wales) was the pursuit only of a tiny minority of the educated classes.

In the first half of the nineteenth century one of the few real bird watchers was another landowner, the eccentric Charles Waterton. Among his eccentricities was to be a pioneer of bird protection; to the scandal of the neighbourhood and the dismay of his gamekeepers he protected owls and provided nestboxes for starlings. Pheasants, which he did not shoot, he preserved by the ingenious device of scattering dummy pheasants about the trees in his grounds, so that the poachers gave themselves away to no purpose. Another of his forward-looking eccentricities was to watch birds from his house windows with a "spy-glass," having put down food to attract them there. He also foreshadowed the modern list-making bird watcher by noting the birds he saw as he travelled across Europe; crossing the Alps he got out and walked by the carriage to see the birds better. The great majority of bird students at this period, however, were more interested in collecting skins and eggs than in watching birds in the field and their habits. Waterton used to refer to them contemptuously as "closet naturalists."

In 1859 the first surviving national bird organisation was founded, the British Ornithologists' Union, originally a group of friends of Alfred Newton, the Professor of Zoology at Cambridge. This has always been the body concerned with the museum and international aspects of ornithology, and has only in quite recent years begun to take an interest in bird watching as a pleasure. Its journal, *Ibis*, has been the principal medium used by British ornithologists to publish the results of their trips or residence abroad, especially in Africa. Since the war, however, it has also carried many important papers on modern developments in bird biology and behaviour. The Union also produces check-lists of the birds of the British Isles (the last one, published in 1952, is now getting rather out of date) and organises expeditions to ornithologically unexplored parts of the world. Two expeditions were sponsored in connection with the Union's centenary in 1959, the main one to Ascension Island and a smaller one to the Comoro Archipelago. At the end of 1960 the Union had 1,153 members who, in the delightful phrase used in the first volume of *Ibis*, must still be "gentlemen attached to the study of ornithology," and may, if they wish, put the letters M.B.O.U. after their names.

In 1892 the Union was supplemented by the foundation of a dining club, the British Ornithologists' Club, which now has 250 members (who must be members of the Union) and publishes its own *Bulletin*, largely concerned with bird taxonomy, i.e. the classification and correct scientific naming of birds. The Union has no direct link with the International Ornithological Congresses, but one of its leading members usually sits on the Permanent Executive Committee that maintains continuity in the four-year intervals between congresses. Since the war, congresses have been held in Sweden, Switzerland, Finland and the United States, England and the Netherlands.

The quarter-century before the First World War produced a great movement away from museum ornithology into the field, and this is when modern bird watching was really born. The collection of records of birds migrating at lighthouses and on the coast had already begun, and before 1914 led to the exciting discovery that Fair Isle, between Shetland and Orkney, and the Isle of May in the Firth of Forth were just as good places to watch birds as Heligoland, where Gätke had made his pioneer observations on bird migration when it was still a British island. Then came a spate of popular books, with W. H. Hudson in the van, from *Birds in a Village* (1893) onwards, until the name itself appeared in Edmund Selous's *Bird Watching* (1901). The dynamic influence of Harry Witherby first made itself felt with the foundation of the magazine *British Birds* (1907), though the war delayed publication of his *Practical Handbook*, forerunner of the monumental *Handbook of British Birds* (see p. 18). In this decade of pulsating activity the British bird ringing scheme was also born, in the offices of *British Birds* under Witherby's inspiration and also at Aberdeen University at the instance of Dr. (now Sir) Landsborough Thomson.

This was the period when people first began seriously to study and practise the art of bird identification in the field. As late as 1906, for instance, Hudson thought it almost impossible to separate common and black-headed gulls in the field in their winter plumage, a feat which nowadays nobody would insult a second-year bird watcher by suggesting he could not achieve. Without this greater skill in field identification, bird watchers could never have abandoned the gun and still have continued to make the important contributions which they have done. This development is due on the one hand to a more extensive use of efficient binoculars and telescopes, and on the other to the more intensive application of the powers of human observation to the practical problems of identifying birds in the field.

The increasing acceptance of records of birds that had only been seen in the field, without the warranty of examining their dead bodies, made possible the development in Britain of annual reports on the birds seen in particular counties or districts, which began in Norfolk and Hertfordshire well before 1900. To-day such reports are issued annually for all but three or four of the counties of England. Books devoted to the birds of a single county, which are less dependent on sight records, started as early as 1866, with J. E. Harting's *The Birds of Middlesex*, and here again every English county has been monographed at least once since 1900. Both annual reports and the latest books on the birds of counties and districts will be found listed by counties in Part Three.

The First World War checked the rapid development of bird watching, not least because so many of the more promising younger bird watchers, such as C. J. Alexander, Gerald Legge and C. S. Meares, were killed. During the middle twenties it began to gather momentum again, and eventually the undue concentration of the B.O.U. on foreign and museum ornithology drove an active group of younger bird watchers, headed by Max Nicholson and Bernard Tucker, with the warm support of Harry Witherby, to found in 1932 the British Trust for Ornithology as the organ of those bird watchers interested in the scientific study of British birds in the field. The Trust plunged at once into a series of co-operative scientific inquiries, drawing on the services of the now rapidly increasing number of younger amateur bird watchers throughout the country. It carried on the annual heron census pioneered by Witherby's *British Birds* with Nicholson as organiser, and ran important inquiries on the food of the little owl, the distribution of the woodcock and the breeding biology of the swallow. As soon as the Trust was firmly established, Witherby transferred to it the *British Birds* ringing scheme, and in fact the Trust rapidly came to occupy the key position in British field ornithology. Its progress was hardly checked by the Second World War, in which its war work consisted of surveys of two birds of economic importance, the rook and the woodpigeon. To-day the Trust has more than 3,000 members and an excellent journal, *Bird Study*, in which reports of its investigations appear.

Shortly after the war the Trust was asked to provide an umbrella for the rapidly growing network of bird observatories, where migration, breeding biology and other aspects of the natural history of birds are studied in the field. Starting almost simultaneously on the Isle of May in the Firth of Forth and the Pembrokeshire island of Skokholm in 1935-36, the bird observatories shot ahead immediately after the war, when Fair Isle, Spurn Head (Yorkshire), Gibraltar Point (Lincolnshire) and Cley (Norfolk) all started up within a few years. By 1962 a score of observatories, all on islands or the coast, were recognised by the Bird Observatories Committee, whose annual conference in Oxford in January is one of the highlights of the year for the active younger bird watchers. At present there is a tendency towards inland observatories and ringing stations, and in a few years' time there will probably be as dense a network inland as there now is on the coast. Most of the observatories are manned by groups of local enthusiasts, but some of the more remote island ones, such as Bardsey, Fair Isle, Lundy and Skokholm, have to have a full-time warden. Probably not less than a thousand keen, mostly younger bird watchers stay at bird observatories, most of which provide some sort of accommodation on youth-hostel lines, in the course of a year, and take part in their activities, mainly the day-by-day recording of migration. Mainland observatories, such as Cley and Dungeness, must be visited by many more still. There is no better way for an up-and-coming bird watcher to learn his birds than a week at a bird observatory under the tutelage of an experienced warden. The seven field centres of the Field Studies Council and the Scottish Field Studies Association all usually have at least one week in the year when bird watching beginners can go and learn the rudiments of their chosen pursuit. Observatories, ringing stations and field centres are all listed under their respective counties in Part Three.

An interesting offshoot of the B.T.O. is the Edward Grey Institute for Field Ornithology, now an integral part of the Department of Zoology at the University of Oxford, but once very much the child of the Trust, which was called into being partly to administer the fund raised in memory of Lord Grey of Fallodon on behalf of the Institute. Here for once Oxford led the way, in compensation for Cambridge's leadership from the days of John Ray to those of Alfred Newton. Cambridge has since redressed the balance by setting up its Ornithological Field Station at Madingley. The E.G.I. has specialised in bird population and migration problems and Madingley in bird behaviour. These two research institutions are appropriately headed by two of our younger ornithological Fellows of the Royal Society, David Lack at Oxford and W. H. Thorpe at Cambridge. The other ornithological F.R.S.'s are that pioneer and doyen of British field ornithology, Sir Julian Huxley, and the eminent student of bird behaviour, Dr. Niko Tinbergen.

Another important national body is the Wildfowl Trust, created by the organising genius of Peter Scott for the study and preservation of the wildfowl of the world. Starting from a small nucleus of captive ducks and geese and the wild flock of white-fronted geese that has frequented the New Grounds at Slimbridge on the Severn estuary for hundreds of years, Scott has since 1948 built up a formidable organisation with over 5,000 members, two fine wildfowl collections, at Slimbridge and Peakirk (Northamptonshire), and a research laboratory that is contributing substantially to our knowledge of the biology and behaviour of wildfowl. The collection at Slimbridge is the best and most comprehensive that has ever existed in the world. Before the war nobody would have cared to predict that five thousand people could be found to support a body devoted to the study and conservation of a single family of birds. In 1959 the Ornamental Pheasant Trust was founded in Norfolk to do much the same for game birds.

Besides the national bodies, there are innumerable local ones. The whole of Great Britain south of the Great Glen is covered by a network of local natural history societies, many of them with ornithological sections, and of ornithological societies and bird clubs (these are listed by counties in Part Three). The natural history societies, which may be either on a county or a district basis, were mostly founded during the nineteenth century, though many new ones have continued to come into existence, for instance, at Seaford, Uckfield and Wantage during 1961. The specifically bird societies, however, are creations of the period since the First World War, the Oxford Ornithological Society leading the way in 1921. Many other districts followed suit, especially where the general natural history societies were too inactive even to appease their bird watchers by allowing them to start a separate ornithological section. Some existing bird societies, such as Newbury, and Leicestershire and Rutland, represent breakaway ornithological sections, but the majority were new creations. To-day the great majority of active bird watchers belong either to a bird club, a bird observatory or the ornithological section of a general natural history society. In Scotland the system is different. There are few local bird societies or ornithological sections, but the Scottish Ornithologists' Club has six branches, at Aberdeen, Dumfries, Dundee, Edinburgh, Glasgow and St. Andrews.

The main activities of local natural history societies and bird clubs are indoor meetings, at which a lecture illustrated by films or slides is given, and field meetings, which range from purely social rambles to serious scientific enterprises. The field meetings are probably the biggest single factor in teaching bird-watching beginners their birds, and much the best advice that can be given to anybody starting out with enthusiasm but little knowledge is to join the nearest bird club or natural history society and attend as many field meetings as he can. He need not fear that he will be the only beginner among a crowd of cognoscenti, but will find both fellow beginners and more experienced bird watchers who are very ready to help. Most bird and natural history societies publish some sort of annual report on the birds of their district, and many now also issue a monthly or bi-monthly bulletin giving the latest news of the unusual birds that have been seen in the district. The national counterpart of these bulletins is the " Recent reports and news " feature of *British Birds*. The " bush tele-graph " is also very active in local bird-watching circles. The result is that when any real rarity turns up and shows signs of staying, bird watchers appear literally from all parts of the country on the following week-end, sometimes causing embarrassment when the site is on private land or needs a permit.

For many years British naturalists were completely unorganised, with the result that their viewpoint often went unrepresented in the national councils. In 1958 this particular gap was plugged by the formation of the Council for Nature, in which bird societies and clubs joined with other natural history societies throughout the United Kingdom to create a body that would represent their interests on the national plane. The Council now has over 300 member societies and has been very active in such matters as the danger of poisonous farm chemicals to bird life, the checking of irresponsible shooting by youths and others, and the saving of im-portant natural history sites threatened by building and other development. The three main long-term activities of the Council are its Conservation Corps, by which young people are mobilised to carry out essential maintenance work on nature reserves; its Intelligence Unit, which edits the Council's half-yearly bulletin *News for Naturalists*, and acts as a general information bureau on natural history in the British Isles; and Brantwood, its conference and holiday centre for naturalists at Coniston in the Lake District. Individual subscribers to the Council's work are also welcomed.

It has been estimated that at least 80,000 individual naturalists belong to the various member societies of the Council for Nature, and of these more than half, say 50,000, are probably bird watchers. These are the really active people. At the other extreme are the five million viewers who watch the B.B.C.'s popular television programme *Look*, compèred by Peter Scott. The B.B.C.'s Natural History Unit based at Bristol and its various sound and TV programmes have played a vital part in the continued progress of the natural history movement since the war. This is now the first contact that many thousands of town dwellers have with wildlife of any kind. Many must go on from just viewing to watching and feeding birds on their own account in parks and gardens, and later perhaps to join the 50,000 front line troops in the natural history societies. Most of the ITV companies too have natural history programmes, on a more popular level than those of the B.B.C., which also play their part in bringing an ever increasing proportion of the citizens of the United Kingdom to an enjoyment of wild birds as part of their natural heritage.

THE BIRD PROTECTION MOVEMENT

It was about a hundred years ago that ornithologists first began to become interested in the protection of wild birds, other than game birds which had been preserved for the privileged from time immemorial. Wholesale slaughter of seabirds for so-called sport and vapid feminine fashions for hats adorned with grebe and other bird skins were threatening several species. The first Act of Parliament protecting any wild birds other than game birds was passed in 1869 for the preservation of seabirds, and this was followed in 1880 by a more comprehensive measure protecting a wide range of less common species. This was frequently amended and added to during the next few years, with the result that for over half a century the efforts of bird protectionists in Britain were hampered by the incredible complexity of the laws they were trying to enforce *ad hoc* Acts of Parliament jostling with orders for individual counties that named birds by such obscure local names as "purre" and "ox-bird" for the dunlin. Small wonder that the police found the law hard to enforce until it was consolidated and clarified by the Act of 1954 (see p. 34).

Spurred largely by the efforts of those trying to dissuade fashionable women from encouraging the large-scale slaughter of birds by wearing their plumes about their persons, the Society for the Protection of Birds was founded in 1889, becoming Royal in 1904. The early successes of the gallant pioneers, among whom W. H. Hudson was outstanding, included the saving as British breeding birds and subsequent great increase of the great skua, once reduced to a handful of pairs in Shetland; the great crested grebe, the chief victim of the wantons of fashion; and the goldfinch, once being steadily decimated by the bird trappers but now once more a common bird in many parts of England. The arrest of the decline of the kite and the careful encouragement of the return of the bittern also stand to the credit of the pre-1914 bird protectors.

During the inter-war period the RSPB lay somewhat in the doldrums, but afterwards, thanks to new brooms on the council and staff, the Society burst into renewed vigour, created a chain of new sanctuaries, established a Scottish office, and safeguarded the return of the avocet to Suffolk, the osprey to Scotland and the black-tailed godwit to a still not publicly named English county. It also played a leading part in securing the enactment of the Protection of Wild Birds Act, 1954, and continues to press for the blocking up of the remaining loopholes in the law which frustrate the aim of fully protecting all wild birds and their eggs that are not either game birds or economic pests. To-day, with over 17,500 members, its excellent magazine *Bird Notes*, its thriving Junior Bird Recorders' Club for young people, and a dozen reserves and sanctuaries, notably Minsmere and Havergate Island on the coast of Suffolk, the RSPB is in a more flourishing state than ever before.

Another outcome of the ferment of natural history activity in the years before the First World War was the foundation of the Society for the

Promotion of Nature Reserves in 1912. In the first thirty years of its existence it did little but brood upon a nest-egg of £50,000, and acquire or contribute towards a number of scattered sites, mainly small and of botanical value, though one, Woodwalton Fen, is now an important national nature reserve. Since 1940, however, it has fostered two developments of great importance, one line of advance leading to the Nature Conservancy, the other to the network of county naturalists' trusts. The S.P.N.R. also made a substantial grant to enable the Council for Nature to be launched.

The groundwork for the creation of the Nature Conservancy, the Government body responsible for the conservation of wildlife in Great Britain, was carried out on the one hand by the British Ecological Society, which appointed the working party that planned the central set-up, and on the other by the S.P.N.R., whose Nature Reserves Investigation Committee, starting from an earlier list drawn up in 1915 (the last echo of the Edwardian ferment), produced the blueprint for the actual schedule of national nature reserves. This joint effort led to the official appointment in 1945 of the Wild Life Conservation Special Committee, with Dr. (now Sir) Julian Huxley in the chair, linked with the Hobhouse Committee on National Parks. The report of the Huxley Committee led directly to the setting up, by Royal Charter in 1949, of the Nature Conservancy, which now has 92 national nature reserves, totalling nearly 180,000 acres, in Great Britain. Those of any ornithological significance are listed by counties in Part Three, along with numerous local and private nature reserves and bird sanctuaries. The Nature Conservancy to-day is playing a vital part in British ornithological research, and among other things grant-aids the B.T.O.'s bird ringing scheme. The Conservancy has six research or field stations of its own: Anancaun, near Kinlochewe, Ross-shire; Furzebrook, near Wareham, Dorset; Merlewood, at Grange-over-Sands, North Lancashire; Monks' Wood, near Huntingdon; Moor House, near Alston, Cumberland; and Speyside, near Aviemore, Inverness-shire.

The first county naturalists' trust was founded in Norfolk in 1926, and resulted in the saving of many important bird sites in the county, including Hickling Broad and Scolt Head Island, for these trusts, unlike natural history societies, can own and lease land. Not till 1948 was the challenge accepted by other counties, starting with Yorkshire; Lincolnshire, Leicestershire and Cambridgeshire soon followed. In the later fifties the trickle became a flood and by the beginning of 1962 twenty-three counties in England and five in Wales were already covered, while hardly a county in England was not at least discussing the formation of a trust. At about the time that it was helping to promote the Council for Nature, the S.P.N.R. also agreed to become an umbrella for the county trusts, and the County Naturalists' Trusts Committee was set up to provide a forum for their discussions. The older established trusts have already done much to save threatened sites of importance to birds; Yorkshire has saved Spurn Head, and Lincolnshire was largely instrumental in the declaration of the local nature reserve at Gibraltar Point by the Lindsey County

Council. All the county trusts, which are listed under their counties in Part Three, are worthy of the support of local bird watchers.

The National Trust, a much older national body, founded in 1895, also has many sites in its care that are of the greatest interest and value to bird watchers; these too are listed in Part Three.

The RSPB, and a dozen other societies less directly interested in bird protection, play their part in international affairs, through the British Section of the International Council for Bird Preservation. This body has to its credit, among other things, the protection from R.A.F. practice bombing of moulting shelduck in the mouth of the Elbe, which is the moulting ground for practically all the adult shelduck in the British Isles. The British Section takes part in the quadrennial world conferences of the International Council itself, usually held immediately before the International Ornithological Congresses, as well as in the intercalary quadrennial conferences of the Council's European Continental Section. Aided by the readers of *The Times*, the British Section has recently selected the robin to be Britain's national bird.

The latest development of all in the field of wildlife conservation has been the foundation at the end of 1961 of the World Wildlife Fund, which aims to raise substantial funds to combat the emergency with which wildlife has to contend in many parts of the world, where it is threatened with extinction. A British National Appeal has now been formed, with H.R.H. Prince Philip, Patron of the Council of Nature, at its head, to raise money in the United Kingdom for the conservation of the world's wildlife. One-third of all funds raised by this appeal may be retained for the benefit of British wildlife.

PART TWO: WHAT TO WATCH FOR

Introductory

This part of the book describes briefly and simply all the birds which occur regularly in any part of the British Isles. Attention is drawn to the quickest and easiest ways of identifying them in the field, but with no attempt at complete descriptions of plumage, voice or any other aspect of behaviour, such as is already given in my *Pocket Guide to British Birds*. The thumbnail sketches of the typical birds in each group are only there as indications of general shape and outline, for full illustrations of all the birds and their various plumages, mostly in colour, will be found in the *Pocket Guide*. In the present book I have arranged the birds in roughly natural groupings, as a useful cross-check to the arbitrary size groupings used in the *Pocket Guide*, though adhering to the broad arrangement of separating land birds from water birds and waterside birds, which most beginners find useful.

LAND BIRDS

Small Seed-Eaters: Finches, Buntings, Sparrows

There are two main groups of small song birds, the thick-billed seed-eaters and the thin-billed insect-eaters. Some, which eat both seeds and insects, have medium-thick bills, but the specialist seed-eaters, the finches, buntings and sparrows, have very distinctive short fat bills adapted to crushing seeds and sometimes even small nuts and fruit stones. Even so, most of their young are fed on insects, a fact which has to be borne in mind when trying to decide whether a bird is harmful or not.

In winter most of our seed-eaters consort together in large mixed flocks in stackyards, arable fields and other places where grain and weed seeds are to be found. The most frequent members of these flocks are house sparrows, chaffinches, greenfinches and yellowhammers, with linnets, bramblings and tree sparrows not unusual, and goldfinches, reed, corn and cirl buntings, and in some parts of the country twites as hangers on. Bramblings also frequently flock with chaffinches under beech trees, while goldfinches, redpolls and siskins form a quite distinct winter association feeding on alders and birches. Of all these seed-eaters house sparrows, chaffinches and greenfinches are the only really frequent visitors to garden bird tables. These three and linnets commonly nest in gardens, being joined in the more countrified ones by goldfinches and bullfinches.

THE SPARROWS AND THE LARGER FINCHES

type: the House Sparrow

HOUSE SPARROW, COCK	grey crown and rump
HOUSE SPARROW, HEN	plain brown
TREE SPARROW	chestnut crown
CHAFFINCH	white patch on shoulders
CHAFFINCH, COCK	blue-grey head, pink breast
GREENFINCH	yellow on wings and tail

47

BULLFINCH	black cap, pink breast, white rump
BRAMBLING	white rump
BRAMBLING, COCK	black head, orange-buff on shoulders
CROSSBILL	crossed mandibles
CROSSBILL, COCK	red or orange plumage
HAWFINCH	huge bill, white wing patches

The House Sparrow is the one bird that everybody knows, for it forces itself on our attention even in the heart of cities. It is indeed almost the typical small bird. Certainly it is one of the few that will actually come indoors, seeking its living even in railway stations, restaurants and the animal houses at zoos.

The first thing to notice about the house sparrow is its thick, seed-eating bill, and the second the fact that the cock is quite different from the hen. The cock house sparrow, when not too grimy, is really quite a handsome bird, with his chestnut mantle, black chin and throat and grey crown and rump. Seen at close range you can hardly mistake him for any other British bird except the tree sparrow. **Tree Sparrows** of either sex look like cock house sparrows with chestnut crowns and a small black patch on each cheek. You can also readily pick out the tree sparrow by its rather . higher-pitched voice, especially the distinctive flight note *teck teck*. In some parts of the world the tree sparrow is a town bird, but in Britain it prefers to breed in places where there are plenty of old trees full of holes, such as parks, orchards, and river banks, but it will also nest in old buildings, disused quarries and even on bleak marine islands.

The hen house sparrow presents more of a problem, for she is so nondescript. Most of the other plain brownish seed-eaters are either appreciably larger or smaller, and it is easier to show how they differ from a sparrow than the other way round. The hen chaffinch, which is about the same size, is readily told by her white shoulder patch and much more conspicuous white wing-bar. If you can see the shape of the tip of the tail, all sparrows differ from all finches and buntings by their square, not cleft, tails. It is worth remembering too that house sparrows do not always nest in holes in buildings or in creeper on house walls, but often, and especially in the London parks, in large untidy nests in trees or tall bushes.

Though the house sparrow is the most familiar British bird, the **Chaffinch** ranks as the commonest over the whole country, sharing this distinction with the blackbird. Chaffinches of both sexes stand out among all other small birds by their conspicuous white shoulder patches, which enable experienced bird watchers to identify them at a considerable range or height on migration. These white patches, coupled with a prominent white bar on each wing and white feathers in the tail, distinguish the hen chaffinch at once not only from the hen house sparrow but also from all other small nondescript brown seed-eaters. The cock chaffinch, on the other hand, is one of our handsomest birds, with his slate-blue head and nape and pinkish-brown underparts. Indeed, a correspondent of *The*

Countryman once related how he saw a mother pointing out a cock chaffinch to her child with the words, "Come and look at this pretty blue tit, it's got a red breast."

If you get a good view of a cock chaffinch, you can't mistake it for anything else, certainly not for a cock **Brambling**, especially when this handsome winter visitor is in his spring plumage of black head and bright orange-buff breast and shoulders. Nor on a close view could the hen brambling, with orange-buff breast and no white shoulders, be confused with the hen chaffinch. But in fact the view you get of mixed winter flocks of chaffinches and bramblings is often only a fleeting one, and then, as they fly up into the trees, you look for the white rumps of the bramblings which pick them out at once. In winter, incidentally, the cock's black head is suffused with brown. Though bramblings are especially fond of feeding under beeches for the beech mast, in years when the mast crop fails they have to resort to the stackyard along with the other finches. In March and April they return to northern Europe again, though it is always worth while keeping an eye open for possible breeding bramblings in the Scottish Highlands from April to July. A pair certainly bred in Sutherland in 1920, there are two or three "probables" and most likely several more have been overlooked.

The gay trill of the chaffinch's song is easy enough to pick out of the bird-song chorus, but it has another note, *pink*, which is remarkably like a similar note of the great tit except that, as Terry Gompertz has recently pointed out, it has a thicker or flatter quality and does not seem to echo. The brambling's call note is a rather harsh *tsweek*, which often enables you to pick out an odd brambling or two in a flock of chaffinches flying by and uttering their own flight note, a soft *tsup*.

Two other finches, the greenfinch and the bullfinch, are about the same size as the house sparrow, while two more, the crossbill and the hawfinch, are appreciably larger. The **Greenfinch** is a common bird, especially among houses with gardens, and it really is green. When it flies off you notice at once the bright yellow patches at the base of its tail and on each wing; no other small bird, except the much smaller and less common siskin, has both these sets of patches. The lazily drawn-out *dzweee* of the greenfinch is one of the characteristic sounds of the spring and summer, but its rather melodious flight note *chi-chi-chi-chi-chit* is not always easy to tell from the similar but more staccato and metallic flight note of the linnet.

The **Bullfinch** is an easy one, for nothing else has the cock's bold combination of black head, grey mantle, white rump and bright rosy-pink cheeks and underparts. Even when you fail to see the whole bird at rest, the white rump seen just as it dives into a hedge will often reveal the bird's identity. The hen is a paler counterpart of the cock. Bullfinches rarely flock in more than family parties and never seem to consort with other finches. They frequent woods, lanes with old overgrown hedges, large gardens and orchards, though the owners of the last two do not always welcome them. Bullfinches are shy, and often the first you know of their presence is their soft piping whistle.

You have to get quite close to a **Crossbill** to see that its mandibles are crossed, so it is advisable to have some other means of naming it. I have always found its sharp metallic cry, *jip jip*, the first indication of its presence nearby; it is a sound that once heard you never forget and has led me to the crossbill in many places from my own garden on the Chilterns to Tresco Abbey in the Isles of Scilly. The owner of the cry, if not flying overhead, will soon be tracked down to a coniferous tree of some kind, pine, spruce or larch, and may prove to have either dull brown (juvenile), yellowish-brown (hen), orange (immature cock) or the predominantly red plumage of an adult cock. A flock of crossbills flashing their colours about the tree as they move from cone to cone, is one of the few almost tropical sights the bird watcher can hope to see in Britain. Crossbills are only irregular visitors to our shores, sometimes coming in large numbers and occasionally staying to breed. When they do invade us, they usually start in June or July. Only in the Breckland of Norfolk and Suffolk and in the Scottish Highlands do crossbills breed regularly, and the Scottish birds have recently been pronounced by the experts to belong to a different species, the parrot crossbill, on account of their large bills.

Our largest finch, the **Hawfinch,** looks very different from all the others, mainly because of its quite disproportionately large beak, which it uses to crush the stones of cherries and other fruits. As with the crossbill, I find I usually first pick up hawfinches by ear, recognising a certain loud robin-like *tick tick* overhead as not coming from a robin. I have comparatively rarely seen a hawfinch at rest, so that I could see its beak properly, but more often when it flies away from me, showing a mixture of chestnut, black and white in its plumage. Actually the bird is mainly chestnut, with black wing-tips, a white patch on each wing and white at the tip of the tail, but the grotesque bill is what settles it. In flight a hawfinch has a very dumpy look, and even if you don't know it, you know at once you have seen something you don't know.

THE SMALLER FINCHES

type: the Linnet

LINNET, COCK	red breast and forehead, grey head, chestnut back
LINNET, HEN	plain brown, bill brown
REDPOLL	red forehead, black chin
REDPOLL, COCK	pink breast and rump
TWITE, COCK	pink rump
TWITE, HEN	plain brown, bill grey or yellow
SISKIN	yellow on wings and tail
SISKIN, COCK	yellow rump
GOLDFINCH	red on head, yellow on wings

Our five smaller finches are all appreciably smaller than the house sparrow. The **Linnet** is the commonest and the cock is easy enough to identify in spring and summer with its crimson breast and forehead, and at all times with its grey head and chestnut back. Hen linnets are more of a problem, and need to be distinguished from both the smaller redpoll and the same-sized twite; they are dull brown birds with little but whitish wing-bars to relieve the monotony. These wing-bars, incidentally, are very conspicuous in both sexes when they fly. Linnets are frequent in larger gardens, as well as on heaths, commons, downs and dunes, and are especially fond of gorsy spots.

Redpolls are commoner in the north and west than in the south and east, but I know of Surrey suburbs where they breed in the gardens and have more than once spotted them there by their characteristic *chuch-uch-uch* flight note, often delivered in a circular song flight. Adult redpolls are easy enough if you can see their red forehead and black chin (neither possessed by a hen linnet), but cocks in breeding plumage with pink breast and rump are easier still. Juveniles are the hardest, and must be told from both linnets and twites mainly by their smaller size and black chins.

Those who live in the north must also allow for the **Twite**, the linnet of the moorlands, which has nothing to relieve its brown streaked plumage except the pink rump of the adult cock. As rumps are not always easy to see, you have to rely on the colour of the bill, which is grey in the summer twite, yellow in the winter twite and the redpoll, and dark brown in the linnet. A winter twite can be told from the smaller redpoll by its yellowish-buff chin.

Fortunately these three rather confusing little birds have very distinct call notes: the twite's *twa-it* gave it its name. Unless you live in hill districts of the north and west, nine out of ten, or even 99 out of 100, spring and summer sightings will prove to be linnets, but in winter both twites and redpolls wander and you can't be so sure. Redpolls in particular come south to feed on alders and birches with goldfinches and siskins, but at a time when linnets prefer to consort with other seed-eaters in the finch flocks on the ploughlands.

The **Siskin** is the least familiar of our finches to the average bird watcher, for it breeds mainly in the pinewoods of the Scottish Highlands and only in winter joins with the redpolls in the alders by our southern rivers. It is our smallest seed-eater, not much bigger than a blue tit, and the cock is like a miniature canary, strikingly yellow-green with a bright yellow rump and black chin and crown. The hen is duller, but shares a yellow wing-bar and yellow at the base of the tail with her mate; these distinguish her from all other finches except the much larger greenfinch. In the poor light of a winter's afternoon it is often hard to detect any colour at all in a mixed flock of siskins and redpolls feeding on the alders, but you may still be able to separate them by the siskin's shorter tail and dumpier appearance.

If a supposed siskin should turn up in an unusual place in the south, it is always worth considering the possibility of its being a **Serin,** a somewhat similar little bird that has spread north-westwards over the Continent in recent years, but has not yet taken the jump over the Channel—it may do so any year now. Serins differ from siskins in having a yellower rump but no yellow at the base of the tail nor any black about the head. Fame will go to the bird watcher who first hears the curious little high-pitched jangling song of the serin in Britain and tracks down its nest and eggs in some tree overhanging a busy street, for in Europe it is very much a suburban bird.

The finch I have left till last is perhaps the most beautiful of them all, the **Goldfinch,** unmistakable with its harlequin plumage: red, black and white head; yellow, black and white wings; brown back and white rump. We have no other bird at all like it. The young birds have no red on the chin or forehead, only the yellow wing-bar. The liquid *tswitt-witt-witt* of its flight note is elaborated into one of our most delightful minor bird songs. Goldfinches, of course, love thistles and often feed on the seeds of dandelions and other tall weeds as well. They represent one of the triumphs of bird protection, for the bird-catchers had made them local and scarce about sixty years ago. Now they are quite common in many areas, such as the Cotswolds, where a pair once nested in a medlar tree in my Burford garden. Fruit trees are among their favourite nesting sites.

THE BUNTINGS

type: the Yellowhammer

YELLOWHAMMER, COCK	bright yellow and chestnut
YELLOWHAMMER, HEN	dull yellow and brown
CIRL BUNTING, HEN	dull yellow and brown
CIRL BUNTING, COCK	black and grey on head, green breast-band
CORN BUNTING	large, plain brown
REED BUNTING, COCK	black and white on head
REED BUNTING, HEN	plain brown

The buntings closely resemble the finches and are all larger than the house sparrow. Far the commonest of our five breeding species is the **Yellow-hammer**, whose brilliant yellow cock is a familiar roadside bird with his handsome chestnut mantle. No other British bird, apart from the very different yellow wagtail, is so yellow. The hens, as so often, are dull beside their spouses and practically impossible to tell from hen cirl buntings unless their chestnut rumps can be seen. Both sexes show white feathers in the tail as they fly.

While the yellowhammer is widespread, the **Cirl Bunting** is distinctly choosy, even in the favoured south and west of England, as to where it will set up residence. You will often find it at the foot of the downs, and in sheltered valleys in the West Country it is not infrequent. There is no mistaking the cock, for his head is strikingly patterned with grey crown, pale yellow cheeks divided by a black stripe through the eye, and black throat, while his breast is crossed by an olive-green band. The hen cirl, on the other hand, differs from the hen yellowhammer only in her olive-green rump.

The day-long song of the yellowhammer, which often continues into August, is the familiar " little bit of bread and no cheese," but some birds are " lazy " and do not get as far as the cheese. These are the tiresome ones whose song can be confused with the flat little trill, " bread " only, as it were, of the cirl bunting. Even living with both species singing on my doorstep, I still sometimes encounter birds which keep me guessing at first. It is always best to try and get a sight of the bird, as the cocks are so distinct.

The **Corn Bunting** is the dullest bird of all, apart from its marital habits, which the late Colonel Ryves proved to be remarkably polygamous. It is just a plumpish, plain brown bird, with no distinctive features about its plumage, not so much as a pale eyestripe, and is the largest British seed-eater. It perches on a post or bush, or sometimes just a clod of earth, and monotonously intones its jangling song all day, interspersed with quick forays to make sure that all its wives are behaving. When it flies it has a characteristic way of dangling its legs, which is not found in any other small British bird. In winter corn buntings collect into small flocks, and may fly over making a liquid *quit* call, but otherwise it is one of our most sedentary birds. Nobody has yet solved the mystery of corn bunting distribution, why some tracts of country have plenty and other apparently identical tracts have none. On the whole, it prefers arable land, downland and rough fields near the coast.

The **Reed Bunting** always breeds near fresh water or at least in marshes, but not necessarily near reeds. About the size of a yellowhammer, the cock's black and white head pattern and rich brown plumage make it an easy one, while the hen is all brown apart from the white in the tail she shares with her mate. The call note *tsweep* is confusingly like that of the yellow wagtail. Reed buntings present no difficulty when they stick to their reeds, but when they wander in autumn and winter and perhaps turn up in finch flocks or as solitary vagrants, the hens especially are a bit puzzling at first, largely because you may not be thinking in terms of reed buntings. Then it sometimes helps to remember that the hens have a buff throat and buff lines on either side of the eye.

Our remaining native bunting, the snow bunting, is discussed with the group of mountain birds on p. 87.

Small Insect-Eaters: Chats, Warblers, Tits, Larks, Pipits, Wagtails, Shrikes, Flycatchers, Swallows

The great majority of our small land birds are insect-eaters, easily told by their thin bills. They fall into six broad groupings: the chats and robin, which are actually the smaller members of the thrush family; the warbler type; the tits; the larks; pipits and wagtails; the shrikes and flycatchers; and the aerial feeders, swallow, martins and swift. Most of these are not very gregarious, though tits band together in mixed parties in autumn and winter, skylarks flock at the same season, wagtails have communal roosts, and swallows and martins flock on migration. The most frequent visitors to gardens are the robin, hedgesparrow, wren and great and blue tits, with the coal and marsh tits, pied wagtail, spotted flycatcher and the aerial feeders in larger gardens, and chiffchaffs and willow warblers looking in on migration.

THE CHATS AND ROBIN

type: the Robin

ROBIN	red breast and forehead
ROBIN, JUVENILE	spotted breast
NIGHTINGALE	rufous tail
COMMON REDSTART	red tail
COMMON REDSTART, COCK	white forehead, black throat, grey back
BLACK REDSTART	red tail
BLACK REDSTART, COCK	black with white wing patches
STONECHAT	black throat
STONECHAT, COCK	black and white on head and neck
WHINCHAT	white at sides of tail
WHINCHAT, COCK	white eyestripe, pink breast
WHEATEAR	white rump

The **Robin**, recently voted into the vacant post of Britain's national bird, is one of the few birds that everybody not only knows but likes. To describe its plumage might seem unnecessary, when its old popular name used to be redbreast, but until you take a close look at a robin you may not realise that its face and forehead as well as its breast are red, nor see the pleasantly contrasting blue-grey border along its flanks. Most commercial artists have clearly not studied robins as closely as this, for robins in advertisements and on Christmas cards are often shown with a red breast only. When seen against the light, you can often tell a robin by its dumpy, perky stance alone. If, when you get a better view, the bird has not got a red breast at all but a speckled one, and the time of year is spring or summer, your bird is a juvenile robin. This is one of the first pitfalls for the tiro bird watcher, but even more experienced ones have been known to confound the shrill hunger cry of the young robin with the normal call note of the spotted flycatcher. The robin's is perhaps the most familiar of all British bird songs, largely because it can be heard almost throughout the year, starting in mid-July after the end of the summer moult and going right on to the middle or end of the following June. It is worth remembering also that the robin occasionally sings at night, and that by no means every nocturnal songster is a nightingale.

Nor for that matter does the **Nightingale** itself sing only by night. From mid-April to mid-June it sings vigorously by day as well; at other times of year a bird singing by night is most likely something else. The nightingale is like nothing so much as an outsize robin, with no red breast but a rufous tail. Indeed its tail is often the only part of the bird you see, for in Britain it has most retiring habits. Though nightingales in the Mediterranean countries will sing out in the open on telegraph wires, in Britain they almost invariably choose the middle of a dense thicket. Fortunately it is easy to learn its song, which is one of the richest and most varied we have, though some performers are less good than others. The famous *jug jug*, a rich throaty note, will turn up sooner or later in any nightingale's song. To hear a nightingale in Britain you must stay in the south-eastern half of the country, which for this purpose extends west and north as far as eastern Devon, the Vale of Glamorgan, the lower Wye valley, the Severn valley, the Trent valley and the extreme south of Yorkshire. Beyond this line any nocturnal songster is more likely to be a woodlark, and even south and east of it people are far too ready to assume that any song heard after dark comes from a nightingale, even at times when this summer visitor is far away in Africa.

Aristotle believed that robins were redstarts in winter plumage. This was because in Greece the **Common Redstart,** which is a summer migrant, disappears to Africa each autumn and is replaced by migrant robins from the north of Europe. A more genuine link between the two is the fact that the common redstart replaces the robin as a garden bird in many parts of modern Europe. In Britain, however, it is a bird of woodland, parkland and riversides, wherever there are large old trees with holes. It can also be induced to breed in nestboxes in favoured large gardens in the country.

The first thing you notice about a redstart is its red tail, which it often quivers to make it even more conspicuous; "start" is an old English word meaning tail. Both the common and the **Black Redstart** look like red-tailed robins, and often the flash of a red tail as they fly off is the first sign of their presence. The cock common redstart is a most striking bird, with his white forehead, black throat, grey mantle and reddish-chestnut underparts to match his tail. He is totally distinct from the cock black redstart, which is coal black all over except for a white patch on each wing and of course his red tail. It is the duller hen birds that are likely to be confused. The hen common redstart is brown with orange-buff underparts, but the hen black redstart is greyer above and greyish-brown also below. Incidentally, young cock black redstarts often breed in their first year in the immature plumage which is very like that of the hen.

The status, and at most times of year also the habitat, of the two redstarts are a great help in separating them. The common redstart is a summer visitor, most unlikely to be seen anywhere in the British Isles between October and March. The black redstart, on the other hand, is primarily a passage migrant in spring and autumn, and a winter visitor in small numbers, mainly on our south-western coasts. But a few pairs, probably not more than 20-30 in most years, breed in towns in south-east England, especially on the bombed sites in the City of London, which are at present vanishing fast as the City is rebuilt, and in coastal towns from Great Yarmouth to Eastbourne. A few pairs also nest in natural cliff sites, while just to confuse the issue the occasional garden-nesting common redstart must also be expected. So summer redstarts, especially in built-up areas, must be scrutinised more closely than winter ones. A final check, if the nest can be found, is that the common redstart builds in a hole in a tree or building or on the ground and lays pale blue eggs like a hedgesparrow's, while the black redstart prefers a ledge or a crevice in a building or cliff and lays pure white eggs.

The songs of both redstarts are quite distinct once you know them. The common redstart's I always find one of the most variable and hard to be absolutely sure of. After the final banquet of the Tenth International

Ornithological Congress in the ancient castle at Upsala, Sweden, diners emerging at 1 a.m. were puzzled by a bird singing from the topmost point of the flagstaff. After some rather blush-making wrong guesses by the very eminent ornithologists all around, it proved to be a common redstart. The normal song of the common redstart has a family resemblance to those of its close relatives the chats and wheatears, but at other times it reminds me of the chaffinch's gay little trill. Moreover, the bird is a great mimic and may incorporate puzzling phrases from other birds' songs into its own. I usually reckon that if I am not in pied flycatcher territory, any mystery song in a wood will in the end turn out to be a common redstart's.

The black redstart has an equally chat-like song, recognisably akin to that of its common relative, but much less variable, and usually incorporating a remarkable sound which the late Bernard Tucker most aptly likened to the grinding together of little metal balls. The practised ear is eventually able not only to pick out this song among the roar of city traffic, but to be sure that it is not made by a canary in a nearby window.

Three kinds of chat breed in the British Isles, but one of them we call a wheatear. The other two, the resident **Stonechat** and the summer visitor **Whinchat,** are also a confusable pair, like the two redstarts. They are alike in being small robin-like birds that perch prominently on bushes, flick their tails up and make grating cries. The cock stonechat is easy enough, for it has a handsome patchwork of black, white and chestnut plumage, with a black head and throat and a white half-collar. The cock whinchat is almost equally easy with its striking white stripes both above and below the eye. Both have deep buff breasts, but the stonechat's is tinged chestnut and the whinchat's pink. It is with the hen and young birds that trouble begins, for both look rather dull brownish birds with a white wing-bar. However, you can always tell the hen whinchat by the white patch on either side of the base of the tail (which the cock also has), while the hen stonechat has a blackish throat. Habitat is not much help in separating the two chats, for both like heathy, gorsy places, though the stonechat is now commoner on the coast than inland and the whinchat is very local in the south-east. Their songs, though separable with practice, are a fairly advanced exercise in birdmanship for those who do not hear them regularly.

Indeed, it may take some time before you can by ear alone distinguish the song of either chat from that of the **Wheatear,** though there is no problem at all in separating them by sight. The wheatear's main field mark is its very conspicuous white rump, the "white arse" which gives it its name. The bird itself is appreciably larger, the size of a chaffinch to the two chats' linnet-size, and the cock wheatear in summer is a handsome creature with his clear French grey upperparts contrasting with his warm buff underparts. The hen and young birds are browner on top, but all have the distinctive white rump. Whereas the two chats often perch on bushes, the wheatear is very much of a ground bird, except occasionally on migration. Some of our migrant wheatears, especially those that go through in late April and early May, are large brightly coloured birds with a more upright stance that are on their way to breed in Greenland. The wheatear is a bird of the hills and moors, and so especially common in the north and west of the British Isles, though frequent enough on migration everywhere.

Brief mention must also be made of the robin-like **Bluethroat,** a scarce passage migrant on the east coast. It gets its name from the bright blue chin and throat of the adult cock, which may have either a red or a white spot. But most of our visitors are brownish hen and young birds.

WARBLERS AND WARBLER-LIKE BIRDS

type: the Common Whitethroat

COMMON WHITETHROAT	white throat, rufous on wings
COMMON WHITETHROAT, COCK	grey head
LESSER WHITETHROAT	white throat, dark spot behind eye
DARTFORD WARBLER	dark above, pinkish-brown beneath
GARDEN WARBLER	plain brown
BLACKCAP, COCK	black cap
BLACKCAP, HEN	brown cap
WILLOW WARBLER	greenish-brown
CHIFFCHAFF	greenish-brown
WOOD WARBLER	yellow breast, white belly
GOLDCREST	tiny, orange or yellow crest
WREN	rufous brown, short tail
HEDGESPARROW	grey underparts, streaked flanks

Many people quail at the warblers at first, for they have the reputation of being difficult, and it is absolutely necessary to learn their songs. But knowing the songs of birds is half the pleasure of bird watching, so this never seems to me a very real objection. Anyway, almost all our warblers are shy and retiring birds, so that it is much easier to learn their songs first and later get a sight of them if you can. All except one of our true warblers are summer visitors, and most of them sing only from mid-April to mid-July, and it is probably this necessity of relearning the songs each year that puts people off. But how dull it is once there are no new songs to learn! Besides, most of our warblers rank as "small brown birds" that are at first especially tiresome to separate from each other, while most of their songs are quite distinct.

I have chosen the **Common Whitethroat** as the type bird not only because it is so common, but because it is one of the least retiring warblers and has a reasonably distinct plumage. This is the small bird that flies up from the roadside hedges in spring and early summer, utters a scratchy little song and dives back into the bush again. If you follow it and catch sight of it weaving its way through the nettles—this habit has earned it the local name of nettle creeper—you will see not only that it has a white throat, but also the warm rufous brown of its wings, perhaps the white feathers in its tail, and if it is a cock his handsome grey head. As so often, there is another warbler with a white throat, the **Lesser White-throat.** But if your bird has an aerial song flight, it is not a lesser white-throat, which is very retiring and usually sings its flat little rattle in thick cover: a single note repeated, which most people would hardly call a song. Getting a sight of the lesser whitethroat, except in late summer when the young birds are about, usually calls for more stalking than the common whitethroat. When you do glimpse it, look out for the dark patch behind the eye; it is also greyer. The common whitethroat is much the more widespread of the two, breeding throughout the British Isles, whereas the lesser is only at all frequent in the south of England and does not penetrate to Scotland or Ireland.

If you are on the gorsy and heathery heathland of Surrey, Hampshire or Dorset, on one of the few patches that the War Office and the Forestry Commission have left to us unscathed, you may with luck come across our only other warbler with an aerial song flight, which also happens to be the only warbler that regularly stays with us all the year round. This is the very local **Dartford Warbler,** no longer to be found at Dartford, or indeed in any part of Kent, and virtually confined to the three counties just mentioned. To catch it singing from the top of a gorse bush or in the air some time between March and June is your best chance of actually seeing the bird. Your second best chance is when it is feeding young in May or June. At all other times, in my experience, all you see is the rear view of a very dark, rather long-tailed little bird diving into a gorse bush or patch of tall heather. When you do get a proper view of it, it is far the handsomest of our warblers, with its pinkish-brown underparts, dark grey head and pale edging to its graduated tail.

Closely related to the whitethroats and Dartford are two of our larger warblers, the misleadingly named **Garden Warbler,** which has no special liking for gardens, and the aptly named **Blackcap,** whose cock's black cap makes it the easiest of our warblers to identify by sight. Hen and young blackcaps have the cap warm brown, and this too is quite distinctive. The garden warbler, on the other hand, is *the* little brown bird. It is a brown bird and nothing more, no eyestripe, no wing-bar, no white feathers in tail, just brown above and paler brown below. What is more, it dislikes showing itself to the public gaze, and when it does so it usually slips back into cover again before you can be quite sure that it has none of those desirable features that so help to separate one bird from another. So there is nothing for it but to learn the garden warbler's song, that pleasant rippling contralto that goes on and on, in contrast to the silvery and much more broken up soprano of the blackcap. If only they would stick to their proper parts, all would be plain sailing, but alas the blackcap is a great mimic. The song thrush seems to be its favourite model, but I am convinced that some blackcaps do also mimic garden warblers. This lends a kind of Marx brothers' air to the task of learning to separate these two, especially as the blackcap also has a quite loud warbling subsong that sounds a good deal more like the true song of a garden warbler than like its own normal song. Altogether much stalking is needed before you can invariably distinguish these two songsters with confidence, and even then there will still be birds that fox you, as they certainly still fox me.

Habitat is no help with these two warblers, for both like open woodland, bushy heaths and commons and large gardens with shrubberies, especially rhododendrons. Their nests are hard to find, but if you should be lucky, Bruce Campbell has pointed out a useful distinction; the blackcap's nest is fastened to surrounding vegetation by "basket handles." Both are common in England and Wales, but much less so in Scotland, where the blackcap goes farther north. In Ireland the situation is reversed. There is an increasing tendency for odd blackcaps to winter in the British Isles, even in hard winters and as far north as Scotland.

The three leaf warblers are the easiest to separate by song and the hardest to tell by plumage. Indeed people who claim confidently to be able to distinguish between the **Chiffchaff** and the **Willow Warbler** in the field by sight alone should be regarded with suspicion in direct proportion to the confidence they display. It can be done, but only by those entering for their final exam in birdmanship. Both are small greenish-brown birds, among the half-dozen smallest we have, with paler underparts but no marked eyestripe or wing-bar (if you see one with either of these features you are on to a real rarity). The one thing you can be sure of is that a bird with flesh-pink legs is a willow warbler, but since some willow warblers have dark legs the fact that all chiffchaffs have dark legs is of limited value. Additional points are that willow warblers, especially in late summer, have their underparts tinged yellow, while chiffchaffs are inclined to be less greenish above and whiter below.

But when it comes to separating these two by ear, it really is a piece of cake, to use the modern idiom, and fortunately they sing a great deal. The chiffchaff's song is just like its name, a monotonous *chiff-chaff*, or *zilp-zalp* as the Germans have it, all day long. The willow warbler, on the other hand, makes that soft, wistful, diminuendo song that forms the backcloth to every woodland scene from April to June. The willow warbler is one of our commonest birds, and millions must have heard that song without ever having heard of the name of its owner. The two birds have much the same habitat, but chiffchaffs like trees to sing from and do not go so far into Scotland. Willow warblers have no special liking for willows and as they do not mind singing from low bushes they are more widespread on heaths and commons.

Our third breeding leaf warbler, the **Wood Warbler** (wood wren in the old books, just as the willow warbler was miscalled willow wren) is fortunately distinct in several ways. It is appreciably larger, and has a yellow breast, white underparts, a marked yellow eyestripe and yellowish legs. Moreover, it is confined to woods, especially beech woods and the sort of oak wood on the western side of Britain where common redstarts and pied flycatchers also abound. Its song is also a good distinction, or rather songs, for it has two. One is a long quivering trill, quite unlike anything else in the repertoire of British bird song (apart from one tiresome blue tit in my garden which has somehow learned to imitate it!), and the other a plaintive single note, repeated in diminuendo, that is also unlike anything else you will hear in the woods. Hence, like most of its relatives, the wood warbler is usually heard before it is seen. It is widespread, but rather local in some areas, including Ireland and south and east England.

Four other warblers breed in the British Isles, the reed, sedge, marsh and grasshopper warblers. They are discussed in the section on reed-bed birds (p. 82).

Though the **Goldcrest** is not a warbler, it does look rather like a tiny leaf warbler, with two whitish bars and a dark mark on each wing to offset its greenish plumage. It is in fact the smallest British bird, with a tiny needle-like bill. The crest that gives it its name is orange in the cock and yellow in the hen, with a black border on each side. If you should chance to see a goldcrest with a white stripe above the eye and a black stripe through it, then you are on to a **Firecrest,** an uncommon autumn and winter visitor, mainly to the south of England. It is in fact probably less rare than records suggest, since few people scrutinise goldcrests really closely. The song of the goldcrest is as needle-like as its bill, and is well worth learning, as is its normal high-pitched little call-note, which can with practice be distinguished from those of the treecreeper and coal tit, which it often accompanies in winter foraging parties. Though goldcrests are especially fond of conifers and usually nest in them, they are often found, particularly in winter, in completely broad-leaved woods.

The older books call the goldcrest the golden-crested wren, but, like the so-called wood wren and willow wren, it is not at all closely related to the true **Wren,** our second smallest breeding bird. The wren's rufous brown plumage, barred darker in places, its whirring flight and its habit of cocking up its tail are so familiar and distinctive that no more need be said, but its song, curiously enough, is sometimes confused by beginners —I remember it was by me—with that of the hedgesparrow. The wren's song, however, is much higher-pitched and more vigorous than the flat, rather tuneless little ditty of the hedgesparrow. No British bird is more ubiquitous than the wren, which may be found almost anywhere from the inner suburbs of cities to high mountain glens and gullies and remote marine islands.

The **Hedgesparrow** is neither a warbler, though it looks like one, nor a sparrow, as a glance at its thin bill soon shows. It is fashionable nowadays to abandon this well-established name, which was good enough for Shakespeare, in favour of the old folk-name "dunnock," but personally, out of sheer conservatism, I prefer to go on calling it a hedgesparrow. Even apart from its bill, the hedgesparrow is easily told from the house sparrow by its grey underparts and streaked flanks. It also behaves quite differently, shuffling about in hedge bottoms, pottering among flower-beds and rarely leaving the ground except to fly up and utter its dull little warbling song. It also has a shrill *tseeep* note that is often tantalising, for its owner is so retiring that hopes are often raised of something more interesting nearby. In habitat the hedgesparrow is almost as ubiquitous as the wren.

THE TITS

type: the Blue Tit

BLUE TIT	blue and yellow
GREAT TIT	large, black head with white cheeks, black bib on yellow underparts
COAL TIT	black cap, pure white patch on nape
MARSH TIT	black cap
WILLOW TIT	black cap
CRESTED TIT	black and white crest
LONG-TAILED TIT	long tail

Eight species of tit breed in the British Isles, all spending the whole year with us; five of them are common, one local and two rare. The great and blue tits are regular members of the garden association of birds, the coal tit a frequent one, and the marsh and long-tailed tits visitors to the more countrified gardens. Apart from the two long-tailed members of the group, the tits can be told by their dumpy forms, their short sharp thin bills and their intense activity, constantly searching for food. All except the marsh and willow tits are easy to identify by sight, but at first less so by sound, for they have such a wide range of notes and the cries of young tits are especially hard to disentangle. In autumn and winter tits of different species band together in parties, often accompanied by such hangers on as treecreepers, nuthatches, goldcrests and in late summer also leaf warblers, and forage through the woods.

The **Blue Tit** is our commonest tit, found in gardens, town parks and squares and almost every kind of wooded country, and in winter also in such treeless places as the reed-beds on our east coast marshes. It is easy to recognise, for it is our bluest wild bird, its head, wings and tail being bright blue, offset by yellow underparts, yellowish-green mantle, white cheeks and a white patch on the nape of the neck. There is really nothing you can confuse it with, while its typical call note and song, once learnt, are also among the most distinctive tit cries.

The **Great Tit** is also an easy one, and another town dweller. To start with, it is much the largest of our tits, being nearly the size of a sparrow where the blue tit is little bigger than a willow warbler. Then it has boldly marked plumage, especially the black bib down the centre of its primrose yellow underparts and the white cheeks on its black head. Young birds are much yellower all over, especially on the white parts, and are also brownish on the black parts. The great tit has a most extensive vocabulary, including some notes apparently mimicked from other tits. One of its most frequent calls, *pink pink*, is remarkably like a chaffinch, but with a more echoing quality, while even its highly characteristic song, the so-called saw-sharpening or *teacher teacher* note has a counterpart in the coal tit's *ticha ticha*. I usually reckon that any particularly puzzling call heard in woodland will eventually prove to be made by a great tit. Patient learning is therefore the order of the day with the great tit, and even then, when you have learned the range of variation in your local birds you may have to start all over again in another district.

The **Coal Tit** is our smallest tit and has a simple plumage pattern, just plain olive-grey above and buff beneath, with black crown and throat and white cheeks and nape. In fact, the white patch on the nape is what you look for; no other small tit has a white nape with a black crown. Young coal tits have this patch yellowish, and could then possibly be confused with great tits, which also have yellowish nape patches and black crowns, but of course are much larger. The coal tit's vocabulary is rather like the great tit's in miniature, but it also has a thin high-pitched note not unlike the goldcrest's. Coal tits are especially fond of coniferous trees, and may be the commonest tits in pine or spruce plantations, but they also frequent broad-leaved woodlands. However, if you have a pine or even a larch in your garden, you will find that sooner or later the local coal tits, if any, will gravitate to it.

The **Marsh Tit** and the **Willow Tit** present the only real identification problem among the British tits. They are such a problem indeed that it was not until the turn of the century that anybody realised that there are in fact these two distinct species in Britain, and for years after that veteran ornithologists would stoutly maintain that the whole idea was a mare's nest. They are both only slightly larger than a coal tit, with similar brownish plumage, paler beneath and on the cheeks, and black on the crown and chin. They lack, however, the coal tit's white nape patch and double white wing-bar. The marsh and willow tits are thus easy enough to tell from all other tits; it is in separating them from each other that A-level bird-watching standards are needed. For the only two visual field characters available are a pale patch on the willow tit's wing that the marsh lacks (but in some willow tits this patch is rather faint), and the glossy black cap of the adult (but not the juvenile) marsh tit compared with the dull sooty black cap of the willow. If this were all we had to go on, we might as well pack up and go home, unless we happened to be carrying not only a gun but an official licence to shoot protected birds.

Luckily there are in fact several excellent differences between the voices of the two species. The marsh tit makes two very characteristic calls that the willow never does; a scolding *chickabee-bee-bee-bee* and a spluttering *pitch-ü-ü*. The willow, on the other hand, has a very harsh grating *tchay* or *aig* note which is absolutely diagnostic once you know it, though you must first learn to distinguish it from a somewhat similar but much less nasal note of the marsh tit. The willow tit also has a thin *eez-eez-eez* note which is quite distinct from the high-pitched *si-si* common to most other tits. The songs of the two birds, both heard mainly in the first half of the year, are also quite different. The marsh has a rather hard flat *schip schip schip* call for its song, but the willow is the only true songster among the tits. Like the wood warbler it has two songs, one the repetition of a single, quite melodious *piu* (curiously enough not unlike the wood warbler's), the other a full-blooded, almost canary-like warbling song, which unfortunately is much less often heard. There is thus much less difficulty with marsh and willow tits if only they will give tongue, and you rarely have to wait long for a marsh tit to make some sort of sound. Willow tits, in my experience, are more silent.

Both these tits frequent the same type of wooded and bushy country, the marsh tit not being especially fond of marshes nor the willow tit of willows. If anything, the willow tit prefers damper woods, especially where it can excavate its own nest holes in rotten alders or other trees. A black-capped tit found actually excavating its own nest hole is much more likely to be a willow than a marsh. Over most of the south of England and Wales the marsh tit is much the commoner of the two, but in the north of both countries it becomes less common, so that the chances of a black-capped tit being a willow are higher. In Scotland the marsh tit is only found in the extreme south, in Berwickshire, but the willow is thinly scattered northwards over the Lowlands, and even more thinly in the Highlands. One last word of warning: both marsh and willow tits could be confused with the occasional wintering cock blackcap, which will sometimes visit a bird table. A blackcap, however, is appreciably larger, great tit-size, and greyer, with a longer bill and no black chin.

Our only other short-tailed tit is the attractive little **Crested Tit,** rather like a coal tit with a prominent black and white crest, which is confined to the pinewoods of Strathspey and adjacent valleys in the Highlands of Scotland. In these woods it often flocks with coal tits, from which it also differs in having no wing-bars and in its characteristic short trill, which with the usual high-pitched *si si* contact note seems to comprise its entire vocabulary.

Much the commoner of our two tits with long tails is the **Long-tailed Tit** itself, and indeed its fantastic tail, longer than its whole body, is all that is needed to identify this otherwise tiny woodland bird, with its black, white and pink plumage and very short bill. Strings of long-tailed tits can often be seen passing from tree to tree with their weak, dipping flight. It is useful, however, to learn their spluttering call note and the high-pitched cries that usually accompany it. In country districts, where it is widespread, the long-tailed tit used to be called the bottle tit, from the oval shape of its domed nest, which is carefully woven of moss, cobwebs and lichens and lined with anything up to 2,000 feathers.

For our other tit with a long tail, the bearded tit, see under reed-bed birds on page 82.

Larks, Pipits, Wagtails

The chief reason for linking these three fairly distinct groups of insecteaters together is that the pipits look more like larks, but are in fact more closely related to the wagtails. Both larks and pipits fall neatly into the category of tiresome small brown birds, but the wagtails are distinctive with their long tails and more varied and attractive plumage.

THE LARKS

type: the Skylark

SKYLARK   plain brown, prominent crest
WOODLARK   plain brown, less prominent crest, short tail

The **Skylark** is the largest of the whole group, and fortunately has one very easy field character, familiar at least to poets, its aerial song flight. Apart from the woodlark, it is the only British bird that regularly hovers almost out of sight while singing, and its song is both distinctive and easily learned. It will also sometimes sing from the ground or even from a perch. Seen on the ground, the skylark is a rather slim, fairly large, small bird (if the paradox may be excused), with a thin sharp insect-eating bill, despite the fact that half its food consists of seeds and other vegetable matter. Apart from a few white feathers in the tail, its brown plumage is relieved only by some darker streaks, but it does have a crest, which can be conspicuous. When they fly skylarks usually make a kind of liquid *chirrup*, which is a useful guide when you can see no colour in the murk of a winter's afternoon. In autumn and winter skylarks regularly go in flocks, often of considerable size, and one of the first signs of hard weather on the Continent is the sight of westward-flying skylarks over the eastern half of England. Incidentally the term "skylarking" derives from the frequency with which skylarks chase each other in the flocks, especially just before they break up in the spring.

The skylark is common throughout the British Isles, and is especially welcome over downland, sand dunes, shingle tracts and other places which have few song birds because there are no trees or bushes for them to sing from, but the **Woodlark** is much more local. Though it has increased in recent years, the woodlark is still largely confined to the southern half of England and Wales, and except in East Anglia is especially local north of the Thames. Woodlark territory is usually heathy and bushy, with scattered trees, but there are extensive tracts of country of this sort that have no woodlarks. Its song, which connoisseurs of bird song esteem as even sweeter and more melodious than the skylark's, is also usually delivered on the wing. It is often heard at night and is probably the cause of more false alarms about nightingales than the song of any other British bird. The woodlark's call-note *tit-looeet* and its much shorter tail, which often gives it an almost bat-like appearance, both readily distinguish it from the appreciably larger skylark. But beware young skylarks in late summer and autumn, when their tails are noticeably shorter than their parents' but nevertheless still longer than a woodlark's. At close range you can also see that the woodlark has a dark brown and white mark on the leading edge of the wing, buff eyestripes meeting at the back of the head, and a tail with a white tip but without the skylark's white feathers. Though the woodlark does also have a crest, it is less often obvious than the skylark's.

Our only other native lark, if such a term can be applied to a regular winter visitor, is the shore lark, discussed with other birds of the saltmarsh and sea-wall on page 88.

THE PIPITS

type: the Meadow Pipit

MEADOW PIPIT	white outer tail feathers, song flight starts from ground
TREE PIPIT	white outer tail feathers, song flight starts from tree
ROCK PIPIT	greyer, greyish outer tail feathers, song flight starts from ground or rock

Pipits, wrote the late T. A. Coward, perhaps the finest field naturalist of the last generation, are almost hopeless in the field and not much better in the hand. Though he was probably thinking mainly of the rarer pipits that are only vagrants to our shores, his lament also partly reflects an age before skill in the field identification had reached modern heights. Three species of pipit breed in the British Isles. All are small brown birds with streaked breasts, lark-like in their plumage but more wagtail-like in their stance, but once you have learned their voices you should have little difficulty with them.

The **Meadow Pipit** is much the commonest; indeed in the north and west of Britain it may well be the most numerous bird, for it breeds all over the hills and moors. The meadow pipit is with us all the year round, but the **Tree Pipit** is only a summer visitor, and is commoner in the south than in the north. In plumage both resemble miniature song thrushes, but their breasts are streaked instead of spotted, and they have white outer tail feathers. Although the meadow pipit has a long hind claw and the tree pipit a short one, this can only be seen at very close range; and although the tree pipit is slightly larger and has pinker legs, immature meadow pipits also have pinker legs than the adults. I do not therefore recommend anybody to try and separate the two species by sight alone. Luckily their voices are quite different. The meadow pipit has a shrill *pheet* call note, usually uttered three times over, while the tree pipit makes a louder and harsher *teez*. The two songs are more similar, but the tree pipit usually has a terminal flourish *see-er see-er see-er* (though some tiresome birds are too lazy to finish their song), which can often be heard at a greater distance than the rest of the song. Both have a special aerial song flight, but whereas the meadow pipit usually starts from and finishes on the ground, the tree pipit nearly always both starts and finishes from a tree, bush or other elevated perch. This is one reason why the meadow pipit is the commoner of the two, for there are vast areas of moorland which provide no song posts for the tree pipit. In winter meadow pipits visit both freshwater margins and seashores.

Our third pipit, the **Rock Pipit,** is much more easily identified. To start with, except for a few vagrants inland in the autumn, it almost always stays within sight of the sea, on rocky coasts in the breeding season and along muddy ones as well at other times. It is slightly larger and greyer than the two others, with greyish instead of white outer tail feathers. Its call note *phist* is less high-pitched than the meadow pipit's and is usually uttered singly, but its song is more similar and is also delivered in a flight starting from and finishing on either the ground or a rock.

THE WAGTAILS

type: the Pied Wagtail

PIED WAGTAIL	black, white and grey
GREY WAGTAIL	grey above, yellow below
GREY WAGTAIL, COCK	black on throat
YELLOW WAGTAIL	shorter tail; yellow on face and underparts, very bright cock.

Wagtails as a group are easy, for they have a characteristic dipping flight and long tails, which they wag up and down when excited. The commonest of the three is the **Pied Wagtail;** its old name of water wagtail is not a very good one, for it is no more attracted to water than the other two, and in the breeding season rather less so. In plumage the pied wagtail is black, white and grey, the amount of black decreasing progressively from adult cock to adult hen down to immatures and juveniles. Young birds in their first plumage are almost entirely grey and are then liable to be confused with the white wagtail, the Continental form of our pied (actually it would be less insular to say that the pied is the British form of the white). A good many white wagtails from Iceland pass through the British Isles on migration every year, especially on the west coast, and in spring the cocks at least are not too difficult to tell. One constant difference between the two forms is that the pied has a dark rump and the white a grey one, but this is not always easy to see, even at quite close range. Easiest to distinguish are the cock pied, which is black on both head and back, and the cock white with black head and grey back. In the autumn, however, there are numerous grey-backed young pieds to confuse the issue. A pied-type wagtail with grey head as well as back but no juvenile-type bib is certainly a white; one with a black or blackish back is certainly a pied.

The pied wagtail's call note *tschizzick* often enables you to pick it out at a distance or in poor light from the two other wagtails. Of these, the **Grey Wagtail** has a longer tail than the pied, but the **Yellow Wagtail** is smaller and has a shorter tail. Because some pied wagtails are grey and all grey wagtails are partly yellow, there is a good deal of semantic confusion between the three wagtails, and in particular between the grey and the yellow. This is reflected most often in the reports of yellow wagtails seen in winter, when all our yellow wagtails are in Africa, and which obviously refer to greys. In fact the chief difference between the two, apart from size and tail length, is the greyness of the grey wagtail's upperparts, while the cock yellow wagtail can look an almost completely yellow bird.

The general pattern of the grey wagtail's plumage is grey above and yellow below, paler on the breast than under the tail, but in spring and summer the cock has a handsome black gorget on his throat. Juvenile grey wagtails look very grey and are less yellow beneath, but always have enough yellow under their tails to separate them from young pieds. The grey wagtail's call note is not unlike the pied's, but is louder and more metallic and often consists of a single note.

The grey wagtail is rarely seen away from water at any time of year. In the breeding season it is especially a bird of the hill streams of northern and western Britain, but in recent years it has colonised many lowland rivers as well, particularly where a mill-race or an artificial waterfall creates a small patch of the fast running water it really likes. In autumn and winter, when many grey wagtails turn up on rivers and brooks in parts of the country where they do not breed, slower running water is acceptable. During and just after the war grey wagtails used quite often to frequent the static water tanks that were part of London's fire defences. The yellow wagtail, on the other hand, does not seek running water in the breeding season, but prefers marshy meadows of various kinds, and in some districts may even nest in quite dry habitats, such as heathland and farm-land. Mainly a southern and eastern bird, it is almost absent from south-west England and much of Wales and Scotland, and has recently become extinct in Ireland.

With its brilliant yellow head and underparts, the cock yellow wagtail vies with the cock yellowhammer for the title of our yellowest bird; hens and young birds are also yellow or yellowish beneath, with greenish-brown upperparts. The blue-headed wagtail is an uncommon migrant, most often seen on the east side of Britain; cocks have a blue-grey head with a white eyestripe, but the hens are indistinguishable in the field from hen yellow wagtails. The blue-headed wagtail does occasionally breed in eastern England, and though hybridisation with the yellow wagtail is not easy to prove, owing to the similarity of the hens, it probably does occur and produces the aberrant birds that have grey heads with or without white eyestripes which are sometimes found among colonies of yellow wagtails, especially in south-east England. The call note of the yellow wagtail, *tsweep*, recalls that of the reed bunting.

Shrikes and Flycatchers

The only justification for grouping the shrikes and flycatchers together is that they share the habit of flying out from a perch to catch winged insects and back again. A good many other birds, including starlings, house sparrows, whinchats and especially leaf warblers, may be seen chasing after flies or even hovering to catch them, but only shrikes and flycatchers make a living out of sitting on a perch and waiting for insects to fly by. All our breeding species are summer visitors only.

THE SHRIKES

type: the Red-backed Shrike

RED-BACKED SHRIKE, COCK	blue-grey and rufous
RED-BACKED SHRIKE, HEN	brown
GREAT GREY SHRIKE	grey, black and white

The shrikes are half-way to the birds of prey in habit, though not at all closely related to them. They have slightly hooked beaks, and prey on small mammals and birds, especially nestlings, as well as on bees, beetles and other insects. The fruits of their hunting can often be seen impaled in " larders " on thorn bushes, or even on barbed wire if no suitable bush is available. These larders are used especially when they are feeding their young and demand for food outstrips the supply.

The **Red-backed Shrike,** our only breeding shrike, is a summer visitor, arriving in early May, rather later than most of our summer migrants. Its habit is to perch in prominent places on the lookout, but it is a very watchful bird, and often the first you know of its presence is when it flies off, showing the conspicuous large white patches on either side of the base of its tail. The cock is most handsome, resembling (for it is no bigger than a skylark) a miniature kestrel in plumage: rufous brown above with blue-grey head and rump, black stripe through the eye, white throat and creamy underparts. Hen and young birds are plain brown above, with crescent-shaped marks on their paler underparts. Red-backed shrikes frequent heaths, commons and other places with thick bushes and dense scrub, and nowadays are scarce and local except in Surrey and the coastal counties from Norfolk to South Devon.

As our red-backed shrikes depart to winter in Africa, very much smaller numbers of the **Great Grey Shrike** arrive from northern Europe to spend the winter here. This is much larger, blackbird-size, and frequents the same type of habitat, also perching prominently on thorn and other bushes on the lookout for its larger prey. It has even been known occasionally to kill birds of its own size, such as blackbirds and thrushes. Its plumage is grey, with black on the wings and longish tail, a broad black eyestripe, and white underparts, wing-bar and sides of the tail. Though a great grey shrike may turn up anywhere, most bird watchers count themselves lucky if they see one in the course of five or ten years: I have seen five, in four counties, in thirty-five years' bird watching, and one of those was a bird that returned to a Chiltern common for two years running, a not infrequent habit.

Another shrike, formerly thought to be a great rarity but seen more often in recent years, is the **Woodchat** from the Mediterranean. It is the size of a red-backed shrike, but has conspicuously black and white plumage with a chestnut crown, and is most likely to turn up in the southern counties in spring.

THE FLYCATCHERS

type: the Spotted Flycatcher

SPOTTED FLYCATCHER   plain grey-brown
PIED FLYCATCHER   black and white

With the **Spotted Flycatcher** we are back in the realms of the small brown bird, for the adults are little bigger than a whitethroat and have nothing to relieve their plain dull grey-brown plumage and paler underparts but a few dark streaks on the head and breast. Only the young birds have the spotted appearance that gives the bird its somewhat misleading name. The normal call note of the spotted flycatcher is remarkably like the hunger cry of a young robin just out of the nest, while its song is one of the most curious of any British bird. It is so squeaky and spasmodic that it is easy to fancy you are hearing several different birds at once, and not to realise for some time that you are in fact listening to what passes for song in the spotted flycatcher. The bird is well distributed throughout the British Isles, and is one of our few summer visitors that will breed in parks and quite small gardens in the middle of towns. It often builds its nest in a creeper against a house wall, and will also use an open, robin-type nestbox.

The **Pied Flycatcher** is much more appropriately named, for the cock is a very black and white bird, indeed the only black and white British bird that is so small, for it is no bigger than a goldfinch. Hens and juveniles are browner and more like a spotted flycatcher, from which they can always be told by their white underparts and outer tail feathers, and especially by their white wing-bars. Though the pied flycatcher breeds almost exclusively on the west side of Britain, especially from the Forest of Dean to the Solway, but also in the North York Moors in the east, it not infrequently turns up elsewhere on migration, even in the middle of London. The pied flycatcher always nests in holes and can readily be induced to use a tit-type nestbox. Its flycatching habits differ slightly from the spotted, for it nearly always returns to a different perch from the one it started at.

A rare flycatcher visitor is the **Red-breasted Flycatcher** from Central Europe. Adult cocks with the robin-like red breast are extremely rare, but hens and especially immatures are more frequent, particularly along the east coast in autumn, and can then be picked out by the prominent white patches at the base of the tail, which the bird frequently flicks up to reveal them. The red-breasted is slightly smaller than the pied flycatcher, and also lacks its white wing-bars.

THE AERIAL FEEDERS: SWALLOW, MARTINS, SWIFT, NIGHTJAR

type: the Swallow

SWALLOW	long forked tail, blue-black above, chestnut forehead and throat
HOUSE MARTIN	white rump, blue-black above
SAND MARTIN	brown above
SWIFT	all black
NIGHTJAR	larger, brown, nocturnal

Five of our breeding birds specialise in feeding on flying insects caught on the wing and do in fact spend much of their lives in the air. These are the swallow, the two martins, the swift and the nightjar. All are summer visitors, because there are not enough insects on the wing here in the winter to sustain them. The swallow and the two martins, collectively known as hirundines, are closely related to each other and belong to the great assemblage of song birds, but the swift and the nightjar belong to two quite different orders of birds, and have evolved a likeness to the hirundines because of the similarity of their way of life. Hirundines and swifts often flock together, especially over lakes and rivers.

The **Swallow** is one of the most familiar British birds, but most of the general public hardly realise that it needs to be distinguished from the martins and the swift. In fact, of course, you can readily tell the adults from all three by their long tail streamers, though young swallows with their shorter tails can be confused with martins if no plumage details can be seen. Swallows are all blue-black above, with a reddish-chestnut forehead and throat, a blue-black breast-band and underparts that vary in colour from creamy-buff to a quite deep buffish-chestnut. But in the air and against the light it is their long pointed wings and long forked tails that separate them from the other three.

The **House Martin** is easily told by the white rump that is the only break in its otherwise uniform pattern of blue-black above and white below; young birds are brownish on the blue-black parts. It is surprising, however, how often a house martin will fly in such a way that this key recognition feature is hidden from the watcher. Then you must rely on its dumpier shape, with shorter wings and tail, to separate it from the swallow, as well as on learning its call note, which is flatter and more spluttering than the swallow's melodious twitter.

Under such circumstances, when the bird is above you and against the light, the reedy voice of the **Sand Martin** is also the best means of telling the two martins apart. When light permits, its sandy brown upperparts with no white rump, and the brown breast-band on its otherwise white underparts, separate it even more quickly.

The **Swift** has a most distinctive outline, with much longer wings and shorter tail than any of the hirundines. Its plumage is simple enough: sooty black all over, with a pale patch under the chin that you can only see at close range. Swifts are the birds that fly screaming "round the houses" on summer evenings. They are with us for a much shorter time than the hirundines, which may be seen from the end of March till late October. Swifts on the other hand rarely arrive before the very end of April and are almost all off again before August is out.

The three hirundines and the swift all have quite different nesting arrangements. The most conspicuous nests, made of mud and affixed under the eaves of houses are those of the house martin. Swallows prefer to nest on a ledge or beam inside a barn or shed; boathouses on the Thames and other rivers are also favourite sites. Their nests are open at the top, whereas the house martin's has only a small hole at the side for the bird to get in. Swifts nest in holes and crevices in walls and buildings, and especially on the rafters of old houses with open eaves, but they make next to no nest, and lay their two or three white eggs in a shallow saucer made of feathers and other fragments they find floating in the air, stuck together with a glue made of their saliva. The colonial sand martin has the most distinctive nesting arrangements of the four, for it burrows into the sides of sand and gravel pits, or the sandy banks of north-country rivers.

All these four birds are common and widely distributed throughout the country, but one rare visitor needs to be briefly mentioned, the **Alpine**

Swift, which looks like a giant swift-shaped sand martin. This large brown swift is easily told by its white underparts, crossed by a brown breast-band, but you will be very lucky indeed to see one.

The **Nightjar** is the fifth of our native specialised aerial feeders and the only nocturnal one. Most people's introduction to the nightjar is the sound of its extraordinary churring "song" as it sits across a branch in the dusk—it is little use listening for nightjars till about forty minutes after sunset. Sometimes the churring, which resembles a distant two-stroke motor bike, appears to change pitch; this is when the bird turns its head in another direction. If you stalk the churring noise, you may eventually see a shadowy long-tailed and long-winged shape fly away, making sudden darts to snap up moths or beetles, and perhaps also hear the curious whip-like noise it makes by clapping its wings together. A sight of a nightjar by day is usually a sheer accident as you walk over one of the heathy, gorsy or brackeny places it frequents. Then you will see that the rather hawk-like long-winged shape is mottled brown all over, though the male also has three white spots on the outer wing feathers and white tips to its outer tail feathers. You can, of course, at once tell it from a hawk by its not having a hooked beak, and from the young cuckoo by its having no pale patch on its nape. The nightjar is one of the latest arrivals among our summer visitors, rarely here before mid-May and away again in early September. It is found all over the British Isles in woods and on heaths and moors.

Medium-Sized Insect-Eaters

THRUSHES AND STARLINGS

type: the Song Thrush

SONG THRUSH	brown, dark spots on pale breast
MISTLE THRUSH	larger, greyer, white tips to outer tail feathers
REDWING	pale eyestripe, reddish-chestnut flanks
FIELDFARE	blue-grey head and rump, chestnut back
BLACKBIRD, COCK	all black, yellow bill, long tail

BLACKBIRD, HEN	dark brown, speckled breast
RING OUZEL, COCK	black, white throat
RING OUZEL, HEN	brownish-black, white throat
STARLING	blackish, iridescent in summer, pale spots in winter; short tail

The thrushes are a well-defined and easily recognisable group of fairly stocky birds, with brown or black plumage and thickish bills that are intermediate between the thin warbler type and the stout finch type. The blackbird, song thrush and mistle thrush, together with the superficially similar but unrelated starling, are familiar garden birds that penetrate to parks and gardens even in the middle of cities; all four are with us all the year round. Though the prime food of both thrushes and starlings is insects, earthworms and other small invertebrates, the thrushes especially do rely heavily on both wild and domesticated fruits in summer. Though gardeners do not then regard them as their friends, the good they do at other times of year should be remembered.

The **Song Thrush** is one of the most familiar of all our native birds, for its loud clear repetitive song brings it constantly to our attention. It was Robert Browning who wrote, " That's the wise thrush; he sings each song twice over," but actually it repeats the individual notes or phrases, not whole song patterns. Occasionally these repeated notes sound remarkably like the calls of other birds: a day or two before I wrote these words I heard an Oxfordshire song thrush give a remarkable imitation of the curlew. The alarm chatter of the song thrush is similar to, but flatter than, the better known chuckling note of the blackbird.

The song thrush's plumage is simple enough, with olive-brown upperparts and dark spots on its creamy underparts. At first glance the larger, greyer-brown **Mistle Thrush** has just the same plumage, but a closer look will show that its spots are actually larger and more numerous. When it takes wing the mistle is easy to tell, for the white patches under its wings flash on and off as it flies past, while the whitish tips to the outer tail feathers are also conspicuous as it flies away. Young song and mistle thrushes can both be readily told from their parents by the pale specklings on their backs.

The song thrush has a fairly direct flight, but the mistle's is much heavier, the wings appearing to pause in the closed position, though there is no woodpecker-like undulation. Mistles usually make a churring call note as they fly, best reproduced by drawing a hard object along the teeth of a comb (if you don't value your comb!). Their loud ringing song is quite distinct from the song thrush's, with no repetition, and sounds rather like what might happen if a song thrush tried to sing a blackbird's song. Indeed, when distance mellows it, even experienced bird watchers can mistake a mistle thrush's song for a blackbird's. Both song and mistle thrushes flock together on migration, but at other times are rather solitary birds, except that mistles tend to go in small family parties in summer, often on downs or moorland where they do not breed.

Each October huge flocks of **Redwings** and **Fieldfares** cross the North Sea to spend the winter with us, the redwing being the northern counterpart of the song thrush and the fieldfare of the mistle thrush. Redwings are actually slightly smaller and darker than song thrushes, and can readily be told from them by the prominent pale eyestripes as well as by the chestnut-red on their flanks that gives them their English name. Both redwings and fieldfares are rather shy birds and rarely come to smaller gardens except in hard weather, but they are easy enough to watch when feeding in grassy fields or on their favourite hawthorns. Since the winter light is often poor, it is also useful to learn their call notes. The redwing's high-pitched *seee-ih* needs a little practice, for the blackbird and song thrush both have rather similar notes. The blackbird's *seeeep* is more vibrant, and the song thrush's *seep* shorter and less often heard than its softer call note *sipp*. It is most important to learn to distinguish between these three call notes before trying to identify, as many people do with much too great confidence, flocks of redwings flying over at night. In October and November, when these nocturnal cries can most frequently be heard, huge flocks of blackbirds and song thrushes are also arriving here from the Continent.

The redwing also has a communal warbling song, often heard just before the migrating flocks return to Scandinavia, and a clear fluty, but rather staccato true song, a single note repeated three times. This is not often heard in Britain except in snatches amid the communal warble, but it is worth keeping an ear alert for it in the north-western Scottish Highlands from April to June, for the redwing is known to have bred there more than a dozen times in the past thirty-five years, and has probably done so many more times unobserved.

The fieldfare is like the mistle thrush both in size and in its heavy flight that shows up the white patches under its wings, but its plumage is very different. It is in fact easily our handsomest thrush, with its blue-grey head and rump, chestnut back, black tail and deep buff underparts with well-spotted breast. The grey rump shows up well in flight. Its chuckling call note *chack chack* is also very distinctive; with its aid you can identify fieldfares flying almost out of sight or against the light with great confidence. The fieldfare has never been satisfactorily proved to breed in the British Isles, but since it does nest in Europe as far south as Switzerland and Austria, it may well do so one day.

Turning now from our four brown thrushes to our two black ones, we must first take note that only the cocks of these are really black, the hens and young birds being confusable with the brown group. The cock **Blackbird** is the smallest of our half-dozen all-black birds (the cock black redstart being disqualified by its fiery tail and white wing patches) and is indeed coal black all over, with a fine orange-yellow bill. Its long tail, which it often cocks up on alighting, gives it quite a different shape from the starling, which in poor light also looks all black, and it hops where the starling usually runs. Hen and young blackbirds are dark brown and thrush-like, but are larger than song thrushes, have longer tails, and breasts less clearly marked with distinct dark spots. Incidentally the frequent reports of alleged blackbird-thrush pairings nearly always turn out to be perfectly ordinary pairs of blackbirds, seen by somebody who did not realise how different from her mate the hen blackbird is. Juvenile black-birds also look more rufous than both thrushes and their own mothers. Partially white blackbirds are by no means rare, though I have never seen a complete albino.

The blackbird's mellow, fluty contralto song is neither repetitive like the song thrush's nor loud and challenging like the mistle's, and it is heard for a shorter period of the year, mid-February to late July, compared with November to July for the song thrush and January to June for the mistle. The most often heard call note of the blackbird is its loud *chook chook*, representing mild alarm, which degenerates when the bird is really alarmed into the loud chattering scream which I have already compared to the corresponding cry of the song thrush. Before going to roost black-birds often utter a continuous and sometimes highly irritating *pink pink*, and this note is also used when they are mobbing an owl or other predator. Indeed, one of the best ways of locating an owl's daytime roost is to follow up blackbirds "pinking."

The nests of the blackbird and the song and mistle thrushes are among the best-known nests of British birds, partly because they are large, bulky structures anyway, partly because they nest early in the spring when few leaves are on the trees, and partly because they are found in parks, gardens, roadside hedges and other conspicuous places. You can tell the song thrush's from the other two even before the eggs appear, by the lack of any inner lining of dried grasses on its mud cup. The eggs of the three are quite distinct: blackbird's greeny-blue with brown specklings; song thrush's clear blue with black spots; and mistle's white with brown spots.

In hill districts, and sometimes surprisingly near busy mill towns in the Yorkshire and Lancashire Pennines, another kind of blackbird, the **Ring Ouzel**, is not uncommon. The cock is easily told by the conspicuous white shirt-front offsetting his otherwise dark brownish-black plumage. Hens and winter cocks are browner with grey flecks and a duller white gorget, while juveniles are greyer with a speckled breast. Just occasionally a partially albino adult blackbird will turn up with a white breast like a ring ouzel, and sometimes young blackbirds show a pale band on the breast. Then it is useful to have other ways of separating them from ring ouzels, such as voice, the paler wings of the ring ouzel, and the facts that ring ouzels are summer visitors highly unlikely to be seen here from mid-October to mid-March, and do not breed at all in the south-eastern half of England. Genuine ring ouzels do, however, sometimes turn up in the south-east on migration, and contrariwise there are plenty of blackbirds in the hill districts where ring ouzels are most frequent. The ring ouzel's chief call notes are a loud clear pipe, of which its song is merely an elaboration, and a hard *tac tac tac*, the equivalent of the blackbird's *chook chook*, which may similarly run into a harsher chattering note.

The **Starling** is the only other bird at all likely to be confounded with a blackbird, and then only by those who have had a very inadequate view of it. For the starling is not all black, but spangled with whitish spots and shot with iridescent green and purple tints, the spotting being more prominent in winter and the iridescence in spring and summer, while its bill is yellow in spring and summer only. In flight the short-tailed, almost triangular appearance of the starling quickly separates it from the long-tailed blackbird, and its hurrying, walking gait, jabbing its beak into the turf at random, contrasts strongly with the blackbird's more leisurely hops and quizzical pauses when it listens before digging for its worm. Another point is that though blackbirds do flock together, especially at night, they never fly around, like the starling, in immense flocks during daylight. Nesting habits too are quite different, for the starling lays its pale blue unspotted eggs in a hole in a tree, cliff or building.

Young starlings in their first few weeks out of the nest look quite different from their parents, being dull mousy brown all over with a paler throat, but even then they can be told from the same-sized song thrush by having no black spots on the breast. The hunger screams of young starlings, both in and out of the nest, are among the most familiar bird sounds of both town and country from mid-May to mid-June. The old birds make a wide range of nondescript sounds; being great mimics they pick up almost anything from a vacuum-cleaner to a curlew or a boy whistling, and their song, often delivered in chorus, sounds more like a general conversation or, as Kenneth Williamson has well described it, a "one-man band" than a bird singing. Starlings are highly gregarious at all times, and as is well known come in vast numbers to roost on buildings in the middle of London and many of our other cities.

One of our more conspicuous rarities is closely related to the starling and occasionally turns up in starling flocks: the **Rosy Pastor** or rosy starling. The adults are easily identified, for their plumage is markedly pink and black, the black parts being the crested head, wings and tail. Unfortunately, however, most of the rosy pastors that do reach our shores are immatures, which differ from the mouse-brown juvenile starling only in their paler plumage and pink legs.

Special Habitat Groups

TREE CREEPERS AND PECKERS

type: the Pied Woodpecker

GREEN WOODPECKER	large, green, red crown, yellow rump
PIED WOODPECKER	medium, black and white, red under tail
PIED WOODPECKER, MALE	red nape
BARRED WOODPECKER	small, black and white
BARRED WOODPECKER, MALE	red crown
WRYNECK	small, grey-brown
TREECREEPER	smaller, brown, curved bill
NUTHATCH	small, blue-grey above, buff and chestnut below

Certain birds have especially adapted themselves to running up and down trees and feeding on the insect life of the bark and timber. The woodpeckers are the largest and most important of these among British birds, but two small song birds, the treecreeper and the nuthatch have, as it were, qualified as honorary woodpeckers. The true woodpeckers all have a markedly dipping flight, and inhabit wooded and park-like country.

The **Green Woodpecker** is the largest (jackdaw-size) and most gaudily coloured of our four native woodpeckers. Indeed, it is so colourful, with green plumage, red top-knot, yellow rump, and in the male also a moustachial stripe, that many people, on first seeing one on their lawn, and not realising that woodpeckers often feed on the ground as well as in trees, think they must have seen some escaped tropical cage bird—I have even heard a toucan suggested! The green woodpecker often announces its presence with its loud yelping or "yaffling" cry. It is common in southern and midland England and in Wales, but much more local north of the Humber. Though it is now spreading into southern Scotland, the green woodpecker still ranks as a rare bird north of the Border, and in Ireland it has not been seen for over a hundred years.

Second in size comes the **Pied Woodpecker,** now the most widespread of the four. Most of the books still call it the great spotted woodpecker, but as this name is rather misleading—the bird is neither spotted nor particularly great—I prefer the name pied woodpecker, which is descriptive and has been strongly advocated by Max Nicholson, among others. This woodpecker is no bigger than a song thrush, and its plumage is all black and white, except for some red under the tail; males also have a red nape and juveniles a red crown. If size is not enough to separate the pied from the sparrow-sized barred woodpecker, then its prominent white wing patches should settle the matter. The main call of the pied woodpecker is a sharp *tchick*, but when excited it can make a very mistle thrush-like churring sound. It also makes, mechanically on dead branches, a curious resonant sound known as drumming. This is what passes for song in the pied woodpecker and is only likely to be heard in the first half of the year. The pied woodpecker is found over the whole of Great Britain, though very local in the far north of Scotland, but not at all in Ireland. It is the most likely woodpecker to be seen in gardens, for in recent years it has taken to visiting bird tables.

The **Barred Woodpecker,** which more descriptive name I again follow Max Nicholson in preferring to the lesser spotted woodpecker of the books, is our only other black and white woodpecker, and is no bigger than a house sparrow. The black and white of its plumage has a barred rather than a spotted effect, and its only red patches are on the crown of the adult male and of juveniles of both sexes. It has a weak *pee-pee-pee-pee* call, a *tchick* that is weaker and more sibilant than the pied's, and a feebler drumming note which, however, is more prolonged than the pied's. It is a remarkably local bird, even in the south of England where it is commonest; in West Wales, Yorkshire and Lancashire it becomes increasingly scarce, and is unknown in Scotland or Ireland.

The **Wryneck** is both our only summer-visitor woodpecker and our only brown one, and is also well on the way to becoming our rarest breeding bird. Only fifty years ago it was widespread in the south of England, and the 1899 edition of Howard Saunders's *Manual* describes it as a rare breeder north to Northumberland. To-day you will be lucky indeed to find a breeding pair outside Surrey, Sussex and Kent, and even in those favoured counties there are now fewer than fifty pairs all told. Indeed, there may now be fewer breeding pairs of wrynecks in Britain than there are of the collared dove (p. 96), a bird which only began nesting here in 1955. Seen away from trees—and every year some hundreds of migrants reach our east coast, often in treeless places—the wryneck does not look

F

particularly like a woodpecker, but more like a small brown shrike or a large warbler (it is about the size of a nightingale). Its plumage is all grey-brown, mottled darker and paler, and its straight bill quickly separates it from the much smaller treecreeper. Its *quee-quee-quee* cry, louder and more ringing than the barred woodpecker's, is reminiscent of the similar calls of kestrels and other birds of prey.

The **Treecreeper,** our only other small brown bird that creeps up trees, which it does jerkily and like a mouse, is quickly told by its downward curved bill and tiny size, nearer the blue tit than the great tit. Its plumage is entirely brown above and silvery white below. This is another bird whose very distinctive song pattern it is desirable to learn, for in the first half of the year you can more often pick it up by ear than by eye. It is also worth learning to separate its prolonged high-pitched *tseeee* note from similar ones of the tits and goldcrest. The treecreeper is resident, breeding almost throughout the British Isles.

The second song bird addicted to woodpecker habits is the **Nuthatch,** whose distinctive plumage, blue-grey above, buff and chestnut below, with a black eyestripe, coupled with its small size, that of a great tit, prevent its being confused with any other British bird. The nuthatch has as varied a repertoire of calls as the tits, but the most characteristic are loud ringing or piping calls, one of which is very like the wryneck's *quee-quee*; the most often heard can be rendered *twitt-wit-wit*. Like the treecreeper the nuthatch often accompanies foraging tit parties in the winter woods and, unlike it, it is an occasional visitor to bird tables where its specialised taste for nuts is catered for. The nuthatch is another primarily southern bird, found mainly south of the Mersey and the Humber, and is only a vagrant to the Lake District, Scotland and Ireland. It is sometimes found in town parks, even in Kensington Gardens in London.

REED-BED BIRDS

REED WARBLER	plain brown, whitish throat
MARSH WARBLER	plain brown, whitish throat
SEDGE WARBLER	pale eyestripe
GRASSHOPPER WARBLER	graduated tail, streaked rump
BEARDED TIT	rufous, grey head, black moustaches
WATER RAIL	long red bill, barred flanks
BITTERN	large, brown, long neck

Extensive reed-beds, such as are found by the Norfolk Broads and many other inland waters, as well as on many coastal marshes, have their own specialised bird fauna, most notably the reed warbler itself, and including the bearded tit, the bittern, the water rail and two kinds of harrier. For convenience three more brown warblers of damp habitats are also discussed here.

The **Reed Warbler** is one of the few British birds strongly associated with one plant, the common reed (*Phragmites communis* or, in the older books, *Arundo phragmites*). It is a help, therefore, in identifying the warbler to get a botanist friend to acquaint you with the differences between this, the true reed, and various species of grass, especially the reed-grass *Phalaris arundinacea*, rush and sedge that are liable to form similar extensive beds at the edge of fresh water. None of them, incidentally, except quite locally, form extensive beds of tall (over 6 ft.) stems as the common reed does.

The reed warbler, its close allies the sedge and marsh warblers, and the grasshopper warbler bring us back, for the last time in this book, to the small brown bird that plagues bird-watching beginners. All are among our smaller warblers, and the reed warbler and **Marsh Warbler** compare with the marsh and willow tits in difficulty of identification for the beginner (and for many experienced bird watchers too). Both are plain brown birds, with whitish throats and pale underparts. Early in the season, if you are very familiar with both, you may be able to separate the adults by the slightly rufous tinge and dark brown legs of the reed compared with the slightly olive tinge and flesh-pink legs of the marsh. But you do need to be pretty expert to be able to do this with confidence, and once the young are fledged you are foxed by the rufous tinge on the young of both, and the pale flesh-pink legs of the young reed.

So even experts in the end fall back on song, habitat, distribution and the structure of the nest to distinguish these two. The reed warbler has a fairly distinctive song that sounds not unlike somebody rather monotonously rubbing two pebbles together, *churr, churr, churr . . . chirruc, chirruc, chirruc*, for minutes on end. The pebble-rubbing is sometimes interspersed with snatches mimicked from other birds' songs. With the marsh warbler this mimicry is carried to greater lengths than with any other British bird, and indeed the greater part of the song output of most marsh warblers seems to consist of imitations, often very excellent and deceptive, of other birds' songs. Interspersed with these it has some fine liquid warbling notes of its own, with none of the reed warbler's pebble-rubbing—unless, of course, it happens to be mimicking a reed warbler! The marsh warbler has a very restricted song period, from the last few days of May until early July. The harsh churring alarm notes of the reed, marsh and sedge warblers are all so much alike that it needs a very practised ear indeed to distinguish them.

As for habitat, it is unusual, though by no means unknown, for reed warblers to be found away from reed-beds. Marsh warblers, on the other hand, much prefer osier beds and other places where tall, lush, coarse vegetation, such as meadowsweet and hairy willow herb, grows up among young trees. They also frequent quite dry habitats much more often than reed warblers, and in my experience rarely if ever resort to reed-beds. Distribution is also a help, for the reed warbler nests widely over southern and midland England, and more locally in the south-west, South Wales and northern England. In Scotland and Ireland it is only a vagrant. The marsh warbler, on the other hand, is an extremely local bird of southern England only, and much the most likely places to find it are the valleys of the lower Severn and Stratford Avon and parts of Dorset and Somerset; it also seems to breed sporadically in Kent, the upper Thames valley and a few other places. Both are late arrivals, the reed usually appearing about the last week in April, the marsh not till nearly the end of May.

Finally, if you do find a nest, you can often identify the owner by its method of construction. The reed warbler makes a deep cup and almost invariably weaves it on to the stems of reeds. The marsh warbler's is much shallower, more like a whitethroat's and is attached to the stems of nettles, willowherb and other tall plants by "basket handles" like the blackcap's.

The **Sedge Warbler** is commoner and more widespread than the reed warbler, and may be found throughout the British Isles in almost any spot where there is fairly coarse vegetation close to fresh water, from a small brook or pond to a large lake or river, or even a marsh. You can tell it at once from both reed and marsh warblers by its distinct pale eyestripe, as well as by the darker markings on its upperparts. Its song, much more varied than the reed warbler's, is a medley of diverse notes, both harsh and melodious, all mixed up with still more frequent snatches of mimicry of other birds' songs and calls. My own notes on sedge-warbler song include imitations of the blackbird, swallow, house and tree sparrow, chaffinch, nuthatch, yellow wagtail, linnet, lapwing, house martin and greenshank. The sedge warbler's nest is shallower than a reed warbler's and usually not attached to plant stems; it may be found in almost any kind of thick vegetation within a few yards of fresh water.

The fourth member of the damp-habitat warbler quartet, the **Grasshopper Warbler,** is much more often heard than seen. Its song is one of the most singular and unbirdlike of any British bird, for it sounds like a continuous angler's reel or a loud bicycle freewheel, or even some Continental species of grasshopper. It is nearly always delivered from thick cover, but if you should get a glimpse of the bird, look for the dark streaks on the upperparts, especially on the rump (the sedge warbler's rump is unstreaked) and graduated tail. The grasshopper warbler frequents dry habitats, such as the sites of felled woodland, heaths and commons, as often as damp ones like osier beds and marshes; an abundance of coarse vegetation for cover is its chief requirement. It is distributed rather locally over the whole of the British Isles except the north of Scotland.

Even more local than the marsh warbler is the attractive **Bearded Tit,** now confined in the breeding season to the Norfolk Broads and the coastal marshes of East Anglia. In the past few years the breeding population has been so high that many birds have emigrated in autumn to reed-beds in other parts of southern England, often in counties where no bearded tit had been seen for fifty years or more. This great build-up of bearded tit population is a feather in the caps of the Royal Society for the Protection of Birds and the Norfolk Naturalists' Trust, the bodies chiefly responsible for the bird's protection. In Britain the bearded tit is even more restricted to reed-beds than the reed warbler, and requires much more extensive ones if it is to breed successfully. The cock bearded tit is a striking little bird, with its mainly rufous plumage, grey head, black moustachial stripes (the "beard") and black and white marks on the wings. The hen has the wing markings but not the head ones. Both have a long rufous tail, which distinguishes them from all our other small reed-bed birds. Listen out also for their characteristic metallic *ching ching* call note.

The only other small bird especially associated with reed-beds in the breeding season is the reed bunting (p. 54), though blue tits and wrens often feed there in winter.

A larger and excessively retiring reed-bed bird is the **Water Rail,** which looks rather like a moorhen with a long red bill. You usually learn of its presence by hearing a series of curious squealing, clucking, grunting or even miaowing notes coming from a bed of reeds or sedges, though of course it is desirable to be familiar with the range of moorhen and coot vocabulary first before diagnosing water rail. If you do see the bird, the chances are that you will merely glimpse a dark form slipping through the reeds, but when hard frost drives the water rails out of cover to feed on the open mud, you can see that they are brown, streaked black above and barred black and white on the flanks and belly, with grey cheeks and breast and, like the moorhen, conspicuous white feathers under the tail. A sight of the long red bill will, of course, settle the matter. Water rails like very wet marshes with thick reeds or other cover; there are probably more of them in Britain in winter than in summer, but nobody really knows.

There are also three much rarer small crakes, all with shorter bills. The **Spotted Crake,** about the size of a common sandpiper, may still occasionally breed in the West Country and along the Welsh Border, but is nowadays mainly a scarce passage migrant. It is most likely to be detected by its call note, an extraordinary sound like a whiplash, but if by good fortune seen in the open looks like either a small brown moorhen or a small dark corncrake with whitish spots. Baillon's and the little crake are rarer still, and not much bigger than a sparrow. They both look like miniature short-billed water rails, and are quite hard to tell apart in the brief views that they usually offer the observer.

Moorhens (p. 135, coots (p. 135) and great crested grebes (p. 152) also rank as reed-bed birds in the breeding season.

One of the most characteristic reed-bed birds is the **Bittern,** which is largely confined to the same area in East Anglia as the bearded tit, but in recent years has shown some tendency to recolonise other extensive marshy areas in England and Wales. It is one of the three marsh birds which ceased to breed with us in the nineteenth century but has since come back; the two others are the avocet and the black-tailed godwit. Like several other reed-bed birds the bittern is far more often heard than seen; its curious dull booming "song" is sufficiently like a distant lowing cow for an eminent Oxford ornithologist once to have identified a lowing cow as a bittern for a group of admiring undergraduates. The most usual view of it is a large broad-winged brown bird that flies up from the reeds and soon drops down again, but occasionally one will stalk out into the open and reveal its true nature as a brown heron. Even then, if it crouches down, it looks at first sight more like a brown farmyard goose. In flight you can tell it from other large brown broad-winged birds, such as harriers and owls, by its long bill and trailing legs.

Two species of harrier, Montagu's and marsh, are especially associated with marshes and extensive reed-beds, but they are more conveniently discussed with the other large birds of prey (p. 109).

BIRDS OF RIVERS AND STREAMS

DIPPER   white breast
KINGFISHER   blue-green above, chestnut below

Only two of our land birds are so closely linked with rivers and streams that they spend most of their lives there: the dipper and the kingfisher. Several others, however, including the grey wagtail (p. 69), the sand martin (p. 74 and the common sandpiper (p. 120), are inseparably associated with our upland streams during their breeding season from April to July. Many of our freshwater birds, such as moorhens (p. 135) and coots (p. 135) are also frequently found on rivers and streams at various times of year, while most bird watchers are more likely to see some of the reed-bed birds (p. 82), notably the reed bunting (p. 54) and the sedge and reed warblers, beside the broader lowland rivers than actually in reed-beds, which are often less accessible.

The **Dipper** is quite unmistakable, if you get a satisfactory view, though a briefly glimpsed common sandpiper could be confused with it. It is our only small bird with a white "shirt-front" that stands on stones in rivers, bobbing up and down with apparent impatience. Common sandpipers may also bob impatiently, but their white is more on the underparts and beneath the tail, and of course they have long bills and a quite different, wader-like stance. The dipper is like nothing so much as an outsize wren —its closest relative among British birds—and the rest of its plumage is dark or blackish, with a chestnut band below the white breast. Dippers are completely adapted to aquatic life in swiftly flowing streams, and can swim both on and under the surface, as well as walking along the stream bed underwater. They also sometimes dive in, either from a stone or from the air. Their loud warbling song is distinctly wren-like. It is no good looking for dippers beside sedate lowland rivers in the south-eastern half of England—if you do see one, in winter, it is likely to be a wanderer from the Continent with no chestnut band—for apart from a few pairs in the Cotswolds, they live, in both summer and winter, only by the swift streams and torrents of the hill country on the west side of Britain, from Cornwall to Sutherland, and in Ireland and the Isle of Man; on the east side they are only found from Yorkshire northwards.

The **Kingfisher** is completely unmistakable, for no other British bird has its harlequin combination of brilliant blue-green above and reddish-chestnut below, while its short-tailed dumpy form and long thick bill are also uniquely coupled in our avifauna. Even so, I think I most often pick up a kingfisher by hearing its loud shrill call note, *chee* or *chi-kee*, when a quick look will often reveal a blue speck speeding away downstream or making a wide detour across a field to avoid me as it follows the stream. Unlike the dipper, the kingfisher is a bird of the lowlands, not of the uplands, so you will not often find the two together on the same stream. In the autumn some kingfishers go down to the sea to winter along the estuaries or sometimes even on open shores.

MOUNTAIN BIRDS

SNOW BUNTING	small, black and white
DOTTEREL	medium, white eyestripe and breast-band, chestnut lower breast
PTARMIGAN	large, grey-brown and white (summer) or mostly white (winter)

Not many British birds breed really high on mountains, at or above the 2000-foot level, and nowhere else, though a good many hill birds do go above this height on some mountains. Our only really montane species in this sense are the snow bunting, the dotterel, which is a wader, and the ptarmigan, which is a grouse. Among the other birds that may be seen above the 2000-foot level with them are the ring ouzel (p. 78), the meadow pipit (p. 67), the dunlin (p. 118), the golden plover (p. 116) and various birds of prey (p. 103), not to mention foraging gulls (p. 137).

The **Snow Bunting** is one of our rarest breeding species, nesting on a handful of the highest mountains in the Scottish Highlands; nobody really knows if they breed on the same tops every year, though probably they do on some of them. Nothing but a partially albino finch or bunting of some other species could be confused with a cock snow bunting in summer, for it looks very black and white, but there are decreasing amounts of white and increasing amounts of brown in the plumage of the winter cock, hen, immature and juvenile birds, in that order. In winter, flocks of immigrant snow buntings occur along our eastern seaboard, and sometimes also on hills inland, for instance in the Pennines. A flock of these "snow-flakes" as they are often called, flashing white as they open and close their wings in flight, is one of the high spots of the bird watcher's winter. A flock will present no difficulty in identification, but a solitary immature bird might, for it looks very like any other small brown bird until it flies and reveals its white wing-bars.

The plover-like **Dotterel** also breeds on some of the highest mountain tops in the Highlands and still also very sparingly indeed in the north of England. At one time it used to be not uncommon on migration in the south, but nowadays it is very rarely seen, though there is still one farm in Cambridgeshire where migrant parties halt regularly in spring and a few autumns ago a small party spent a few days on London Airport. The thing to look for in a dotterel is the white eyestripes, which meet in a V on the nape of its neck; the yellowish legs; and the distinctive pattern of its underparts, white throat, grey-brown upper breast divided from reddish-chestnut lower breast by a narrow white band, black belly and white again under the tail. Birds seen on autumn passage in the south are likely to be in the winter or juvenile plumages on which the white stripes and bands are fainter and the chestnut lacking. In size the dotterel is larger than a dunlin but smaller than a golden plover, the only two confusable waders likely to be seen on a mountain top.

The **Ptarmigan,** which is also confined to the Scottish Highlands and rarely found below 2,000 feet, is like a red grouse with much or most of its plumage white. In winter it is all white, except for a black tail and a dark spot near the eye in the cock. In summer and autumn it is mostly pale grey-brown, with the white confined to the wing-tips and belly, though it shows very conspicuously when the bird flies. Like grouse, ptarmigan have feathered legs and red wattles over the eyes, but if you have got near enough to see these, you will be in no doubt as to what you are seeing.

SEAWALL AND SALTMARSH IN WINTER

SHORE LARK	black and yellow on head
LAPLAND BUNTING	pale stripes down back, yellow bill

A very distinct winter bird habitat is the seashore from high-tide mark up to the seawall or saltmarsh, where a good many small birds gather to feed on the seeds of the saltmarsh plants, both in the marsh and washed up by the tide, and on various small animals that live among the tide-wrack. Finch flocks include especially greenfinches (p. 49), linnets (p. 51), twites (p. 51) and snow buntings (p. 87), and occasionally an uncommon species, the Lapland bunting. Larks and pipits include both meadow (p. 67) and rock pipits (p. 68), the skylark (p. 66) and another uncommon species, the shore lark.

It is only on the east coast between Fife and Kent that you are at all likely to see a **Shore Lark,** and much the best place to make its acquaintance is the north coast of Norfolk, where it usually stays close to the shore but occasionally strays on to nearby stubbles. At a distance it looks remarkably like a skylark, but at close range you can see its distinctive black and yellow face pattern, and sometimes also the black "horns" that have given rise to its American name of horned lark. Its call note *tseep* is more like a wagtail's or pipit's than a skylark's.

The **Lapland Bunting** is rather a "bird-watcher's bird," for once you have learned its very distinctive call note you can often pick it out under light conditions which prevent identification by sight. This note, a hard flat little rattle *tr-r-r-ik*, is often coupled with a rather flat toneless *teuk*; the two together are diagnostic. This is just as well, for its winter plumage, the one we usually see in Britain, is so like a hen reed bunting that, if the bird is so disobliging as not to call, you must see its yellow bill and two pale stripes down the back to be certain of it. Summer cocks are easy enough, with head and breast black, nape chestnut and a whitish stripe back from the eye, but most birds seen in Britain are on autumn migration, when these distinctive features are dulled over. Lapland buntings usually turn up on the coast, especially in places frequented by snow buntings, but like them are also occasionally found on hills inland.

Game Birds

type: the Common Partridge

COMMON PARTRIDGE	brown, horseshoe on breast, rufous tail
RED-LEGGED PARTRIDGE	barred flanks, black and white on head, red legs, rufous tail
QUAIL	small, brown, buff streaks on head, tail not rufous
CORNCRAKE	small, chestnut on wings, longish bill and legs
STONE CURLEW	black and white on wings, long legs, yellow eyes
WOODCOCK	warm brown, very long bill
RED GROUSE	dark rufous brown
BLACK GROUSE, COCK	larger, blue-black, white wing-bar, lyre-shaped tail
BLACK GROUSE, HEN	dark grey-brown, forked tail
CAPERCAILLIE	huge, tail undivided
CAPERCAILLIE, COCK	grey-black, no wing-bar
CAPERCAILLIE, HEN	grey-brown, chestnut patch on breast
PHEASANT	large, long tail
PHEASANT, COCK	harlequin plumage
PHEASANT, HEN	brown

Most of our game birds stick closely to the ground, rarely flying except when compelled to do so, though pheasants regularly roost in trees and blackgame and caper also resort to trees to feed on the young shoots. The cocks of these three are our only game birds whose plumage is not some shade of brown, which is no doubt an adaptation for concealment on the ground. Most of our game birds have rather short, stout but pointed bills. They range in size from the quail, which is no bigger than a starling, to the capercaillie, almost our largest breeding land bird. Young game birds resemble the hens.

Partridges are in many ways our most typical game birds, and the **Common Partridge** is a plump compact brown bird with a whirring flight, that is widespread on farmland throughout the British Isles, but especially on the east side of England, where on certain "manors" it forms almost the most important crop. Its cultivated habitat alone should serve to distinguish it from the red grouse, a bird almost confined to heather moors, but partridges do also frequent such wilder places as sand dunes and wide tracts of shingle. From the introduced **Red-legged Partridge,** often called the French partridge or Frenchman from its country of origin, the common or English partridge can easily be told by the chestnut horseshoe on the breast of the adult. The Frenchman is distinctly larger and also differs in having its flanks strongly barred with blue-grey, its legs red and a conspicuous black and white pattern on the head and neck (white chin, cheeks and stripe above eye; black stripe down through eye to lower neck, where it widens out into a bib). At a distance or in poor light you can often tell a Frenchman by its more upright, almost pheasant-like stance, and by its habit of standing up on a post and crowing with a loud challenging *chucka, chucka* or *chik-chik chikar.* The shyer common partridge usually utters its creaky *keev-it keev-it* note from cover; when the bird is flushed this degenerates into a spluttering cackle, ending in . . . *it-it-it.* Red-legged partridges are much more local than the native birds, being almost confined to England and there only at all common on the east side from Yorkshire to Essex. In parts of Essex and East Anglia, however, they may outnumber the common partridge.

Young partridges can be confused with the uncommon **Quail,** a summer visitor mainly to the southern chalklands, which is very shy indeed and usually only betrays its presence by its persistent, subtly liquid *quip-ip-ip* call note, popularly rendered as *wet-mi-lips.* I have heard this call in the Cotswolds, the Chilterns and Wiltshire, but the only time I ever set eyes on a wild quail was on a barren Spanish hill-side, where there was no vegetation for it to hide in. If you do see a quail, perhaps flushed during a shoot (when there should, of course, be no partridges young enough to confuse it with), the buff streaks on the head and lack of chestnut under the tail should suffice to identify it. Cock birds at close range can be seen to have dark stripes on the throat, curling back to the nape.

Nowadays the **Corncrake** is so unfamiliar in the south, where its rasping *crex crex* call was once as much a part of the summer's day as the humming of the bees, that one seen by chance on migration might be momentarily taken for a quail or a young partridge. It is in fact a much slimmer bird, with a longer bill and much longer legs than either and chestnut in the wings, not the tail. Moreover, when the corncrake does fly, it dangles its legs, which neither of the others do. To-day, except for one or two favoured areas in the south, such as the Avon valley near Tewkesbury, corncrakes must be sought in the far western fringe of the British Isles, especially the western Highlands, the Hebrides and Ireland. Here, unless you are prepared to trample down somebody's hay crop, you must be content with that everlasting sound like a grated comb, which can be as damnably iterating as the cuckoo. The best chance of actually seeing a corncrake is on its return journey to Africa in the late summer, when the grass is shorter and it sometimes turns up in places where it has not bred for fifty or sixty years.

The corncrake is not strictly a game bird, nor is another ground-loving brown bird with quite different habits, that is more likely to be confused with a curlew than a partridge. The **Stone Curlew** or Norfolk plover is actually more closely related to the bustards. A very distinctive bird when seen close to, with long legs, much shorter bill than a curlew (black at the tip and yellow at the base) and staring yellow eyes, it shows its difference from the curlew again when it flies and reveals the conspicuous black and white marking on each wing. Its only really curlew-like feature, apart from the superficial ones of size, long legs and brown plumage, is its wild, shrill wailing call, best heard in the dusk. As a bustard rather than a wader, it is a bird of dry country, mainly nowadays on the Wessex chalk and the sandy heaths of the East Anglian Breckland north-east of Newmarket, though small colonies do survive in a few other spots on the chalk and limestone uplands of southern England. One of the best times to see stone curlews is in late summer or early autumn, when they assemble in parties prior to migrating.

A game bird by custom but zoologically a wader is yet another brown bird, the **Woodcock**, which is actually more likely to be mistaken for an owl than for either a wader or a partridge. Most people's first view of the woodcock is either when they flush a dark russet-brown bird in walking through the woods or when, from March to June, it passes overhead in the curious "roding" flight with which it patrols its territory at dusk. If there is still light enough you may be able to see the woodcock's long probing bill, carried almost vertically downwards as it pursues its slightly hesitating way, but in any case you will hear one of the two characteristic notes it utters while roding, a sibilant *twissick twissick* and a curious little low growl. Most woodcock seem to take five or ten minutes to complete their patrol, so if you have just missed one, wait where you are and it should come back again. Woodcock breed locally in woods in most parts of the British Isles, and in winter, when they do not rode, are much more widespread, for thousands of immigrants come to us from across the North Sea.

The **Red Grouse** is not really red, but a dark mottled rufous brown, and in the poor light of a dull winter's day it just looks dark. You really identify it by the fact that it is rarely seen off a heather moor, except in hard weather, and by the cock's gruff summons to the moorland walker to *go-bak, go-bak, go-bak*. It also has a pheasant-like *kok-kok-kok*. Larger than a common partridge and more the size of a Frenchman, the red grouse inhabits heather moors all over Scotland, north and mid-Wales and the north of England, and occurs more sparsely in Ireland, South Wales and midland and south-western England, where a line drawn from Flamborough Head to Exeter marks its south-eastern limit. Its mountain counterpart, the ptarmigan, was discussed earlier, under Mountain Birds (p. 88).

The **Black Grouse** is now found in roughly the same area as the red grouse, but is decreasing almost everywhere, except in parts of mid-Wales, Staffordshire and Scotland. There are still a few on Exmoor, but none have been seen for many years in the New Forest or on the Surrey heaths, despite the fact that our ancient game laws still prescribe a special close season for New Forest blackgame. The black grouse is intermediate in size between the capercaillie, with which both sexes could be confused, and the red grouse, for which the hen might also be mistaken. The dark bluish-black blackcock, as the male is called, is much smaller than the cock caper and differs also in its conspicuous white wing-bar and lyre-shaped tail. The dark grey-brown female, usually known as a greyhen, differs from both red grouse and hen caper by her inconspicuous white wing-bar and forked tail, and from the caper also in having no rufous patch on the breast. Habitat is also a help, for though you do see black-game out on the open moor, you much more often find them near or among trees, especially on the woodland/moorland edge, than you do red grouse. A great help, of course, is the tendency of greyhens to accompany blackcocks. Both blackgame and capers will occasionally cross with pheasants in the wild, and the resulting hybrids can be very puzzling. Blackgame have a remarkable habit of communal courtship, which includes mock battles, on a traditional courting ground called a lek; a visit to a lek is one of the "musts" for all bird watchers, even though it means getting up rather early in the morning.

The **Capercaillie** is the nearest thing to a wild turkey we have in the British Isles. The explosive effect of flushing a family party of these huge birds can be quite startling. The cock, if you need any plumage details to identify the monster, is greyer than a blackcock, with no wing-bar, but green on the throat and upper breast and white on the flanks. The hen caper is like an outsize greyhen, with no wing-bar, tail not forked and a large chestnut patch on the breast. Capers breed in pine and other coniferous woods in the eastern Highlands and very locally elsewhere in Scotland. The original native stock of Scottish capers was exterminated by shooting and deforestation in the eighteenth century; the present population descends from a stock of Swedish birds imported about 125 years ago.

With its gaudy plumage, long tail and often a white neck-ring, the cock **Pheasant** needs no further clues to its identity. Hens, if their long tails are obscured, can be puzzlingly like partridges, and young birds before their tails have fully grown even more so, but of course they have no chestnut about the tail and are usually chaperoned by an adult bird. Young pheasants have a remarkable call that sounds like a loud bullfinch's pipe, repeated and followed by a creaking third note. The familiar crowing call of the old males, *korr-kok*, is often provoked by a gunshot or other loud report.

All our pheasants were originally introduced from abroad, and most of them now live a highly artificial life, being reared and fed by game-keepers, so that they really should not rank as wild birds at all. But sometimes they will escape into some more natural habitat such as a reed-bed and maintain a completely feral existence. There are really no pure-bred pheasants left in the British Isles, for many different strains have been brought here from Asia in the past 200 years. The most distinctive of these is the ring-necked or Chinese race; birds lacking the white neck-ring are likely to approximate to the so-called "old English" pheasant, introduced from western Asia about 900 years ago. Much more recently the admixture of Japanese pheasants into our breeding stock has produced some very dark coloured hybrids, misleadingly known as "melanistic mutants." There is no evidence that these are mutants in the true genetical sense.

In a few districts there are a good many golden and Lady Amherst's pheasants at large in the coverts; these two are closely related and hybridise readily, so they cannot be put down in the same area. Their cocks are highly distinctive, the golden with its brilliant red and yellow plumage and golden cape over its neck, and Lady Amherst's with its plumage dark green and white and cape barred black and white. The two hens, however, are hard to tell apart unless the colour of the legs, bill and eyes can be seen; both are paler than hen common pheasants with a more barred tail. Golden pheasants are most likely to be seen in the Norfolk and Suffolk Breckland around Thetford and Brandon, and in parts of Galloway. Lady Amherst's have established themselves both in the New Forest and around Woburn Park, Bedfordshire. Not long ago I came across two fine cock Lady Amherst's in a wood some six miles from Woburn. Both species are often turned down by landowners wishing to embellish their estates, so might be seen almost anywhere.

Pigeons and Doves

type: the Woodpigeon

WOODPIGEON	large, white patches on wings and neck
STOCK DOVE	black wing-tips, small black wing-bars
ROCK DOVE	white rump, larger black wing-bars
FERAL PIGEON	plumage varied
TURTLE DOVE	chestnut back, tail black with white tip
COLLARED DOVE	black half-collars, tail white with black base

There is no real distinction between pigeons and doves; it is just that some, usually rather large, doves are called pigeons, rather as some narcissi are called daffodils. All our native pigeons and doves are modestly coloured, with some pastel shade of grey or brown; all have smallish heads, short bills and longish tails. Most of their crooning or cooing voices have a family resemblance. All except the turtle dove are resident with us all the year round.

The **Woodpigeon** is both our commonest and our largest dove (rook-size). You can easily tell it by the conspicuous white patches on its wings, often visible at a great distance, while adults also have a white patch on each side of the neck, which gives them their alternative and now somewhat outmoded name of ring dove. Other plumage features are the black tip to the rather long tail and, at close range, the iridescent green and purple patches above the white on the neck. The woodpigeon's song is the familiar soothing *coo coo coo coo coo*, and in its distinctive display flight the bird flies up at a steep angle and then glides down again. Seventy years ago the woodpigeon was exclusively a shy country bird, but from the 1890s onwards it has colonised the parks of London and other towns, so that it is now one of the most familiar town birds. It is still also widespread in wooded districts throughout the British Isles, nesting in trees, hedges and thick shrubs.

The next dove size-group contains the stock dove, the rock dove and the feral pigeon, all about as big as a jackdaw. The **Stock Dove** is the commonest and most widespread of these, and frequents a much wider variety of country than any of our other doves, for it nests in holes in cliffs and rocks as well as trees, and so is found on rocky hill-sides, both inland and sea cliffs, and downs and dunes (where it uses rabbit burrows), as well as in wooded and park-like country, where it is especially partial to pollard willows and other old scattered trees. It is easily told from the woodpigeon by its smaller size, shorter tail and lack of any white patches; and from the otherwise very similar rock dove and feral pigeon by its black wing-tips, two *small* black bars on each wing, and no white rump. Its song is a distinctive double coughing or grunting coo. It is worth remembering that stock doves feed with woodpigeons in the fields much more than feral pigeons do.

The true **Rock Dove** is a bird of the far northern and western rocky coasts of the British Isles, confined nowadays to Scotland, Ireland and the Isle of Man, where it nests in holes in cliffs and on ledges in sea caves. On many English and Welsh cliffs, as at Flamborough Head in Yorkshire, there are colonies of feral pigeons, some of them scarcely distinguishable from genuine rock doves, but there is in fact no pure-bred rock-dove population left south of the Border. Rock doves look just like stock doves with a conspicuous white rump, no black wing-tips and larger black bars on the wing. Beware, incidentally, of stock doves nesting on sea cliffs, which may even be called rock doves by the locals. The coo of the rock dove is the same as that of the pigeons in Trafalgar Square.

All the pigeons of our dovecots have in fact been domesticated from the wild rock dove, and **Feral Pigeons** are merely descendants of dovecote pigeons that have escaped and readapted themselves to living in the wild. Many of these escaped birds live on cliffs, both sea and inland, in England and Wales, but some penetrate even into the fastnesses of the wild rock doves in Scotland and Ireland. The great majority of our feral pigeons, however, are to be found in the streets of London and other towns, where they breed on ledges and in holes of buildings instead of cliffs. Identifying a feral pigeon in Trafalgar Square presents no problem, but on a sea cliff it is not quite so easy. Some are identical in plumage with wild rock doves, and these can only be told by their urban habitat or if they accompany some different looking birds. For the salient feature of our feral pigeon population is its protean mixture of plumages. Besides the minority of the wild rock dove or "blue rock" type there are innumerable "blue chequers" with the grey parts mottled black; "mealies" with cinnamon-red instead of blue-grey, and white wing-tips; "red chequers" with the mottling white instead of black; and many variations on black, white and pied. If you see any of these oddities on the cliffs, you almost certainly have a feral pigeon colony. If, however, there are only a few blue chequers among many blue rocks, it is possible that these are genuine natural variations in a wild rock dove colony.

The **Turtle Dove** is our smallest native dove and the only summer visitor. A tree-nester, it differs from all the preceding species in both plumage and voice. The first sign of the turtle dove's arrival, late in April or early in May, is its soothing *turr turr* song. When it flies, you at once notice its striking tail pattern, black with white edges and tip. At rest the chestnut upperparts contrast with the blue-grey head and neck, with a black-and-white barred patch on each side of the neck. Young birds lack this patch and are generally browner. Like the woodpigeon, the turtle dove has a display flight involving a steep upward flight and a downward glide. It is commonest in south and east England, becoming more local as you go west and north through the Midlands. In Scotland and Ireland it occurs only as a rare and presumably lost migrant.

Until a few years ago there was nothing else that could reasonably be confused with the turtle dove, but now the **Collared Dove** has arrived. In the past thirty years this remarkable bird has made a headlong advance north-westwards over Europe from the Balkans, and in 1955 jumped the North Sea to breed in north Norfolk. Since then it has been spreading over Britain too, and has already penetrated as far north as Morayshire and south to Kent. Within a few years it will probably be breeding in almost every mainland county in Great Britain, and should certainly be keenly watched for everywhere. The collared dove comes between the woodpigeon and the turtle dove in size, being about as big as a stock dove. It looks like either a small, slim, sandy grey woodpigeon, but with sooty-brown wing-tips and black half-collars instead of the white neck patches; or a rather large turtle dove, sandy grey instead of chestnut above, with black half-collars instead of barred black-and-white neck patches, and its tail white with a black base instead of black with a white tip. Its call is a triple *du-duh-du* or *du-duh-druuuh*, much more like the woodpigeon and stock dove than the turtle dove, but quite distinct from all three. One should also bear in mind the possibility of escaped Barbary doves, a favourite cage bird. These have the same black half-collars as the collared dove, but are smaller than a turtle dove, with more buff-coloured plumage, no dark wing-tips and blue-grey instead of black in the tail. Collared doves are especially likely to turn up in suburbs and villages, frequently near chicken runs, on a free supply of food from which they largely rely for their living. Often the first you hear of the collared dove in a new district is when a neighbour says he has a strange dove feeding with his chickens, flying up afterwards to perch on his TV aerial. Like turtle doves, collared doves nest in trees; unlike them they stay with us all the year round.

The Crows

type: the Rook

ROOK	all black, bluish sheen, bare patch at base of bill
CARRION CROW	all black, greenish sheen
HOODED CROW	black and grey
JACKDAW	grey patch on nape
RAVEN	large, all black, heavy bill

CHOUGH	red legs and bill
MAGPIE	black and white, long tail
JAY	pinkish-brown, white on wings and rump

Five of our seven species of crow are all, or almost all, black in plumage, though one, the carrion crow, has a largely grey form, found in Scotland and Ireland, that is called the hooded crow and has until recent years been regarded as a separate species. Our two remaining crows, the magpie and the jay, have much diversified plumage. All seven are resident with us, and have fairly stout bills, for most are in greater or less degree eaters of flesh.

The **Rook** is our commonest and most familiar crow; indeed our ancestors hardly distinguished between it and the carrion crow, or if they did the rooks were crows and the carrion crows corbies. Shakespeare shows the general confusion by his reference to the crow making wing to the rooky wood. The rook is one of our five all-black crows; superficially it is very similar to the same-sized **Carrion Crow**, though there are several good ways of telling them apart. Adult rooks, for instance, always have a bare patch at the base of the bill, which is completely diagnostic. Juvenile rooks, however, have feathered faces, like carrion crows. If they are not accompanied by adults, they can be identified (as can the adults too) by the bluish-purple rather than green gloss on their plumage, and by the rather baggy, "plus-four" appearance of their thigh-feathers instead of the tighter "knee-breeches" effect of the crow.

Voice is also a useful guide. The rook has a wide range of notes in its vocabulary, but its cawings are always more deliberate and less raspingly harsh than the crow's, while it can also misleadingly mimic the croaking of a raven and the yelping of a herring gull. The crow usually repeats its notes three times, and has at least one call reminiscent of the old-fashioned motor-horn, but I have never heard it make raven-like or gull-like notes like the rook. The best known distinction between rooks and crows, that rooks are gregarious and crows not, is good as far as it goes, but it does not go far enough. Rooks are certainly gregarious at all times of year, nesting in rookeries, feeding in flocks and resorting to communal winter roosts, but even the most sociable bird is sometimes seen alone, and isolated rooks' nests, in particular, are by no means uncommon. The crow, on the other hand, while it never nests colonially, can and does flock in winter and uses communal roosts—there is or used to be one in Ken Wood adjoining Hampstead Heath. So gregariousness in winter is a less sure guide than in summer; it is always advisable to check by looking at or listening to some individual birds. Rooks, incidentally, never nest on cliffs, though occasionally on buildings; crows regularly nest on both as well as in trees.

While rooks are found throughout the British Isles, wherever there are trees for them to nest in, carrion crows breed only in England, Wales and south and east Scotland. In north and west Scotland, Ireland and the Isle of Man they are replaced by the partially grey form known as the **Hooded**

Crow, which also visits the rest of Britain as a winter visitor from the Continent, though it is a good deal less common now than formerly. In quite recent years a small number of carrion crows have also started to breed in Ireland, especially near Dublin and in Cos. Antrim and Down, so that more caution is needed nowadays in identifying rooks in Ireland.

The hooded crow is an easy one, for its grey body contrasts strongly with its black head, neck, wings and tail, but it is surprising how often the reflection from the sheen of a rook's or carrion crow's feathers in strong sunlight can give the momentary impression of a hooded crow. In the zone that stretches right across Scotland from Galloway to the Moray Firth in which the hooded and carrion crows interbreed and hybridise, some very puzzling intermediate plumages can be seen. In most of their habits and behaviour hooded and carrion crows are virtually identical, though I have sometimes noted that the voice of the hooded crow seems a little less harsh and more hoarse than the carrion's.

Jackdaws often consort with rooks, especially in feeding and roosting flocks in winter, but sometimes even at rookeries in spring, when they may make their own nests in the bases of large old rook nests. When you see one side by side with a rook, its much smaller size is an easy distinction, as are also its conspicuous grey nape-patch, the feathered base of its bill and at close range its white eyes. The jackdaw's more buoyant flight picks it out quickly in a mixed flock, and so does its much higher-pitched voice. Its chief calls are the *tchack* that gives it its name and *kow* or *kyow*. These notes are often mixed together, and a single jackdaw, by using them antiphonally, can give the impression that several birds are conducting a conversation. Jackdaws are essentially hole-nesters, using cliffs, rocks, buildings or old trees in all parts of the country. Like rooks, they are highly gregarious at all times of year.

The **Raven** is our largest black bird, and like the carrion crow is black all over, on bill and legs as well as plumage. Given a good view, it is quite distinct from the crow, but you do not always get a good view and young birds especially can be confusing. The best field character is the voice, a deep croak like nothing else in the British bird world except the similar note of the rook mentioned above. At reasonably close range you can also see the raven's heavy head and bill and longish neck, which give it a much more Maltese-cross appearance in the air than the crow or rook. In spring ravens will indulge in remarkable aerobatics, tumbling and nose-diving in a surprisingly agile way for so large a bird. Ravens rarely wander far from their breeding sites, which are on sea cliffs from the Isle of Wight west and north round Cape Wrath to eastern Scotland, and in Ireland, as well as in the wilder hill country of the north and west of both countries. The great majority of ravens nest on ledges of inland and sea cliffs, but tree nests, formerly frequent when the raven bred inland in southern England, are still by no means unknown. Away from its normal haunts, any raven is under suspicion of being an escaped cage bird. At one time one of the ravens in the Tower of London used to fly around the

London suburbs, causing great excitement among unsuspecting bird watchers.

The only remaining black crow is much the rarest, the **Chough,** which should really be called the red-billed chough, both to distinguish it from the yellow-billed Alpine chough and to give the best possible clue for identifying it. Choughs do in fact look like smallish rooks with red legs and a slightly down-curved red bill. Among several rather high-pitched notes, one has earned the bird its odd name, another is jackdaw-like and a third gull-like. To see a chough in the British Isles to-day, you must go to the sea cliffs of the west of Ireland, the Isle of Man, the extreme west of Wales or some of the Inner Hebrides, notably Islay and Jura. In Cornwall and on the Scottish mainland it is virtually extinct, and the only remaining inland localities in Great Britain are a few quarries and disused slate mines in Wales. In a few favoured parts of western Ireland choughs are still as common as jackdaws are in the rest of the British Isles.

Besides these five crows, there is only one other British land bird whose plumage is all-black, the cock blackbird (p. 77), which is much smaller than any crow, but there is, of course always the chance of a melanic (or albino) specimen of any kind of bird turning up to confound the bird watcher.

The **Magpie** is by far our largest black and white land bird, and its pied plumage and long graduated tail make any further description unnecessary, for there is no other British bird you can possibly confuse with a magpie. Having said this, perhaps I should refer the reader back to the cautionary tale on p. 16. The magpie breeds throughout the British Isles, though rather locally in Scotland; its nest is much the largest domed nest made by any British bird and is a conspicuous feature of the hedgerows in poorly-keepered areas. The magpie has not yet become a town bird in Britain, as it has in parts of the Continent.

The **Jay** is our least crow-like crow, and one of the most attractively decorated British birds, with its pinkish-brown plumage, blue and white wing-patches, white rump and black on wings and tail. Its most conspicuous feature is the white rump, which shows up clearly as the shy bird makes for the nearest thicket with its rather dipping flight. Often you will first hear its harsh screeching call in the woods, perhaps protesting at the presence of a tawny owl. At close range you can see its black and white crest. The jay is more of a woodland bird than any of our other crows, though it has colonised some London parks and suburbs. It breeds throughout the British Isles, but is more local in Scotland and Ireland.

The Owls

type: the Tawny Owl

TAWNY OWL	brown, black eyes
BARN OWL	buff above, white on face and below
LITTLE OWL	small, grey-brown, yellow eyes
LONG-EARED OWL	brown, yellow eyes, ear tufts
SHORT-EARED OWL	brown, yellow eyes, shorter ear tufts

The owls are largely, but by no means exclusively, nocturnal birds of prey. Their salient features are their very rounded wings and their distinct "faces," in the thick feathers of which their hooked beaks are usually more or less hidden. Only the lapwing among our other breeding birds has wings as rounded as an owl's, though in the dusk conditions in which it is usually seen, the blunt wings of the woodcock (p. 91) can lead to confusion. All our owls except the short-eared are resident and non-migratory.

Over most of Great Britain (it is absent from Ireland) the **Tawny Owl**, sometimes known as the brown or wood owl, is the commonest species. Frequenting mainly wooded country, it is the owl which has most successfully adapted itself to town conditions, and may often be heard hooting in the Inner London parks as well as in the more wooded suburbs with large gardens and parks. At one time a tawny owl used to roost regularly in one of the tall plane trees that overlook Piccadilly in London's Green Park. Except when it can be traced to its daytime roost by the urgent chatter and protest of jays, blackbirds, chaffinches and other small birds, the tawny owl is far more often heard than seen. This is the owl that hoots, with a long wavering *hoo-oo-oo* (its song) and cries *ke-wick* around the house on autumn evenings. These two calls, which can incidentally both sometimes be heard in full daylight, are presumably the basis of the traditional owl call *tu-whit tu-whoo*, but in fact tawny owls never seem to repeat them in succession, nor does any other owl make anything like this combination of sounds. If you do see a tawny owl, it will be a large brown round-winged bird gliding softly away in the dusk, or exceptionally flying in the open on a winter afternoon. It has shorter wings than our other brown owls, the long-eared and short-eared, lacks their ear tufts (which are not always visible in the other two) and at close range can be told from both of them by its black eyes. Tawny owls usually breed in holes in trees, including suitable nestboxes, but also in a wide variety of other sites, from old nests of other birds and ledges on cliffs or in buildings to rabbit burrows or even on the ground.

The **Barn Owl** is our only common white owl, and is in fact white only on its face and underparts, though it is surprising how completely white it can nevertheless look in a car's headlights at night. Its upperparts are golden-buff mottled with grey. Barn owls fly by day much more often than tawnies, and in February and March it is by no means unusual to see them abroad in late afternoon; at this time food (mainly mice and voles) must often be very scarce, hence the lengthening of the hunting period. The barn owl does not hoot, but hisses and snores and has as its main cry a fearful screech in the best blood-curdling tradition. It is widespread throughout the British Isles and breeds in other old buildings besides barns, as well as in holes in rocks, hollow trees and even haystacks.

Going about the country by day, the only owl you are likely to see frequently is the **Little Owl**, a species introduced from the Continent, which has spread over almost the whole of England and Wales since it was released by landowners in Kent and Northamptonshire about eighty years ago. It is now just beginning to colonise the Scottish Lowlands. The little owl is much the smallest of our owls, about the size of a song thrush; it is grey-brown with paler spots all over, and often perches on roadside posts, fences or telegraph wires, glaring at passers-by with its yellow eyes. If you stop and return its stare, it will sometimes start bobbing up and down like a dipper, or waggle its head from side to side, before taking off and flying away with a conspicuously bounding flight. It will also hover, especially in the dusk, when catching moths and other flying insects, for its diet is mainly insectivorous. The little owl's chief call is a loud ringing *kiew, kiew*, often answered by another little owl not far away; it also has a "song" that sounds remarkably like the opening sequence of a curlew's song. This is another hole-nester, preferring treeholes to other kinds.

The **Long-eared Owl** looks like a smaller, slimmer edition of the tawny owl, with longer wings and yellow eyes. When at rest it sometimes raises its distinctive ear tufts (they are not, of course, true ears), which are much longer than those of the short-eared owl. Its hoot is more drawn out and wavering than the tawny's. To get a really good view of the long-eared owl you must track it down to its daytime roost, often against the trunk of a tree; these roosts are sometimes communal. The long-eared owl is thinly spread over the British Isles, being distinctly local in southern and midland England; it is the only brown owl that breeds in Ireland. Like the tawny, it is primarily a woodland bird, but sometimes frequents open country, such as heaths, sand dunes and marshes.

The **Short-eared Owl** is nearly as big as a tawny, but has longer and more pointed wings, yellow eyes and short ear tufts which, however, are not very often erected. In general it flies by day much more often than any of our other larger owls. If there is any doubt as to its identity, a sight of the buff and black patch on the upper side of the "elbow" of the wing and a black mark in the corresponding place underneath may help to settle the matter, but a large day-flying brown owl in open country is much more likely to be this species than any other. The short-eared is not a woodland owl, except in very young plantations, and it normally frequents open, grassy or heathery country, especially moors, downs and sea-walls, where its favourite food the field vole abounds. When there is a local plague of voles, a large number of short-eared owls may congregate and breed in quite a small area of moorland. They breed more or less regularly in Orkney and other parts of Scotland, Wales, East Anglia and the north of England, but are much more widespread in winter, especially near the south and east coasts, thanks to arrivals from across the North Sea. Because these migrants come at about the same time as the woodcock, they used to be known as woodcock owls.

Of several rare species of owl that visit Britain from time to time, the **Snowy Owl** is the only one at all likely to come the way of the ordinary bird watcher, and that only if he is fairly often in winter in northern Scotland, East Anglia or Co. Mayo in Ireland. It is a huge owl, rather bigger than a buzzard, and has indeed a buzzard-like rather than an owl-like flight. White all over, with more or less dark specklings or barrings, it completely lacks the golden-buff upperparts of the barn owl.

Diurnal Birds of Prey

The diurnal birds of prey are first listed in ascending order of size (measured by length, and rather approximate in the case of the buzzards and their neighbours), for there are so many of them and they are so rarely seen together that it is sometimes difficult to remember their relative size. All birds of prey are variable, and there may be some overlapping with each adjacent pair in the list.

Merlin, male
Sparrowhawk, male

Gyrfalcon, male
Goshawk, male

Hobby, male
Merlin, female
(Cuckoo)
Hobby, female
Kestrel, male
Kestrel, female
Sparrowhawk, female
Peregrine, male
Montagu's harrier
Hen-harrier, male
Peregrine, female
Hen-harrier, female

Common buzzard, male
Rough-legged buzzard, male
Honey buzzard, male
Gyrfalcon, female
Marsh harrier
Osprey
Buzzards, female
Goshawk, female
Red kite
Sea eagle
Golden eagle

SMALL HAWKS AND FALCONS

type: the Kestrel

KESTREL	rufous, long tail
KESTREL, MALE	blue-grey head and tail
SPARROWHAWK	shortish blunt wings, long tail, barred underparts
SPARROWHAWK, MALE	slate-grey above
SPARROWHAWK, FEMALE	grey-brown above
CUCKOO	blue-grey above, barred underparts, long white-spotted tail, no hooked beak
MERLIN, MALE	blue-grey above
MERLIN, FEMALE	brown above
PEREGRINE	slate grey above, short tail, dark moustachial streak
HOBBY	short tail, dark moustachial streak

HOBBY, MALE   slate-grey above
HOBBY, FEMALE   dark brown above

At close range the smaller diurnal birds of prey can readily be told by their hooked beaks, but at greater distances their long pointed wings (except the sparrowhawk) and long tails (except the peregrine and hobby) are more useful pointers. Their typical outline is mimicked by the cuckoo, which is why this bird, in no way related to the hawks, is considered along with them. In all our smaller birds of prey the female is larger than the male, sometimes appreciably so.

Nowadays the **Kestrel** is much the most familiar small diurnal bird of prey, being widespread except in the eastern arable counties of England, where in recent years it has been heavily reduced in numbers, apparently as a result of eating prey which had been poisoned by toxic seed-dressings. It owes its familiarity largely to its well-known habit of hovering while searching for its prey, usually mice or voles, which shows up its typical outline of long pointed wings and long tail. It is the only small bird of prey which habitually hovers in daytime, though the merlin does so occasionally. At closer quarters you can see the kestrel's generally rufous plumage, with a dark tip to the tail. Female and young birds are rufous barred darker all over, but the slightly smaller males have both head and tail blue-grey. The kestrel is catholic in its choice of habitat, ranging from city centres and town parks to farmland and wild coastal cliffs. It usually nests in old crows' nests or on cliff ledges, and sometimes ledges on tall buildings.

Fifty or sixty years ago one would have had no hesitation in saying that the second commonest small British bird of prey was the **Sparrowhawk**. But the fact that it is our only unprotected bird of prey has led gamekeepers to concentrate their attack on it to such an extent that, especially in eastern England, it has become virtually extinct over wide tracts of country where it was once frequent. The sparrowhawk's outline, rather short broad blunt wings and a long broad tail, is very different from the kestrel's, and its barred underparts are also a useful distinction from the kestrel, which has streaked underparts. The male sparrowhawk, which is slate-grey above, is our second smallest diurnal bird of prey, little bigger than the mistle thrush or turtle dove. The female is not only significantly larger (grouse or partridge size), but has grey-brown plumage and still broader wings. The sparrowhawk is a fast-moving bird, and as with the kestrel its mode of flight is often the best key to its identity; it dashes along hedgerows, and often whisks up and over the other side in time to surprise a flock of finches or other small birds. In spring, like the kestrel, it may soar, but it never hovers, though it may hang in a stiff breeze on a hill-side; another typical flight technique is the "flap and glide." Sparrowhawks are birds of woodland and farmland in the breeding season, but in winter they may also go down to the shore to hunt the coastal marshes. They nearly always nest high up in trees.

Should the **Cuckoo** be mistaken for a bird of prey, it would be for the male sparrowhawk rather than the kestrel. Though at close range its straight bill identifies it at once, at a distance, especially when it is flying away, its blue-grey plumage can cause momentary confusion with the sparrowhawk. A front view shows the uniform grey of the throat and upper breast (though the lower breast and belly are barred like a sparrowhawk) and a side view at once picks out the long wings and tail, even more rakish than the kestrel's, the tail also adorned with distinctive white spots and tips. Young cuckoos are slightly more confusing, having their grey-brown or red-brown plumage barred all over and no white on the tail, but they do have a fairly conspicuous white patch on the nape, which at once separates them from all birds of prey. In spring, of course, the male cuckoo is constantly calling to announce its identity, but the liquid bubbling note of the female is less well known. I can remember putting it down as a nightingale the first time I heard it myself. Young cuckoos have a remarkable shrill wheezy scream, which attracts passing song birds to feed them even after they have left the nest. If you see a hawk-like bird flying along and being mobbed by small birds, it is much more likely to be a cuckoo than a hawk, for its persecutors seem to know that it can do them no real harm. Cuckoos are, of course, summer visitors, and breed in all parts of the British Isles, their principal victims being meadow pipits, hedgesparrows, reed warblers and pied wagtails. A huge young cuckoo, overflowing the frail nest of one of these involuntary foster parents and opening its orange mouth wide to be fed, is certainly a remarkable sight.

Our smallest bird of prey is the male **Merlin**, which like the male sparrowhawk is scarcely bigger than a mistle thrush; the female is larger, but smaller than a male kestrel. The merlin is our least distinctive smaller bird of prey, rather like a kestrel in shape, but with a somewhat shorter tail. In plumage, the male is blue-grey above like a male sparrowhawk, but with streaked underparts and a single black bar at the tip of the tail instead of three spread out along it. The female is more like a female kestrel, but has no rufous tinge to her brown upperparts and is paler beneath. On the whole habitat is a better clue to the merlin's identity than with most birds of prey. In the breeding season it is found only in the hill country of the north and west, very rare in south-west England but increasing as you go north or cross the Irish Sea. In winter most merlins forsake the uplands and, joined by immigrants from Iceland and the Continent, take to the coastal marshes and dunes all round the British Isles.

The **Peregrine** can only be marginally classed as a small bird of prey, for though the male is about the same size as a female sparrowhawk, the female is larger than two of the harriers and can be nearly as big as a buzzard. A hunting peregrine stooping on a duck or a pigeon is certainly one of the finest sights a day's bird watching in Britain has to offer. To see it in summer you must go to the rugged cliffs and hill country of the north and west, or to certain favoured cliffs along the south coast, though in winter it will join the merlin and sparrowhawk in seeking easier game along the marshes of our low southern and eastern shores. But the peregrine is well named "the wanderer" and may turn up almost anywhere; I have seen it three times over my home in the Chilterns and once even flying high above the Palace of Westminster. Its distinctive outline in the air, long, pointed, almost scythe-shaped wings and short tail, like a monstrous swift, at once distinguishes the peregrine from all other birds of prey except the much smaller hobby. It is indeed the exact opposite of the female sparrowhawk, which has a long tail and short blunt wings, so no confusion need be caused by their similar size. Plumage is less important, but adults are slate-grey above and buff streaked and barred darker below, while juveniles are dark brown above; all have a distinctive dark moustachial streak. Peregrines nest on cliff ledges, both inland and by the sea.

Our fifth small diurnal bird of prey is a summer visitor only, the **Hobby,** which is just like a miniature peregrine in outline, with the same long curved wings, short tail and dashing flight. Being so much smaller, however, it looks like an outsize swift, especially when attacking swallows and martins, its favourite prey. The hobby's plumage is also much like the peregrine's, including its moustachial streak, but females as well as young birds are dark brown above, and the adults differ from all our other breeding birds of prey in having rufous thighs. The male hobby is a little bigger than a male sparrowhawk, but the female is not much smaller than a male kestrel. Hobbies do not arrive in this country till well on in May, and then build their nests in trees, usually in the old nest of another bird. They occur mainly in the south, and even there are very local, preferring well wooded districts, or at least numerous scattered trees, such as are to be found on Salisbury Plain. Unfortunately this is one of the rare birds most harried by egg collectors, who thus deprive more law-abiding bird watchers of the chance of seeing this beautiful little falcon become more widespread.

LARGER HAWKS AND FALCONS

Our larger diurnal birds of prey range in size from Montagu's harrier to the golden eagle, which is the largest land bird still breeding in the British Isles. A sight of their hooked beaks is hardly necessary to identify them, for they are readily told by their broad and usually long wings. As they are often seen only at a distance, it is highly desirable to become familiar with their general outline as well as with the more detailed features of their plumage.

type: the Common Buzzard

COMMON BUZZARD	brown, short tail
ROUGH-LEGGED BUZZARD	brown, feathered legs
HONEY BUZZARD	brown, longer tail
RED KITE	forked tail
GOSHAWK	short blunt wings, long tail
GYRFALCON	long pointed wings, short tail
HARRIERS	long wings, long tail
MONTAGU'S HARRIER, MALE	grey, black wing-tips, black wing-bar, streaked flanks
MONTAGU'S HARRIER, FEMALE	brown, pale rump
HEN-HARRIER, MALE	grey, black wing-tips, whitish rump
HEN-HARRIER, FEMALE	brown, whitish rump
MARSH HARRIER, MALE	brown, grey on wings and tail
MARSH HARRIER, FEMALE	brown, pale crown
OSPREY	dark above, whitish below, pale crown
SEA EAGLE	very broad wings, white wedge-shaped tail, pale head
GOLDEN EAGLE	dark tawny brown, square tail

The **Common Buzzard** is now the commonest of our larger birds of prey, though at the turn of the century it was still a comparatively scarce bird. To-day it is almost common in south-west England and parts of west Wales, and breeds at least sporadically almost everywhere in Great Britain, except the eastern seaboard counties of England south of the Humber and some of the inland counties of the East Midlands. In Devon, for instance, you can often see half a dozen or more buzzards in the air at once. There are, however, no buzzards in Ireland or the Isle of Man. The common buzzard frequents mainly wooded country, especially woods in hill districts, where it nests in trees, but will also breed on rock ledges, especially on sea cliffs. Buzzards are most familiar as large birds with broad blunt wings, soaring in wide circles overhead. Their brown plumage, with rather variable patches of dark, pale and white, is of little value in identification.

In districts where the common buzzard is not often seen, two other kinds of buzzard need to be ruled out before it is named with real confidence. These are the **Rough-legged Buzzard,** an irregular winter visitor, mainly to north and east Britain, and the **Honey Buzzard,** a very rare breeding species and passage migrant, which formerly bred in the New Forest. At close range the rough-legged can easily be told from the common buzzard by its feathered legs, but in practice rough-legs rarely allow themselves to be so closely examined. One must therefore fall back on such unsatisfactory plumage details as the rough-leg's generally whiter underparts (bearing in mind the wide range of variation in the common buzzard), its more well-marked dark patch at the "elbow" of the wing, and its tail pattern. The underside of the rough-leg's tail is largely white, whereas the common's is uniformly barred; both have a dark band at the tip. Rough-legged buzzards are most likely to be seen on northern moors or eastern coastal marshes in winter. They often hover while hunting, but so, rather less often, do common buzzards. On the whole, the best advice to one wishing to identify a rough-legged buzzard is to seek the company of an experienced bird watcher!

The honey buzzard is a little easier, for it has a distinctly longer tail and more pointed wings than the common buzzard, as well as a second broad dark bar half-way along the underside of its tail. It also has a shriller call note, quite different from the gull-like *pee-oo* of the common. However, you need a good deal of field experience before you can confidently identify a honey buzzard in Britain on your own.

Buzzard-like also in its general outline is the now very rare **Red Kite,** confined to-day to the hills of central Wales, though once widespread and a common scavenger in the streets of medieval London. Its longer and deeply forked rufous tail at once identify it if you get a proper view, and in a good light you should also see its more rufous plumage and pale head. Those who wish to make the acquaintance of the kite in Wales are urged not to try to do so during the nesting season, from April to July, for our dozen or so pairs of breeding kites are very shy birds and have been known to desert their nests merely because of some picnickers nearby. Moreover, they are still threatened by egg collectors, and swarms of rubber-necking bird watchers make the task of wardening the nests much harder. Red kites are occasionally seen on migration, especially in south-west England, but all large fork-tailed birds of prey seen away from mid-Wales need to be checked against the possibility of an extremely rare vagrant, the **Black Kite,** which is darker and has a much less deeply forked tail. The black kite has only been seen in the British Isles five times, and I mention it here largely because I myself saw one of these, in the Scilly Isles in September 1938. At the time I had never seen the bird on the Continent, and did not even notice that this one had a forked tail; its true identity was not discovered till somebody shot it after I had left the islands.

Two more rare birds of prey deserve a brief mention: the goshawk and the gyrfalcon. The **Goshawk** is like a buzzard-sized sparrowhawk, with the same short, broad blunt wings and long tail. In recent years a few pairs, perhaps escaped falconry birds or possibly genuine immigrants from the Continent, have bred in wooded districts in the south of England, and an odd bird might turn up in almost any extensive tract of woodland. The **Gyrfalcon**, on the other hand, is an outsize peregrine, paler and with shorter wings and no moustachial stripe. The forms most frequently seen in Britain, mainly in the far north and west of Scotland and Ireland, hail from Iceland and Greenland. Some of these Iceland and Greenland falcons, as the books call them, are very pale indeed, and Greenland birds can be almost completely white.

Harriers are long-winged, long-tailed birds, which can be picked out at a good distance by their rakish outline and characteristic habit of gliding short distances with their wings canted slightly upwards. They range in size from Montagu's harrier, which may be smaller than a female peregrine, to the marsh harrier, which is buzzard-sized. All are at least uncommon in Britain, and the marsh harrier, after a few years of relative increase, seems once more to have become almost our rarest bird of prey—it would be the rarest if the osprey had not nipped in from abroad to take the title.

Montagu's Harrier and the **Hen-Harrier** (which takes its confusing name from its former habit of harrying hens) comprise one of those tiresome species pairs, like the marsh and willow tits, reed and marsh warblers and common and arctic terns, that so vex the bird watcher when he is learning his trade. Both males are magnificent ash-grey birds with black wing-tips, but at a reasonable range the slightly smaller cock Montagu can be told by its more pointed wings, black wing-bar, rufous-streaked flanks and less conspicuously pale rump. Of these the two positive characters of the wing-bar and streaked flanks, though not always easy to see, are more satisfactory than the two relative ones, which are not much good except to somebody already familiar with both. Single female Montagu's and hen-harriers are emphatically not to be identified in the field, even by professing experts, because nothing but the slenderer build of Montagu's and the whiter rump of the hen-harrier distinguish them; both are brown with barred tails, whence the name ring-tail by which they are often collectively known. Juveniles are easier, because young Montagu's are easily told by their deep chestnut-buff underparts, whereas young hen-harriers are indistinguishable from their mothers.

Fortunately season and habitat are useful supplementary ways of identifying this confusing pair. Montagu's is a summer visitor, mainly to the south of England, whereas the hen-harrier breeds in Britain only in the Highlands and islands of Scotland, especially the Orkneys. In winter many hen-harriers come south to frequent coastal marshes on the south and east coasts, but October and April are the only months where there is a serious overlap between the two species in the south. Look for Montagu's in rough, open, heathy places, including very young forestry plantations; for the hen-harrier on moors and other open country in summer, and in winter on coastal marshlands.

Whereas these two, and more especially Montagu's, look at times like a huge kestrel in outline, the **Marsh Harrier** might more readily be mistaken for a rather slender buzzard, for its flight is heavier and much less graceful than its relatives'. The male marsh harrier is a grey and brown bird, grey on the wings and tail, brown on the back and underparts. The female and young birds are brown, with a fairly conspicuous pale creamy crown; this separates them from all other buzzard-sized birds of prey except the osprey, which has very different habits. At present the marsh harrier breeds only on a few coastal marshes in East Anglia, and occasionally in other parts of the country. Like Montagu's it is a summer visitor only, though odd birds occasionally winter with us.

The **Osprey,** now the pride of Speyside, where its eyrie near Loch Garten is the best known rare-bird site in Britain, visited by some 20,000 tourists every year, is one of the four British birds that have re-established themselves as breeding species here during the present century; the others are the avocet, bittern and black-tailed godwit. Any loch in the Highlands is now liable to an occasional visit from an osprey during the spring and autumn migration periods, and so is almost any large lake or reservoir in the south. You are most likely to see it first while it is perched on a post or by the water, awaiting its luck, but when it flies its long wings flap slowly over the water. Then, if you are lucky, you will see it stoop feet first to the water and fly heavily off with a fish; this plunging habit is unique among British birds of prey, though carrion crows will sometimes pick dead fish off the water in this way. The osprey's plumage is dark above and whitish below, with a pale crown like the female marsh harrier.

Our only other large bird of prey associated with water is the **Sea Eagle,** now one of our rarer visitors, though at one time it bred all round our coasts, even as far south as the Isle of Wight. It is a huge bird with great broad wings, and a pale, often almost white head. Its tail is wedge-shaped, dark in young birds but white in the adults, whence its book name of white-tailed eagle. You need to see both the shape and colour of an eagle's tail, for if it is all-white and wedge-shaped the bird is an adult sea eagle; if white with a dark tip and square-ended, an immature golden eagle; if dark and wedge-shaped, an immature sea eagle; and if dark and square, an adult golden.

The **Golden Eagle,** our largest and most impressive bird of prey, is still a comparatively frequent bird in parts of the Highlands and islands of Scotland. In recent years it has also been striving to re-establish itself in Galloway and Northern Ireland, and has even been seen in the Lake District. It is easy enough to identify a golden eagle in its native Highlands; if you get a proper view you will be in little doubt as to what the monstrous bird can be. Its whole plumage is dark tawny brown, and even at long range its longer head and tail give it a distinguishable outline from the buzzard. The majestic soaring flight of a golden eagle is worth going a long way to see.

Brightly Coloured Rarities

WAXWING	brown crest, yellow tip to tail, yellow and red on wings
GOLDEN ORIOLE, COCK	black and yellow
GOLDEN ORIOLE, HEN	yellowish-green
HOOPOE	black and white crest and barred wings, curved bill
BEE-EATER	blue-green, chestnut, yellow and black; long tail

There are certain special rarities that every bird watcher hopes to see in Britain one day, even if he has already seen them on the Continent. Some, like the waxwing, occur here frequently enough to offer a reasonable chance of success, but many people watch birds all their lives without seeing a hoopoe or golden oriole in Britain, though a few do cross the Channel every year. With others, such as the bee-eater, roller and nutcracker, most bird watchers have barely a one per cent chance of achieving their ambition.

The **Waxwing** is a very distinctive crested cinnamon-brown bird, about starling-size, that invades Britain, often in some numbers, in autumn and winter at irregular intervals. The last notable invasion was in the winter of 1959-60. When it does come, it is as likely to be seen in town and suburban parks and gardens as anywhere, for it feeds on such berried shrubs as cotoneaster, pyracantha and hawthorn. Besides the crest, you should be able to see at close range (for the birds are usually quite tame) the black chin, the yellow tip to the tail, and the curious waxy red and yellow blobs on the wings that have given the bird its name.

The main difficulty with the **Golden Oriole** is that it is so shy and retiring that unless you are familiar with its distinctive call, a loud mellow flute-like *weela-wee-o*, you can very easily overlook it. If seen, or more likely glimpsed in the foliage of a tree, the cock's combination of bright yellow body with black wings and tail is unmistakable. Hen orioles are dull yellowish-green birds, especially liable to be wishfully confused with young green woodpeckers, which have no red on their heads. An oriole, however, is rather smaller than a mistle thrush, whereas a green woodpecker is nearly as big as a jackdaw; nor would an oriole ever creep up tree trunks or branches like a woodpecker. May is about the best month for a chance of seeing a golden oriole in Britain, and winter the most unlikely time. Occasional pairs have bred in the south.

Every bird watcher looks out on his lawn in the morning hoping at last to see a **Hoopoe** strutting there. At least I know I do. For lawns are much favoured by hoopoes, which are perhaps the most striking of the various exotic-looking rarities that an ordinary bird watcher may hope to see. At close range, with its fantastic fan-like crest raised, it is unmistakable, but if all you have seen is a brief view of a cinnamon-coloured bird about the size of a mistle thrush slipping into cover, then you must wait till it comes out again. For once it has selected a lawn or other feeding place, it usually returns there after being disturbed, so long as you can persuade the owner of the garden to desist from gardening! When it does come back, look for the black-and-white barred and rounded wings, which make it look just like a huge moth in flight, and the curved bill. Its call is a distinctive triple *hoo-hoo-hoo*, not to be confused with the cooing of the stock dove or the collared dove. Hoopoes may turn up almost anywhere in the south, but mainly between spring and autumn, and have bred here quite a few times.

The **Bee-eater** vies with the kingfisher as the most brilliantly plumaged wild bird likely to be seen in the British Isles. About the size of a mistle thrush, it has a slightly curved bill, long tail with the central feathers projecting, and harlequin plumage compounded of blue-green, chestnut, yellow and black. Its flight is rather swallow-like and its liquid bell-like *quilp* note is easily recognised again when you have once heard it. Spring and autumn in the south are the most likely time and place for the extreme good fortune of the sight of a bee-eater in Britain; a few years ago two pairs actually bred in Sussex.

You have even less chance of seeing a roller or a nutcracker in Britain than you have a bee-eater. The **Roller** is a jackdaw-sized crow-like bird combining generally blue-green plumage with a chestnut back. The **Nutcracker** actually is a crow; it is also jackdaw-sized and is brown, spotted white all over. Other brightly coloured rarities include the bluethroat (p. 58), the woodchat shrike (p. 71), the red-breasted flycatcher (p. 73) and the rosy pastor (p. 79).

A few birds often imagined to be brightly coloured rarities when first seen by bird watching tiros should perhaps also be mentioned briefly, though they are in fact perfectly ordinary resident British birds and not rare at all. The green woodpecker (p. 80) is pre-eminent among these native "exotics," and probably gives rise to more rumours of golden oriole and other rarities in a year than any other single native bird. The gaudy jay (p. 99) and the brilliant kingfisher (p. 86) are probably both well enough known to most people not to be mistaken for anything else on a good view, but confusion is likely to result from the garbled reports of people who have had only a poor view of them. Budgerigars, blue or green with long tails, are the most frequent of many cage-birds that are liable to escape.

9. BUILT-UP AREAS: *a*, House Sparrow; *b*, Great Tit; *c*, Black Redstart; *d*, Starlings

a b

14 & 15. FARMLAND: *a*, Little Owl; *b*, Barn Owl; *c*, Kestrel; *d*, Partridge; *e*, Yellowhammer

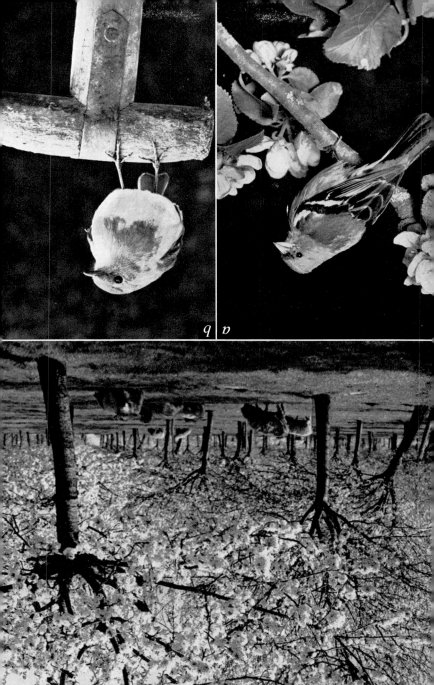

q v

10 & 11. TOWN PARKS AND SQUARES: *a*, Woodpigeon; *b*, Tawny Owl; *c*, Greenfinch; *d*, Blackbird

16 & 17. DOWNLAND: *a*, Stone Curlew; *b*, Stonechat; *c*, Wheatear; *d*, Skylark

18 & 19. LOWLAND MOORS AND OPEN HEATH: *a*, Linnet; *b*, Dartford Warbler; *c*, Nightjar; *d*, Red-backed Shrike

20 & 21. INLAND CLIFFS AND QUARRIES: *a*, Raven; *b*, Jackdaw; *c*, Peregrine; *d*, Buzzard

a *b*

c d

22 & 23. UPLAND MOORS AND ROUGH GRAZING: *a*, Cuckoo (juvenile); *b*, Merlin; *c*, Meadow Pipit; *d*, Greenshank; *e*, Red Grouse

e

24. MOUNTAIN TOPS: *a*, Golden Eagle; *b*, Dotterel; *c*, Ptarmigan (in winter plumag

WATERSIDE BIRDS

Waders: Plovers, Sandpipers, Snipe, etc.

Most waders are long-legged, long-billed birds that feed in marshy places and shallow water. Bill and leg length can, however, vary greatly within the group, and the plovers, for instance, are all relatively short-billed. Many of them, such as the lapwing, golden plover and dotterel, also regularly breed at some distance from water or marshy ground, while a few, such as the stone curlew and the woodcock, are almost entirely terrestrial in their way of life. All the waders that breed regularly in the British Isles nest on the ground. Waders are most easily seen during the migration periods in spring (mid-April to early June) and autumn (late July to early October), when many Arctic breeding species halt for a time at inland marshes, sewage farms and freshwater margins, and again in the winter, when large numbers of dunlins, redshanks, ringed plovers, curlews and other species feed on mudflats all around our coasts. A few non-breeding individuals of all the Arctic breeding species may spend the summer on our shores, especially in Scotland, and some, such as the turnstone and purple sandpiper, have been suspected of breeding with us, but so far without proof.

In identifying waders, you should pay attention, not only to the length of leg and bill, but also to the shape of the bill (whether curved or not) and the pattern of bars, spots and patches on the wings and tail. Voice is also a useful guide, the calls of all species being quite distinctive.

In the following list the British breeding and migrant waders are given in ascending order of size:

Temminck's stint	Common snipe
Little stint	Golden plover
Little ringed plover	Grey plover
Kentish plover	Ruff
Dunlin	Common redshank
Curlew sandpiper	Spotted redshank
Ringed plover	Greenshank
Jack snipe	Lapwing
Common sandpiper	Stilt
Wood sandpiper	Bar-tailed godwit
Sanderling	Whimbrel
Purple sandpiper	Black-tailed godwit
Green sandpiper	Avocet
Turnstone	Oystercatcher
Knot	Curlew

SHORT-BILLED WADERS (PLOVERS)

type: the Ringed Plover

RINGED PLOVER	black and white head pattern, whitish wing-bars, legs yellow
LITTLE RINGED PLOVER	like ringed plover with no wing-bars
KENTISH PLOVER	like ringed plover with less or no black on head, legs blackish
TURNSTONE	black, white and chestnut; orange bill
LAPWING	black and white, rounded wings, crested
GOLDEN PLOVER	yellowish; black cheeks, throat and underparts in summer
GREY PLOVER	greyish; black patch under wing; black cheeks, throat and underparts in summer

The plovers as a group are more likely to be seen away from marshy ground or the margins of fresh or salt water than most other waders. The lapwing regularly both feeds and breeds on dry farmland, downland and moorland; the golden plover joins the lapwing on the farmland in winter and on the moorland in spring and summer; the dotterel breeds on mountain tops and is seen on migration in dry habitats much more often than in wet ones; even the ringed plover breeds in dry places in a few areas. The little ringed plover is mostly seen by fresh water; the grey and ringed plovers and turnstone by salt water; and the lapwing and golden plover by both.

When I was aged about ten I used to see small parties of shore-birds flying up and down the then deserted beach at West Worthing in Sussex, and because they used to turn sharply and fly back again, I imagined they must be terns. It was only some time later that I learned that they were in fact ringed plovers. The **Ringed Plover** is a small short-billed sandy brown wader, most easily identified by its black and white head pattern and the white bar it shows on each wing in flight. Adults have their crown, cheeks and breast-band black, with a white forehead and collar, which is the ring that gives the bird its name, and yellow legs. Females are browner and young birds greyer on the black parts. Bill colour is important in comparing the ringed with both the little ringed and Kentish plovers; it is orange or dull yellow with a dark tip in adults, and blackish with a yellow base in young birds. The liquid, musical *too-i* call is another useful distinction. Ringed plovers both breed and winter widely around the coasts of the British Isles, breeding especially on sandy and shingly shores and wintering on muddy ones. They also occur at fresh water inland on migration and in a few areas also breed inland, but not south of the Trent, except in the Breckland of Norfolk and Suffolk.

The **Little Ringed Plover** is a relative newcomer to Britain. Before 1938, when a pair nested at Tring Reservoirs in Hertfordshire, the bird had been recorded barely a dozen times, but since 1944 it has bred every year. Around 100 pairs now breed in England each year, the great majority of them south and east of a line drawn from the Humber to Poole Harbour. They do in fact breed, or at least have bred, in every county except Rutland north and west to Yorkshire, Cheshire, Staffordshire, Warwickshire, Gloucestershire, Berkshire and Hampshire. The favoured breeding site is a working gravel-pit, but sometimes a pair will nest by other kinds of fresh water or even in a ploughed field a little distance away. The sites it prefers on the Continent, shingle banks in rivers, such as are commonly found on the Loire for instance, are scarce in the part of England it has so far colonised. The little ringed plover is now a summer visitor to the parts of England where it breeds, and is also a spring and autumn passage migrant to inland freshwater margins and sewage farms in the same general area. Since the ringed plover itself also sometimes breeds inland, you cannot assume, without specific identification, that a pair of "ringed plovers" nesting inland in England belong to the smaller species.

Fortunately, the smaller size, detectable by those reasonably familiar with both species, is not the only point that separates them. When it flies, the little ringed plover at once reveals its identity by the absence of its larger relative's pale wing-bar, and if it calls, its very different *pee-oo* note will also betray it. On a close view you can also see that its bill is yellow only at the base of the lower mandible, while immediately around the eye is a narrow yellow ring, called the orbital ring.

The only other bird likely to be confounded with the ringed plover is the now very rare **Kentish Plover,** which is as small as the little ringed plover and is best told by its black bill and legs and the much smaller amount of black about its head. The females indeed have only brown on the head. Their call note is also quite different. The Kentish Plover probably now ranks as our rarest breeding bird, rarer even than the osprey, for it may not nest every year. It used to breed in small numbers on the extensive shingle tracts on the south-east coast between Hythe and Hastings, and a pair or two may still do so, both here and elsewhere.

The **Turnstone** is a dumpy little black and white (in winter) or black and tan (in summer) wader, most often seen on seaweed-covered rocks. Though most frequent in the winter half of the year, it can in fact be seen in the British Isles throughout the summer too. The turnstone derives its name from its habit of turning over small stones and seaweed in search of food. It is one of the most distinctive of our smaller waders, looking very black and white both at rest and in flight. Its short black bill, revealing its kinship to the plovers, and its orange legs are both useful clues to its identity. Inland it is one of the scarcer passage migrants to reservoirs and sewage farms.

The dotterel, though a true plover, is now so rarely seen in Britain away from its mountain breeding haunts that it has seemed more appropriate to deal with it as a mountain bird (p. 87).

Much the most familiar of our three larger plovers is the **Lapwing** or peewit, also known in books as the green plover. Though at a distance it looks a black and white bird, in bright sunshine the black of its mantle turns to a brilliant green, whence the book-name. The names peewit and lapwing derive respectively from the bird's call and from the remarkable lapping sound its wings make during the courtship flight in spring. No other British birds, except the owls and the larger birds of prey have such rounded wing-tips as the lapwing, and this is the bird's most important field character. Next comes its crest (no other British wader is crested), which is most conspicuous in spring and summer. Finally most of its calls make some variation on the *pee-wit* or *p'weet* theme. The lapwing is much the most varied of our waders in its habitat, breeding in many types of open country from coastal marshes and damp rushy fields inland through ordinary farmland, both arable and pasture, to heaths, moors and mountains. In autumn and winter it frequents freshwater margins, estuaries and coastal mudflats. During hard weather on the Continent or in eastern Britain many lapwings fly westwards and may then sometimes be seen passing over London and other large towns.

In winter flocks of lapwings, especially on the eastern side of Britain, you will often find smaller sharp-winged birds, contrasting strongly with their round-winged companions. If these are not dumpy enough to be starlings, they will almost certainly prove to be **Golden Plovers**. Large flocks wholly composed of golden plovers also occur, both in eastern Britain and in the more northerly parts of the west. The golden plover is really golden only in spring and summer, when its plumage is mainly golden brown spangled with black and white. Our native breeding birds have blackish cheeks, throat and underparts, but the northern breeding birds, which winter with us and begin to acquire their full nuptial plumage in March, look strikingly different, with the black parts much darker and bordered by a conspicuous white line. These northern birds may be seen in flocks in many parts of Britain in March and April, just before they leave for Scandinavia and Iceland. Our own golden plovers breed on moors and mountains throughout the northern and western highland zone of Britain, though very sparsely in south-west England; their mournful liquid cry is one of the most typical sounds of our hill country. In autumn and winter, when our own birds and the northern ones are not separable in the field, they are found in the same types of habitat as the lapwing, and are perhaps more frequent on the shore.

Winter golden plovers on the shore, which are much duller and more uniform in plumage than the summer birds of the moors, need to be distinguished from a somewhat larger relative, the **Grey Plover**. Though the ground colour of the golden plover's plumage is yellowish-brown and the grey plover's silvery grey, any colour is hard to see in poor light on the winter mudflats. So they are most easily told apart when they are in flight, for then the conspicuous black mark under the grey plover's wing is plain to see and its wing-bar and whitish rump are also easier to detect. When in flight too, the grey plover more often utters its distinctive triple call note, *phee-oo-ee*, which contrasts with the golden plover's single pipe; the grey plover's can sound remarkably like a boy whistling. Grey plovers are quite common on estuaries and mudflats in winter, often scattered singly over the mud as far as the eye can see, but they are uncommon by fresh water inland. When they do turn up inland, it is likely to be in spring, in perhaps the handsomest breeding plumage of any of our waders, the black, white and gold of the breeding northern golden plover being replaced by a similar pattern of black, white and silver.

One other British bird that has been given the name of plover, though it is not one, is the stone curlew (p. 91), sometimes known as the Norfolk plover.

SMALL AND MEDIUM-SIZED LONG-BILLED WADERS (SANDPIPERS AND SNIPE)

type: the Dunlin

DUNLIN	brown above, with white in tail; white below in winter, black in summer
LITTLE STINT	like miniature winter dunlin but no white in tail
TEMMINCK'S STINT	like miniature common sandpiper, except in flight
CURLEW SANDPIPER	like winter dunlin with conspicuous white rump; red breeding plumage
SANDERLING	very pale grey in winter, warm brown in summer

PURPLE SANDPIPER	very dark, yellow legs
KNOT	grey in winter, reddish in summer
COMMON SANDPIPER	distinctive low flickering flight
WOOD SANDPIPER	rump white but tail barred
GREEN SANDPIPER	conspicuous white rump and tail
RUFF	like common redshank without white wing-bars or rump; bill and leg colour variable; breeding males have ruffs and ear tufts
COMMON REDSHANK	conspicuous white wing-bars and rump, red bill and legs
GREENSHANK	conspicuous white rump and tail, greenish legs
SPOTTED REDSHANK	snipe-like bill, white rump, red legs, very dark breeding plumage
COMMON SNIPE	very long bill, zigzag flight
JACK SNIPE	like small common snipe with shorter bill and different head pattern

This is the group of waders that gives most trouble to the beginner, because at first he does not come across many of them—only common snipe, common redshank and common sandpiper are likely to fall to the glass of the bird watcher on an ordinary country walk, away from marshes, mudflats or the seashore—and he takes longer to become familiar with those that are really only likely to be seen for the six to eight weeks of the spring and two or three months of the autumn migration seasons. Many of them too are more easily identified on the wing than on the ground, because then they show their wing-bars and rump patches and make their distinctive flight calls, but this involves one in the dilemma of whether to go on peering at a bird that is just too far off to be sure of its identity on the ground, or to flush it and risk a poor view and never seeing it again.

The smaller waders may be defined as those up to the size of a knot, which is a kind of median bird, above which come the "shanks," the ruff and the common snipe. **Dunlin** and ringed plovers are the two commonest small waders, the dunlin being very variable in size. Our native breeding birds are among the smallest waders likely to be seen on the shore, while the migrant dunlin from the Arctic are appreciably larger and about the size of a ringed plover. Dunlin are dumpy little birds, with neither bill nor legs exceptionally long. In autumn and winter they are grey-brown above and white below; at this time of year the white sides to their rump and tail, their light wing-bars and their rather weak call *treeep* are their best field characters, and in fact their lack of any of the more striking markings of other small waders is one of the best pointers to their identity. In spring and summer, however, the black belly of their breeding plumage makes them the easiest of all small waders to spot. In late summer and autumn the abundant young birds of the year can be distinguished by their buffish tinge. Dunlins are found on both muddy and sandy seashores and estuaries, though they prefer muddy ones, on marsh pools of all kinds from saltings to sewage farms, and by freshwater margins, especially those of reservoirs. Inland they occur most often during the spring and autumn migrations, but sometimes also in winter. On the shore, however, you may find them in any month of the year, though much commoner in the winter half. To find dunlin breeding in Britain, you must go to the higher peaty and grassy moorlands from South Wales northwards, to coastal marshes northwards from Lancashire, and to both these types of habitat in Ireland.

The only long-billed waders smaller than our breeding dunlin are the two stints, both passage migrants from high northern latitudes: the **Little Stint** uncommon but regular, **Temminck's Stint** much scarcer but a breeding bird *manqué*, for it attempted to nest in either Scotland or Yorkshire three times between 1934 and 1951. The little stint is like a miniature winter dunlin, but with no white in the tail and a distinct call note, *chik*. In spring and summer the little stint's breast is spotted warm brown all over, but in autumn and winter it becomes white in the middle, except for the birds of the year (and many of the little stints seen in Britain in autumn are these juveniles) which have buffish breasts like young dunlins. Temminck's stint, on the other hand, resembles a miniature common sandpiper (p. 120), and differs from the little stint both in its spluttering call *pt-r-r-r-r* and in having white outer tail feathers. Little stints frequent both the seashore and inland pools and marshes, but Temminck's much prefer fresh water to salt.

Often associated with the little stint on the marsh pools in autumn is another high Arctic breeder, the **Curlew Sandpiper,** which is slightly larger than the dunlin that come to us from the Arctic at the same time. It differs from them both in having a markedly down-curved bill (though some dunlin also have their bills slightly down-curved) and especially in its conspicuous white rump. This is essentially a bird that must be flushed to make sure of its identity, when the white rump will show up as clearly as if it were a house martin, but bear in mind that several other waders, notably the green sandpiper (p. 121), which is commoner, also have white rumps. In spring and summer the curlew sandpiper is even more easily identified, for its whole plumage, except for the white on the rump and under the tail, is a beautiful shade of pinkish-cinnamon. Alas, it is much less often seen in Britain in this plumage than in its duller and more dunlin-like winter garb.

In my early bird-watching days I can remember anxiously examining many winter dunlin, trying to turn them into **Sanderling,** the next largest of the dunlin-like waders. I need not have bothered, for I had no doubt about my first sanderling when I did see it, it was such a pale grey. Winter sanderling can look almost white in a bright light, and are in fact white underneath and pale grey above, with a distinctive blackish spot on each shoulder. In spring and summer plumage, less often seen in Britain, sanderling are a beautiful warm brown both above and on the breast, and can, of course, readily be told from dunlin by their white bellies. The sanderling is one of the few birds whose name does help in identifying it. The *Concise Oxford Dictionary* rather helplessly puts (?) for the derivation of the bird's name, but if the brothers Fowler had consulted any bird watcher they would have been told that the sanderling is so called in both English and German because it frequents sandy shores. In Britain you do in fact very rarely see a sanderling on any shore but a sandy one, though on spring passage to the Arctic a few will visit freshwater margins inland, and contrariwise you rarely walk along an extensive sandy beach in winter without coming across a small party of sanderlings scurrying away from you. All small waders scurry, but sanderlings scurry faster than most, and will try to outdistance you without taking wing, even if you chase them, as I did once, on a bicycle.

Slightly larger again is the **Purple Sandpiper,** another bird whose habitat is a good guide to its identity. Unlike all the other dunlin-like waders, you seek it not on the muddy or sandy shore but on the rocky one, including such artificial rocks as groynes and breakwaters, especially where there is a good covering of brown seaweeds; it is more frequent on our northern than our southern coasts. The purple sandpiper is a frequent companion of the turnstone on weedy rocks, but you will probably scan many parties of turnstones before finding one that has one or two purple sandpipers as hangers on. The purple sandpiper is like a large dark dunlin with yellow legs; it is in fact the only small, dark, long-billed wader with yellow legs. The purple gloss on its mantle can be seen only at very close range.

The **Knot** is the largest of the dumpy dunlin-like waders, and shares with the dunlin itself a busy head-down attitude when feeding that helps to pick it out at a distance from other medium-sized waders on the shore. Knots are highly gregarious, even more so than most of our waders, and on some favoured shores, such as those of Liverpool Bay, occur in very large numbers indeed. T. A. Coward wrote of having "seen the Lancashire tide-line, for at least a mile, one continuous ribbon of birds, varying in width from two or three feet to six or more yards." Seen under such conditions knots identify themselves, but sometimes you will see a solitary bird far out over the mudflats, too large for a dunlin, too small and long-billed to be a grey plover. Then its more or less uniform grey plumage, with white underparts but no white in the tail, will help to identify the bird as a knot. In spring and summer the knot is one of our four waders with a reddish breeding plumage, the others being the curlew sandpiper and the two godwits. Knots are uncommon at fresh water inland, even on migration, and for the most part must be sought on extensive mudflats in the winter half of the year, and less frequently on sandy shores.

Having followed the dunlin line as far upwards as it will take us, we must now return to the rather longer-legged parallel line that starts with the common sandpiper (but see Temminck's stint, page 119) and ends with the "shanks." The **Common Sandpiper** is the first migrant wader the average bird-watching beginner is likely to encounter, for it turns up by all kinds of fresh water inland, such as rivers, streams, ponds and even park lakes in towns, much more often than any other wader, large or small. It is the size of our larger dunlins, and its undistinguished plumage is dark above and white below, with white wing-bars and white sides to the tail.

It is therefore easier to identify by its characteristic behaviour; when disturbed, it flies off, low over the water, with a shrill *twee-wee-wee* call and flickering wings. When it pitches, it often bobs its head and tail nervously up and down, like a dipper but quite unlike a dunlin. Common sandpipers breed by rivers, streams and lakes in the hill districts of Wales, northern England, Scotland and Ireland, and exceptionally also by lowland rivers and waters in the south and east.

Slightly larger is the much scarcer **Wood Sandpiper,** whose plumage pattern of dark above and white below is varied only by a white rump and a barred tail. It is, however, more likely to be confused with the still larger but more frequent **Green Sandpiper,** which looks a very black and white bird in the air as it has a very prominent white rump *and* tail. Both wood and green sandpipers tower in the air when flushed and never fly low over the water, but the notes they utter are very different: the green has a loud shrill *weet-a-weet*, but the wood's usually triple *wee-wee-wee* is much weaker and flatter in tone. Both are essentially passage migrants of freshwater margins inland, and if seen by the sea will be in saltmarshes not on the open shore. A few green sandpipers stay the winter in the south, often in the same spot year after year, and both green and wood have bred recently in the Scottish Highlands. It is worth remembering, if you do chance to see one in the breeding season, that the green sandpiper habitually and the wood occasionally lays its eggs in the old nest of another bird in a tree.

The **Ruff** is one of the three marshland breeding birds lost to Britain during the nineteenth century which have not yet returned; the others are the black tern and Savi's warbler. (Those which have returned are the bittern, the avocet and the black-tailed godwit.) Ruffs are remarkably variable in size, the females, known as reeves, ranging in size from knot to redshank, and the males from redshank to greenshank. In autumn and winter, when ruffs and reeves share the same plumage, they are brown, streaked darker above (the streaks having much the same effect as those on a hen pheasant), with a buffish breast and pale underparts, and no distinctive marking except a pale wing-bar and white sides to the rump and tail. Any doubtful looking medium-sized brown wader nine times out of ten turns out to be a ruff or reeve. Leg colour is no help at all, as it may be green, grey, yellow, orange or pinkish; I have more than once spent some time in trying to turn a yellow-legged ruff into a lesser yellowlegs, the North American equivalent of our redshank. In spring and summer male ruffs are a very different kettle of fish, for the fantastic head adornments of their breeding plumage, that give them their name, make them the most unmistakable waders of all. These ruffs on a male ruff's head may be black, brown, buff or white, and either plain, streaked or barred; in addition there are ear tufts, which may be of a different colour. Ruffs and reeves are more often seen at inland pools than on the shore, and show an increasing tendency to stay the winter. They are among the earliest of the wader passage migrants in spring, often arriving in March.

Many a bird watcher has shaken his fist at a **Common Redshank,** as its noisy watchfulness has betrayed his presence to some more interesting bird. Its broad white wing-bars make the redshank one of the easiest waders to identify; you do not even need to see its red bill and legs. Its loud yelping cries you will inevitably hear, for it utters them every time it rises. Redshanks breed far inland, on marshes and in damp riverside meadows, as well as on coastal marshes, and begin to return to their breeding sites as early as February. Immediately after they finish nesting they repair to the nearest freshwater margin, but in autumn and winter they go abroad, or down to the sea, where they are joined on the mudflats and sandy shores by many more redshanks from Iceland and northern Europe.

Though the **Greenshank** is not rare in its Highland breeding haunts, many bird watchers are excited to see it by some inland pool or lake shore in the lowlands. It is a sign that some more recondite rarity may be in the offing. It is well worth learning the loud musical yodel of the greenshank, which has enabled me three times to detect the bird migrating over my Oxfordshire home, far from any marsh or pool, and once actually to see it flying by. When you do see it, it is like a rather large redshank, with no white wing-bars but a very large and conspicuous patch of white rump and tail. In the early stages of a bird-watching career it can be confused with the smaller and darker green sandpiper, as I remember to my own chagrin, but the call notes of the two are quite distinct. This is another wader which may winter in the south of England and Ireland, and it is said to do so regularly as far north as the Solway Firth and the western isles of Scotland. Greenshanks nest widely in the Scottish Highlands, north and west of the Spey valley, and in 1924-25 a pair nested as far south as the Lammermuir Hills on the borders of Berwickshire.

The sight of a **Spotted Redshank** is always enough to make even the most expert bird watcher feel his day has been well spent; if it should be in its handsome breeding plumage, then it is a red-letter day indeed. It is a redshank in the strict sense of having blood-red legs, but its long snipe-like bill and absence of white in the wings make it otherwise very unlike the common redshank. It shares a white rump with both greenshank and common redshank, but in its bill colour, red at the base only, and distinctive double call note *too-it* it differs from both its relatives. Its breeding plumage, which gives rise to its alternative name of dusky redshank, is almost entirely deep greyish-black, spotted with white, a unique combination among British waders. The spotted redshank is another double passage migrant, the first post-breeding birds sometimes getting back from the Arctic as early as mid-July, while a few sometimes overwinter with us, especially in south-west England and southern Ireland.

The two snipes are so different from all our other small and medium-sized waders that I have left them till the last. The bill of the **Common Snipe** is so fantastically long (one-quarter of the total length of the bird) that a sight of it alone is enough to identify its owner. When a snipe dashes up, and zigzags wildly away, uttering a harsh *creech creech*, you cannot always see the bill, but this behaviour is enough to identify the bird as a common snipe, provided its plumage is brown and its size a little smaller than a redshank. In the breeding season they have one other very distinctive habit, of "drumming" or "bleating," when they dive down steeply while in flight, emitting a curious vibrant humming sound from two small feathers projecting at right angles from their tail. No other British bird has such a performance or makes such a sound, which the uninitiated would not recognise as coming from a bird at all. Common snipe breed in boggy and marshy places, including damp meadows in river valleys; in autumn and winter they prefer freshwater margins and marshes to the seashore.

Whereas the common snipe is with us all the year round, the smaller **Jack Snipe** is only a passage migrant and winter visitor, frequenting much the same types of habitat, boggy and marshy places and freshwater margins. It differs from the common snipe mainly in its much shorter bill, the two narrow pale streaks on its head instead of one broad one, and its quite different behaviour when flushed. Instead of dashing noisily away with frequent changes of direction, it gets up silently, flies more directly and drops down again much sooner. Its call, if it does make one, is low and weak.

LARGE LONG-BILLED WADERS

type: the Curlew

CURLEW	brown, white rump, down-curved bill
WHIMBREL	like small curlew with different head pattern
BLACK-TAILED GODWIT	conspicuous white wing-bars, straight bill, red breeding plumage
BAR-TAILED GODWIT	like small curlew with straight bill, red breeding plumage

OYSTERCATCHER	black and white, orange bill, pink legs
AVOCET	black and white, up-curved bill, grey legs
STILT	black and white, immensely long reddish legs
HERON	mainly grey, long legs, broad wings
SPOONBILL	all white, spoon-shaped bill, long legs

The larger waders fall neatly into two divisions, four brown birds headed by the curlew, and three black and white ones, the oystercatcher, the avocet, and as a long shot the stilt. To these may be added two birds that are not strictly waders at all, though they are long-legged, long-billed and wade, the heron and the spoonbill.

The **Curlew** is easy enough to identify at most times and in most places, though at some times and in some places you need to bear in mind the possibility of the **Whimbrel**. The curlew is our largest true wader, and basically is a large brown long-legged bird with a whitish rump and a long down-curved bill, and this is enough to identify it on the moors in the breeding season, and on the shore in winter. During the migration times, however, April-May and August-September, there are often whimbrels about, and in the far north of Scotland and its isles they may even be breeding. Whimbrels are just like small curlews, flying with a quicker wing-beat and uttering a quite different call, a distinctive tittering trill, reputed to contain seven notes, whence the bird used to be called the seven whistler. At close range you can also see that it has three streaks down the centre of its crown, two dark and one pale. The curlew's cry, the *courlee* that gives it its name, is very well known as a result of its being used as the signature tune of one of the B.B.C.'s excellent natural history programmes. Its beautiful bubbling song is also well known, but the whimbrel's not dissimilar song is only likely to be heard on its breeding grounds. The curlew also has many loud and mostly pleasant call notes, and even occasionally makes a sound resembling the whimbrel's tittering trill. So it is always a good idea to check by sight when you hear a whimbrel call, and make certain that the bird that utters it is smaller than a curlew and flying faster. Both curlew and whimbrel are variable in size, though there is an appreciable gap between the largest whimbrels and the smallest curlews; the size differential between average birds is roughly the same as between the common and herring gulls. Oddly enough, it is sometimes possible to confuse curlews for brown immature herring gulls at first glance, for both tend to fly rather lazily in V-formation. But of course one glance at the shape of their bills settles the question.

The curlew is a common breeding bird all over our northern and western moors and coastal dunes, and nests more locally on heaths and in valley grassland in the south, where it has been spreading in recent years, for instance in the Thames valley. In autumn and winter curlews are common by the sea, especially in estuaries and on muddy and sandy shores, but are not often seen by fresh water inland away from their breeding haunts. Migrating whimbrels frequent much the same places as wintering curlews and also breed on bleak moorlands in the Shetlands and irregularly elsewhere in the northern Highlands.

Both the **Black-tailed Godwit** and **Bar-tailed Godwit** can be readily told from the curlew and whimbrel by their straight bills; from each other they are best distinguished by the broad white bar on the wings of the flying black-tail. Indeed a black-tail in flight is much more likely to be taken for an oystercatcher than for a bar-tail. The black-tail is the larger of the two, but godwits are variable in size, and the largest bar-tails approach the smallest black-tails. A more useful distinction is the colour of the tail, which can sometimes be seen before the bird takes flight; as their names suggest, the black-tail has a black tip to its white tail, and the bar-tail a barred tip. In winter godwits are plain brown with white rumps, and look rather like straight-billed whimbrels; in spring and summer, however, they both have handsome reddish breeding plumages, the only larger waders to do so. It is a great pity that godwits are not more often seen in Britain in this plumage.

The bar-tail is a winter visitor, mainly to sandy and muddy seashores, and is rather unusual inland, but the black-tail, which a generation ago was no more than a rather scarce passage migrant, has recently much increased as a winter visitor and has also established a small breeding colony. Black-tailed godwits now winter regularly in some numbers in several south and west coast estuaries, and it is thought that these may come from Iceland, where the bird has recently increased as a breeder. The locality where several pairs of black-tails have bred in England every year since 1952 is a well-kept secret. Occasional pairs have also nested in far northern Scotland during the past twenty years.

The **Oystercatcher** is quite unmistakable, our only large, noisy, black and white bird with a long orange bill and long pinkish legs. Oystercatchers rarely hide their light under a bushel and engage in loud piping contests among each other, often oblivious of the approach of bird watchers along the shore; sometimes a loud *kleep* will draw attention to a party flying low over the sea. Oystercatchers breed on all kinds of seashore, sandy, shingly and rocky, as well as on cliff-tops, and in recent years have shown an increasing tendency to nest inland in the north, on moors and in grassy and arable fields. Except in the Norfolk Broads area, however, they do not nest inland anywhere south of Yorkshire and Cheshire, and outside the breeding season are rare inland anywhere.

Our other large black and white breeding wader is equally distinctive, for no other British bird possesses a long *up*-curved bill like the **Avocet**. Despite their striking appearance, avocets can be surprisingly hard to pick out in a crowd of black-headed gulls, especially if they are wading in water deep enough to hide their long grey legs. At present the only spot in the British Isles where avocets breed is Havergate Island, the now famous bird sanctuary of the Royal Society for the Protection of Birds in the estuary of the River Ore near Orford, Suffolk. They stray on to surrounding estuaries during the summer, and can also be seen in various other estuaries and mudflats during their spring and autumn migration to and from what has apparently become their main wintering ground, the estuaries of the Tamar and other south-western rivers.

One other large black and white wading bird is a rare visitor to Britain, the **Stilt**, a Mediterranean species; two pairs actually bred here in 1945. The stilt's red or pink legs are so fantastically long that very few artists ever paint them long enough, but even these can be obscured when the bird wades in deep water. The stilt has a straight bill.

Herons, though shaped like waders, actually belong to quite a different order of birds. Our only native **Heron**, which if we were less insular we should call the grey heron, is a large bird with long legs, a longish stout bill and immensely broad wings in flight; its plumage is a mixture of grey, black and white. It is much larger than any wader, and quite unmistakable, whether perched immobile while fishing or stalking its prey in a stream or estuary, or flying sedately towards the heronry. Solitary herons' nests are not unknown, but the great majority are in often long-established colonies in trees. Some country folk still call herons cranes, but the true crane, which once bred in the Fens, is now only a very rare visitor to the British Isles, rarer than escapes of various Asiatic species of crane from zoos and private collections. A useful distinction is that cranes always fly with their necks straight out, whereas herons retract theirs in a graceful curve in flight. Storks also fly with their necks straight, but the white stork, which has half its wings black, is even rarer here than the crane. Bird watchers living near Edinburgh may come across a night heron from the free-flying colony at the Edinburgh Zoo. This small and mainly grey heron has a black crown and mantle and is not much bigger than a curlew; it also occurs elsewhere as a genuine vagrant from the Continent.

Another scarce visitor, though by no means as rare as the crane and the stork, is the **Spoonbill,** a large all-white bird with long legs and a long spoon-shaped bill, which is a little smaller than a heron or a stork but still a good bit larger than any true wader. The best chance of seeing a spoonbill is on the estuaries and coastal marshes of the east coast, especially Breydon Water, in the spring and autumn migration periods.

WATER BIRDS

Most beginners at bird watching have been familiar with many kinds of land bird from childhood, but are likely to have become aware of no more than a handful of water birds, mostly those usually seen on the lakes in town parks (mute swan, mallard, moorhen, perhaps also coot and tufted duck), and of course "sea-gulls." Once they start bird watching in earnest, with visits to reservoirs and estuaries, they are likely to be confronted all at once with several species which have hitherto been little more than names in books. Some firm classification is therefore necessary as a preliminary to grappling with the varied array that includes swans, geese, ducks, grebes, divers, gulls, terns, skuas, petrels and auks.

Swans, being large white birds, are easy enough, and the grey geese at least are like enough to the farmyard variety to present no collective difficulty. The ducks, however, distinguished except for the sawbills by their broad blunt bills, are so numerous that they need to be divided, and a useful division is between the surface feeders, which mainly frequent fresh water, and the diving ducks, many of which resort almost exclusively to salt water. This division between divers and surface feeders is also useful in separating the remaining water birds, the gulls, skuas, petrels, shearwaters, phalaropes, moorhen and coot being mainly surface feeders (though the coot does dive a lot), and the grebes, true divers, auks, and in a different way the terns, being divers. Most water birds may be found on either fresh or salt water, but the auks, skuas, petrels, shearwaters, shag, kittiwake and some diving ducks rarely come inland except when blown there by storms, while the moorhen and some surface-feeding ducks only go down to the sea when pressed by hard weather. All our ducks except the eider and the shelduck resort to fresh water in the breeding season, and so do our breeding grebes, divers and the red-necked phalarope.

To anybody wanting to become quickly familiar with our native ducks, geese and swans, the best advice is undoubtedly to visit one of the two collections of the Wildfowl Trust, at Slimbridge in the Severn valley in Gloucestershire, and at Peakirk at the fenland end of Northamptonshire near Peterborough. Here you can study all our breeding and winter migrant species at close range—much closer range than you are ever likely to achieve in the wild—and at Slimbridge in addition, from late September to early March, you stand a good chance of seeing two or three species of wild grey geese together on the Dumbles, the extensive saltmarsh that separates the collection from the estuary of the Severn. Most zoos have a good many of these species, but none are so complete as the Wildfowl Trust's collections, especially the one at Slimbridge. Many town parks also have good collections of waterfowl, especially St. James's Park, London. Many different kinds of wildfowl are liable to escape from time to time, and greatly confuse the beginner—and not only the beginner!—

when they turn up on lakes and reservoirs. Some of the most frequent of these are illustrated and described in my *Pocket Guide to British Birds*, but for a complete conspectus of the wildfowl of the world, all illustrated in colour by Peter Scott, I strongly recommend his *Coloured Key to the Wildfowl of the World*.

Surface Feeders, 1 *Broad blunt bill, large size, long neck*

SWANS AND GEESE

types: the Mute Swan and the White-fronted Goose

MUTE SWAN	large, white, orange bill with black knob
WHOOPER SWAN	large, white, yellow bill with black tip
BEWICK'S SWAN	large, white, yellow bill with black tip
WHITE-FRONTED GOOSE	white forehead, barred underparts, pink or orange bill, orange legs
LESSER WHITE-FRONT	white forehead, barred underparts, small pink bill, orange legs
PINK-FOOTED GOOSE	dark head and neck, pale forewing, small pink and black bill, pink legs
BEAN GOOSE	dark head and neck, black and orange or yellow bill, orange legs
GREYLAG GOOSE	pale forewing, orange bill, pink legs
BRENT GOOSE	head all black, white patch on neck
BARNACLE GOOSE	white face, neck all black
CANADA GOOSE	large, white face and throat
SHELDUCK	black, white and chestnut; red bill, pink legs

Telling our native and resident **Mute Swan** apart from its two winter visitor relatives, the **Whooper Swan** and **Bewick's Swan**, presents no difficulty, for the mute has an orange bill with a black knob at the base, while the other two both have bills with a yellow base and a black tip. Moreover, the mute usually carries its neck in a graceful curve, while the two others have a more erect, goose-like posture. Of course, if you are scanning swans on a loch half a mile away in a bitter north-east wind, your eyes may well be watering too much to see anything at all! It is when it comes to separating the whooper from Bewick's that the trouble starts. Bewick's is appreciably smaller and more goose-like, but size can be deceptive, especially with single birds, and you really need a reasonably close view of the bill to see that the yellow of the whooper's bill ends in an acute angle below the nostril, whereas on the Bewick's bill the yellow ends bluntly and above the nostril, covering a distinctly smaller area. The plumage of the adults of all three swans is, of course, pure white, though when they have been foraging in water stained with iron compounds their necks can look very rusty in colour. The cygnets and immatures all have ash-brown plumage that gradually whitens until their second year. They are harder to tell apart than the adults, for though its more graceful neck should separate the mute, for isolated young whoopers and Bewick's you have to rely entirely on size, except at ranges close enough to see the pattern of the pink which replaces the yellow on their bills. The bills of young mute swans turn from blackish-grey when they are cygnets to dark flesh when they are a year old and dull orange when they are two years old. Not till they are three years old are they fully adult with the bright orange bill and black knob at its base, which is larger in the cob (male) than in the pen (female).

The mute swan is widespread and common all over the British Isles at all times of year, but the two yellow-billed swans are normally seen only in winter, though a few whoopers often stay the summer in the Highlands and sometimes breed. As winter visitors, whoopers are most frequent in the north of England, Scotland and Ireland, and Bewick's, now generally the less common of the two, in Ireland and the south and east of England.

The grey geese usually strike terror into the hearts of bird-watching beginners, for are they not reputed the hardest of all British birds to identify in the field? But in fact the difficulties have been rather overdone, and really amount to little more than the problem of how to get a proper close-up view of the birds. For given this, the differences between our five kinds are straightforward enough. If bill and leg colour can be seen, the following table will give the answer, for no two except the white-front and the rare lesser white-front have these in the same combination:

Pink and black bill, pink legs: *pink-foot*
Pink bill, orange legs: *white-front, lesser white-front*
Orange bill, pink legs: *greylag*
Orange or yellow bill, orange legs: *Greenland white-front*
Orange and black or yellow and black bill, orange legs: *bean*

Grey geese are very wary birds, and much careful stalking is often needed to bring them into view at a reasonable range, frequently in areas where the only available cover is a wet ditch. The faint-hearted will doubtless opt for the Wildfowl Trust's high tower overlooking the Dumbles at Slimbridge, which is equipped with a formidable armoury of high-powered telescopes and binoculars.

The easiest grey goose is the adult **White-fronted Goose,** with its conspicuous white forehead and strong dark barring on the underparts. If these are seen, it can be confounded only with the rare **Lesser White-front,** which has the white on its forehead narrower and extending farther up the crown, a smaller bill, and on a very close view a yellow orbital ring round each eye. Immatures of both the white-fronts lack both the white forehead and the barred underparts, and if not accompanying their parents can best be identified from other geese by their combination of pink bill and orange legs and from each other by bill size. The race of the white-front which breeds in Greenland can be distinguished by its yellow or orange bill.

The **Pink-footed Goose** and the **Bean Goose** can both be picked out at a distance by the strong contrast of their dark head and neck with the rest of the body. After that you must look at their bills and feet. Those of the pink-foot are both pink, the bill being also partly black and much smaller than the bean's in proportion to the bird's head. The bean is a large, portly goose, appreciably larger than the pink-foot, with orange legs and a bill with varying amounts of orange or yellow and black.

Finally the **Greylag Goose,** another large one, has an orange bill and pink legs, and shows a very prominent grey forewing in flight. The pink-foot also shows this grey forewing, but flies faster and more buoyantly. The flight calls of grey geese all sound rather alike to the beginner at first, but can be distinguished with practice.

All grey geese frequent coastal marshes and mudflats, but in some districts may also feed on farmland at a considerable distance from the coast, to which they flight back daily. They are all winter visitors, though a very few pairs of greylags still breed in the northern Highlands and the Outer Hebrides. There are also a number of feral flocks in East Anglia and Scotland, which are apt to wander, to the confusion of bird watchers. The greylags which come to us from Iceland and northern Europe mostly winter in Scotland. White-fronts are the commonest and most widespread grey geese, especially in Ireland, where they are of the orange-billed Greenland form, and on the west side of Great Britain. The lesser white-front is most likely to be discovered as an isolated individual in a large flock of white-fronts. The pink-foot is the special goose of eastern Britain; more than half its total world population breeds in Iceland and winters in Great Britain. The bean goose is now very local indeed, and mainly found in Scotland.

Besides the five grey geese there are the three black ones, brent, barnacle and Canada. The **Brent Goose** is comparatively small, not a great deal larger than a mallard. It can look very black in flight, but in fact only its head, neck, upper breast and tail are black, with the rest of the underparts dark grey in the dark-breasted form which breeds in the eastern Arctic but pale grey in the pale-breasted form from the western Arctic. The black head and neck, relieved only by a small white patch on the neck, readily distinguish it from the barnacle, the only bird it is at all likely to be confused with. Brents are exclusively coastal birds, feeding especially on eel-grass on the mudflats; those on the east coast are mainly dark-breasted, and those on the west, especially in Ireland, largely paie-breasted.

The **Barnacle Goose** is appreciably larger than the brent, being about the size of a pink-foot. Its hall-mark is its white face, with black crown and neck, but despite this distinctive feature an odd bird can be surprisingly hard to pick out among a large flock of grey geese. Barnacles are also mainly coastal birds, frequenting the Solway marshes, the West of Scotland, especially the isles, and parts of Ireland. Any odd bird seen in the south of England is most likely to have escaped from captivity.

Another goose with a black and white head pattern, the introduced **Canada Goose,** is sometimes misreported as a barnacle. It is, however, almost as big as a swan, and the white on its head extends on to its throat, making a much larger patch. This is in fact the most likely wild goose to be seen over a large part of the south of England, except during hard weather. Originally imported from North America as an ornamental waterfowl, it has escaped and firmly established itself as a feral breeding bird in a good many parts of England, including the Thames valley, East Anglia and the meres of Cheshire and Shropshire.

Many visitors to north Norfolk have been puzzled at seeing some curious looking and obviously alien waterfowl at large on the coastal marshes near Holkham Park. These are Egyptian geese, which breed by the lake in the park and are the last survivors of several such feral colonies that used to exist on large estates, mainly in Norfolk. They have a rather variegated appearance, with broad white wing-patches in flight, a dark patch on the breast and round each eye, and pink bill and legs. The superficially similar ruddy shelduck, a frequent escape from collections of waterfowl and an occasional genuine stray from the Mediterranean, has similar white wing-patches, but no dark patches on face or breast, and its bill and legs are blackish.

The true wild **Shelduck** of our shores looks quite different, though in many ways as much like a goose as a duck. It is bigger than a mallard, and looks quite a large black and white bird as it flies around, often in pairs. It has a red bill (with a knob in the drake) and pink legs, and there are green and chestnut in its plumage as well as black and white. No other British bird looks at all like it, but the juveniles, mainly dark above and white below can be puzzling if they are separated from any old birds. It does not consort much with other waterfowl, or even with other shelducks, but may be seen in scattered pairs far across the sandy and muddy shores and estuaries which it prefers. Shelducks are rarely seen on fresh water inland, but exceptionally may breed a few miles from the sea. They are not migratory in the normal sense, but the great majority of our resident birds fly to the Heligoland Bight to perform their annual moult each July, returning in the autumn. A similar but smaller concentration of moulting birds builds up in Bridgwater Bay, Somerset. For this reason very few adult shelducks will be seen around our coasts in August and September.

Surface Feeders, 2 *Broad blunt bill, medium size, shorter neck*

DUCKS

type: the Mallard

The surface-feeding ducks do occasionally dive, but mainly when they are young, or flightless owing to the moult, or wounded. Their diving is in fact a device to save them from enemies, not to search for food as with the diving ducks. The surface feeders may indeed feed below the surface as well as dibbling along it, but they do so only in shallow water, where they can upend and reach the bottom without submerging. Our seven native breeding species all, apart from the gadwall, have drakes with distinctive and more or less brightly coloured plumage. The ducks on the other hand are all rather plain dull brown birds, harder to tell apart, as are the drakes in their moulting "eclipse" plumage, when they resemble the ducks. Both sexes share a coloured patch on each wing, known as the speculum, which is different for each species and so especially helpful in identifying the ducks and eclipse drakes.

The **Mallard** is not only our largest and commonest duck, but the drake with its bottle-green head and neck with a narrow white collar is also one of the most handsome and unmistakable. The other six drakes, in roughly descending order of size, are as follows:

PINTAIL, with dark chocolate brown head, white neck and long pointed tail, much longer than the duck's;

SHOVELER, harlequin-like with its dark bottle-green head and neck, pale-blue forewing, and black, white and chestnut plumage; its large shovel-shaped bill not only gives it its name, but also its permanent head-down appearance;

GADWALL, like a small greyish duck mallard, with a smaller grey bill and a black and white speculum;

WIGEON, with chestnut head and peaked buff forehead;

GARGANEY, with a blue-grey forewing like the shoveler and a prominent white blaze from the eye back to the nape; and

TEAL, with a striking chestnut and green head pattern and a white line along each flank, which can often be seen at a distance when no other marking is visible.

The duck mallard, on the other hand, is a brown bird, distinguished only by her large size, orange bill and white-bordered blue speculum. The speculums of the other surface-feeding ducks are as follows:

Gadwall: black and white
Pintail: bronze
Shoveler: green and white
Teal: green and black
Garganey: green
Wigeon: green

The drake wigeon also shows very conspicuous large white wing-patches in flight, a feature shared with several diving ducks, notably the goldeneye.

Size and head shape are also useful clues to the identity of duck surface feeders: in approximately descending order of size,

the duck *shoveler* shares her drake's blue forewing and large shovel-shaped bill;

the duck *gadwall* is like a small duck mallard with a smaller yellowish bill;

the duck *pintail* is also like a duck mallard, with a smaller bill and pointed tail;

the duck *wigeon* resembles a duck pintail, but is slightly smaller and has a somewhat peaked forehead;

the duck *garganey* is rather larger than a teal, and

the duck *teal*, our smallest duck, is intermediate in size between a moorhen and a coot.

Fortunately, ducks are usually accompanied by their distinctive drakes. The most difficult months for duck identification are July and August, when not only are there many juveniles about (and young mallard, of course, are at one stage no bigger than a teal) but the drakes are mostly in their eclipse plumage, when they can often be told from the ducks only at very close range. Mallard drakes in full eclipse, for instance, are only distinguishable from their ducks because their bills are yellower.

In flight, of course, many plumage features cannot be seen, but the shapes of the shoveler's bill, the wigeon's head and the pintail's long tail can usually be made out. If surface-feeding ducks show a lot of white on the body, they will be shoveler; if a lot of white on the wing, wigeon; if a small white patch on the wing, gadwall; and if a pale blue-grey forewing, shoveler or garganey. A party of small ducks that rise quickly and rather steeply from the water or the reeds and dash off in a body are likely to be teal.

All our surface-feeding ducks breed in Britain, but only the mallard, shoveler and teal do so throughout the country. Wigeon and pintail breed in Scotland, but only very locally in the rest of the British Isles. Garganey are confined to south-eastern England, and gadwall are very local, as natural immigrants in Scotland and as spreading naturalised stocks in East Anglia and the neighbourhoods of London and Bristol. In the breeding season most surface-feeding ducks, except the mallard, seek out fairly secluded lochs and waters. At other times, however, they are widespread on all kinds of fresh water, lakes, lochs, reservoirs and flooded gravel pits, while the mallard, wigeon and pintail are often seen on the sea. The teal is the shyest of them all, preferring waters surrounded by thick sedge or reeds, from the depths of which its presence is often only revealed by the drake's *crick crrick* note. The wigeon's *whee-oo* is another useful duck call to learn, for it often locates the bird in fog or poor visibility. Only the duck mallard makes the traditional quack.

In a few districts you may come across a naturalised species of duck that is strictly neither a surface feeder nor a diver, for it feeds mainly on land. This is the **Mandarin Duck**, whose gaudily variegated drake is equipped with crest, side-whiskers and wing-fans to adorn its red, white, blue, green, purple and orange plumage. The duck, however, is a plain grey-brown. Mandarins like small lakes surrounded by woodland, for they nest in trees, and are especially common in the neighbourhood of Windsor Great Park.

A more widespread pitfall for the unwary is the so-called Cayuga duck, a white-breasted domesticated variety of the mallard, which escapes and often consorts with wild mallards in town parks and on reservoirs, probably interbreeding with them. Sometimes the rest of the mallard plumage is normal, but in other birds it is very dark. These rather artificial urban and suburban mallard flocks also often contain the domesticated breed known as call ducks, which are pure white mallards with white or orange bills. More perplexing still are escaped farmyard Muscovy ducks, in various plumages combining black, white and grey, with a red or black bill and a knob at its base.

Surface Feeders, 3 *Narrow, pointed bill; short wings*

MOORHEN, COOT, PHALAROPES

types: the Moorhen and the Red-necked Phalarope

Two very different pairs of birds fall within this category, the moorhen and the coot which are common, and the two phalaropes which are rare. The coot does not strictly belong here, for it is a great diver, but is included for convenience of comparison with the moorhen, the only bird at all confusable with it.

MOORHEN	red bill and forehead, white under tail
COOT	white bill and forehead, all black
RED-NECKED PHALAROPE	thin black bill
GREY PHALAROPE	thicker bill, yellow at base

The **Moorhen** is perhaps the commonest freshwater bird of all, for it is satisfied with the tiniest pond. Adults are only confusable with the coot, juveniles perhaps with the water rail (p. 85). **Coots** are larger than moorhens, usually prefer more extensive stretches of water, and in winter often go down to the estuaries if not actually to the sea. At rest on the water coots are all black, except for their white forehead and bill, but when they fly they show a whitish line on the wing. Moorhens, on the other hand, have their black relieved by some conspicuous white feathers under the tail, a white line along each flank, a red forehead and a yellow-tipped red bill. Both have greenish legs, but the moorhen has a red garter. Though the adults are easy enough, the juveniles often have beginners guessing, the young coot in particular often being taken for some kind of grebe. Both are browner than their parents, with their throat and underparts whitish, and the young coot also has a white face.

Both moorhens and coots are vocal, restless and aggressive birds, moorhens rarely losing an opportunity to flirt their white under tail

135

coverts at other moorhens while coots are perpetually splashing after each other in the water. Coots dive often, and moorhens will do so occasionally. The moorhen's usual call is disyllabic, but the coot has a laconic single note, from which it is supposed to be named. If so, the namer was a Lancastrian, for it always sounds like *cut* to me.

Phalaropes are actually waders, but waders which have adapted themselves to the aquatic life. On the water they look like miniature gulls, but in flight they are sandpiper-like. Many bird watchers never see a phalarope in their lives. This is not surprising, for the **Red-necked Phalarope**, our only breeding species, nests only in a handful of carefully guarded colonies in the Shetlands, Orkneys, Outer Hebrides and western Ireland. It is rare on migration in other parts of the British Isles, where any phalarope that does turn up is more likely to be a **Grey Phalarope**. Both species spend the winter far out in the Atlantic, and only when they are blown eastwards by autumn gales do we see them here. In winter both are dainty little grey and white birds, with an engaging habit of spinning round and round on the surface of the water. The grey is somewhat the larger, and has a stouter bill that is yellow at the base; the bill of the red-necked is all-black and almost needle-thin. In spring and summer, of course, the red-necked is easy to tell, for it has an orange-red patch on the sides of its neck and throat. The grey phalarope has a most handsome red breeding plumage, like a knot or a godwit, but at this season it is very rarely seen in Britain indeed. With the recent increase in records of the North American Wilson's phalarope on this side of the Atlantic, it is necessary also to take this species into account when a phalarope turns up. It is larger than a grey phalarope and has a white rump and, unlike the other two, no white bar on the wing, so that its wings appear all dark.

Surface Feeders, 4   *Narrow, pointed, often heavy bill; long wings*

GULLS AND SKUAS

type: the Herring Gull

So much depends on size and the colour of legs and bill in identifying adult gulls, that these are summarised below, in ascending order of size and including also the gull-like fulmar for comparison:

	Legs	Bill	Other Points
LITTLE GULL	red	red-brown or blackish	black head and neck in summer
BLACK-HEADED GULL	crimson	crimson	brown hood in summer
COMMON GULL	yellow-green	yellow-green	black and white wing-tips
KITTIWAKE	blackish	yellow-green	black wing-tips
FULMAR	yellow	flesh	tube-nose, stiff wings
LESSER BLACK-BACK SCANDINAVIAN	yellow	yellow	slate-grey wings
LESSER BLACK-BACK	yellow	yellow	slate-black wings
ICELAND GULL	pink	yellow	white wing-tips
HERRING GULL	pink	yellow	black and white wing-tips
GLAUCOUS GULL	pink	yellow	white wing-tips
GREAT BLACK-BACK	pink	yellow	slate-black wings

There are five common species of gull (black-headed, common, lesser black-back, herring and great black-back, in order of increasing size) that are seen together often enough for the bird-watching beginner to be able to learn to tell them all apart as a "first year exercise." Three of them, the black-headed, common and herring, look all-white birds at a distance, but are in fact a beautiful shade of French grey on the back and wings. The two black-backs have varying shades of grey-black instead of the French grey. Immature gulls look quite different from the adults, for they are mostly plain brown, acquiring gradually larger amounts of grey and white as they moult, till they become adult, which may take three or four years in the larger gulls. An assembly of immature gulls can thus look distinctly variegated.

Adult **Black-headed Gulls** are most easily identified in spring and summer, when they sport the chocolate-brown hoods that give them their rather inaccurate name. The only other bird that could reasonably be confused with a black-head in this plumage is the markedly smaller **Little Gull**, which, however, has its whole head and neck blackish-brown and is only a scarce passage migrant in the spring. In winter a black-head looks more like other gulls, and can then be told by its small size, crimson red bill and legs, dark smudges on the head and the black tip and conspicuous white streak along the fore-part of the wing. The winter plumage of the little gull lacks these wing markings, but it can be told at all times of year by its smoky-grey underwing. Young black-heads are much speckled with brown, and have a dark bar at the tip of the tail. Immature little gulls, commoner in the autumn than adults are in the spring, are readily recognised, both by their slightly forked tail (possessed by no other

British gull) and by the conspicuous dark bar diagonally across each wing, recalling the immature kittiwake. Black-headed gulls have a more buoyant flight than the larger species, while the little gull is almost tern-like in the air.

Adult **Common Gulls** and **Herring Gulls** share a very simple plumage pattern, white on the head and underparts and French grey on the back and wings. The yellow-green bill and legs of the smaller common gull quickly separate it from the herring gull with its pink legs and yellow bill, which has a red spot on it. The function of this red spot, incidentally, is to give the young chick something to aim at when its parent arrives with food. Both common and herring gulls have a distinctive pattern of white spots (rather misleadingly called "mirrors" in most bird books) on their black wing-tips; these are especially useful in separating the common gull from the same-sized kittiwake and the smaller black-head.

The **Lesser Black-back** is like a herring gull with a darker grey back and yellow legs. Size, leg colour and shade of grey all distinguish the lesser from the **Great Black-back,** a monstrous bird that dominates assemblies of gulls by its size: its back and wings are dark blackish-grey and its legs pink. Two factors confuse these simple distinctions between the two black-backs. One is the presence in Britain in autumn and winter of a number of lesser black-backs from Scandinavia and the Baltic, which have their grey parts as dark as the great black-back. The other is the fact that the last item of adult attire that immature lesser black-backs acquire is its yellow legs, so that three-year-old lesser black-backs have pale pink legs. The result can be expressed briefly as follows:

Adult lesser black-back: slate-grey back, yellow legs
Scandinavian lesser black-back: slate-black back, yellow legs
3rd-year lesser black-back: slate-grey back, pale pink legs
Great black-back: slate-black back, pink legs

In winter plumage the common and herring gulls and the two black-backs share a common feature in that the pure white of their heads is streaked with dirty grey. The immatures of these four gulls are all very like each other, starting off as plain brown birds with a dark bar at the tip of a white tail, and gradually acquiring more and more of their adult plumage with each successive moult. The immature common gull is, of course, the smallest, and even to start with has more white on it than the other three. Young herring gulls and lesser black-backs literally cannot be told apart until they have enough of their adult plumage to show that one is going to become French grey and the other slate-grey. The immature great black-back again stands out by its great size.

Although gulls are still collectively called "sea-gulls" in common parlance and the old idea that a gull inland means bad weather at sea dies hard, nowadays the five common species are in fact almost as likely to be seen inland as by the sea. This is a development of the past sixty or seventy years, before which flocks of gulls inland outside the breeding season were rather exceptional. In the winter half of the year black-headed and common gulls are scattered all over the Midlands and south of England, feeding on farmland and playing fields and roosting on large inland reservoirs. The black-head is the commonest gull of lakes in town parks at this time, but in some country districts, such as the Cotswolds, the common gull, which usually belies its name, really is the commonest gull. The three larger gulls, particularly the great black-back, are less widespread inland, but are regular in many areas, often feeding on refuse dumps. The lesser black-back is mainly a summer visitor to the British Isles, and is consequently most often seen inland on spring and autumn passage; however it has recently shown an increasing tendency to stay for the winter, especially in London, on the Bristol Channel and in the industrial north. The herring gull is the commonest gull of seaports at most times of year, especially where there is much fish offal to feed on. In the breeding season all five of these gulls are commoner in the north and west of the British Isles, but the herring gull nests on all suitable cliffs even in the south and east. The black-head nests mainly inland, and has several inland colonies in south and east England, including one within a hundred yards of London Airport. Inland common gulleries are also frequent in hill districts, and the three larger gulls show an increasing tendency to nest inland.

The **Kittiwake** looks like a common gull with blackish legs and no white mirrors on its wing-tips, but it is rarely seen inland, being predominantly oceanic in winter. In the breeding season it nests in colonies on cliffs, mainly in the north and west, which resound with the cries that have given it its name, *kit-ee-wayk*. Immature kittiwakes, known as tarrocks, have a dark bar across the nape of the neck and another diagonally across each wing, making a highly distinctive pattern, found otherwise only in the scarce little gull.

The only other gulls that visit British waters regularly are the **Glaucous Gull** and the **Iceland Gull**, both winter visitors from the Arctic. Basically they are herring gulls with no black on the wing-tips; the adults look remarkably white at any distance, but the immatures are oatmeal in colour. The glaucous is a huge gull, often the size of a great black-back, but the Iceland is generally smaller, like a lesser black-back; the two do, unfortunately, overlap. One of the best distinctions between them is that the glaucous has a big heavy bill like a great black-back, while the Iceland's is disproportionately smaller, nearer a common gull's than a lesser black-back's. Another, between the immatures, is that the glaucous has most of its bill pink, while the Iceland's is mostly black with a pink base. The glaucous gull is regular in winter in Scotland, especially the northern isles, but scarce farther south. The Iceland gull is much less frequent in the same areas.

In the winter half of recent years several immature Mediterranean gulls have visited the south and east coasts of England. They are rather larger and chunkier than black-headed gulls in winter plumage, but have no black on the wings and fly somewhat more jerkily.

Fulmars, though they are petrels not gulls, do look remarkably gull-like in plumage. They are in fact rather like herring or common gulls with no black wing-tips that habitually soar and glide with their wings stretched stiffly out. Though they sometimes give a few quick flaps, they never fly with the slow deep wing-flaps of the gulls, preferring to make the maximum use of air currents. At close range their characteristic tubular nostrils betray their relationship to the petrels and shearwaters and make it clear that they are not gulls. Fulmars nest on cliffs all round the British Isles, except in the extreme south-east, and some are present at or near the colonies throughout the year, except for a few weeks in autumn. Fulmars are, however, primarily oceanic birds.

Skuas look like dark immature gulls with slightly hooked beaks, and are easily recognised by their piratical habit of chasing gulls, terns and in the case of the great skua even gannets, and making them disgorge their latest catch. Four species occur in British seas:

ARCTIC SKUA	short straight feathers projecting from tail
GREAT SKUA	large size, white wing-patches
POMARINE SKUA	short twisted feathers projecting from tail
LONG-TAILED SKUA	long feathers projecting from tail

Though there are two British breeding species of skua, most bird watchers see their first skua on the east coast during the late summer and autumn migration, when it is likely to be an immature Arctic skua following the migrating terns southwards. **Arctic Skuas** come between the common and herring gulls in size, and may be either all-dark or dark and light in plumage, in either case with a pale patch on each wing. Adults have a pair of elongated feathers projecting from the middle of the tail, but in young birds these are much shorter and can only be detected at very close range. Arctic skuas breed on barren moorlands in the Hebrides, Orkneys and Shetlands and on the mainland in Caithness.

Our other breeding skua is the large and somewhat buzzard-like **Great Skua,** often known by its Shetland name of bonxie. It comes between the lesser and great black-backs in size, and has only a whitish patch near each wing-tip to relieve its plain dark-brown plumage. Though its flight is sedate enough in its off moments, like other skuas it becomes remarkably agile when a victim heaves in sight. Bonxies now breed in the Shetlands, Orkneys and Outer Hebrides, and represent one of the great triumphs of British bird protection, for in 1880, before protection began, they were persecuted and nested only on Unst and Foula in the Shetlands. In eighty years they have increased from under 70 to over 1000 pairs in Shetland alone.

Two other skuas occasionally turn up off our coasts while on passage from northern seas to the open ocean, but they are not regular anywhere. These are the **Pomarine Skua** and the **Long-tailed Skua,** most easily identified as adults, for the pomarine has twisted central tail feathers and the long-tailed extremely long ones, extending as much as ten inches beyond the rest of the tail. Immature pomarines differ from immature Arctics only by their slightly larger size, so many may be overlooked.

The immature long-tail is distinctly smaller than the Arctic and has a markedly less stout bill. But identifying immature skuas in the field is rather a postgraduate exercise in bird watching.

Surface Feeders, 5   *Oceanic birds, long-winged, tube-nosed*

SHEARWATERS AND PETRELS

types: the Manx Shearwater and the Storm Petrel

MANX SHEARWATER	dark above, pale below
BALEARIC SHEARWATER	browner, both above and below
SOOTY SHEARWATER	larger, all brown
GREAT SHEARWATER	dark cap, white collar
CORY'S SHEARWATER	dark crown, not capped
STORM PETREL	dark, white rump, square tail
LEACH'S PETREL	dark, white rump, forked tail

Unless they visit one of the better-known breeding colonies of the Manx shearwater, such as Annet in the Scillies or Skokholm and Skomer off Pembrokeshire, most bird watchers are only likely to see shearwaters and petrels when they are well out at sea, on a voyage from Penzance to the Scillies, for instance, or in the Irish Sea or the Minch. A voyage across the Atlantic or through the Bay of Biscay also provides excellent opportunities of making the acquaintance of these otherwise rather recondite British birds. Shearwaters are gull-sized, dark above and usually pale below. They are easily recognised by the habit which gives them their name, of shearing low over the wave-tops, with wings stiffly outspread and rarely flapping, tilting first to one side and then to the other. The petrels likely to be seen in British seas and the Western Approaches are all much smaller birds, whose sooty black plumage is relieved only by a white patch at the base of the tail. The fulmar (p. 139) is closely related to the petrels and shearwaters, and shares both their tube-nose (visible only at close range, of course) and their stiff-winged shearing of the waves.

The **Manx Shearwater** is much the commonest shearwater of British seas, and breeds on a good many islands off our western coasts, from the Shetlands to Ireland and the Scillies. In its breeding colonies there is no mistaking it, for though you rarely see it by day, it makes the night resound with a most extraordinary cacophony of coughing and cooing sounds, the principal call having the pattern *it-i-corka*. At night the birds are easy to catch, as they flounder along the ground towards their breeding holes, after spending all day at sea, and are in fact caught and killed in large numbers by great black-backed gulls. In the hand, they prove to be about the size of a black-headed gull, blackish above and white below, with a narrow, slightly hooked bill, which can inflict sharp wounds on ungloved hands. This is also your best chance, apart from a fulmar on its breeding ledge, to see the remarkable tubular nostrils that characterise all the shearwaters and petrels.

At sea the Manx shearwater shows as an alternately dark and white bird as it glides this way and that over the water. Its closely allied Western Mediterranean form, called the **Balearic Shearwater** in the books, is browner, both above and below, and is regularly seen off our southern and south-western coasts in the autumn; Portland Bill is a good vantage point to see it. Elsewhere, however, an all-brown shearwater is more likely to be the **Sooty Shearwater,** the mutton bird of New Zealand, which visits the north-eastern Atlantic for a brief period in late summer and autumn on migration from the Pacific, the greatest traveller of any of our bird migrants. It is larger than a Manx or Balearic shearwater, about the size of a common gull or kittiwake, and on account of its dark underparts might be mistaken for a skua or an immature gull but for its shearwater-type flight.

Another long-distance traveller is the **Great Shearwater,** which includes the north-east Atlantic in its round tour of that ocean from its breeding places in the remote Tristan da Cunha group in the southern seas. It also is most likely to be seen off our western coasts in late summer and autumn. Like a larger Manx shearwater, with its pattern of dark above and white below, the great shearwater is best identified by its dark crown and white collar, which gives it a distinctly capped effect, as well as by the V-shaped white patch at the base of its tail. However, there is a similar but much rarer large shearwater to be taken into account. This is **Cory's Shearwater,** which also has a dark crown and often the V-shaped tail-patch, but lacks the white collar and so the marked capped effect of the great shearwater; it also has a yellow instead of a dark bill. Cory's is only likely to be seen off the Scillies and in Cornish seas in late summer and early autumn. Identifying shearwaters at sea is by no means easy, for the birds are often just too far away or the observer on a deck that is moving up and down, and especial care is needed in distinguishing both Balearic and sooty, and great and Cory's shearwaters.

Three species of small black petrel frequent British seas and the Western Approaches, but only two actually breed with us. Even at their breeding places off our northern and western coasts, however, few bird watchers see either the **Storm Petrel** or **Leach's Petrel** unless they actively search for them, for they are exclusively nocturnal on land, spending the day either at sea or in their nest-holes deep in rocks and boulders. Unlike Manx shearwaters, which assemble a few miles offshore at dusk and sometimes fly close in to headlands during the day, the smaller petrels stay well out to sea till after dark, and it is the rarest thing to see one close inshore. You are in fact more likely to find one blown miles inland by an equinoctial gale. The storm petrel is our smallest sea-bird, if you disqualify the phalaropes for being waders; it is not much bigger than a sparrow but with proportionately much longer wings. It has a white rump and a square tip to its tail, whereas the larger Leach's petrel, almost the size of a song thrush, has its tail forked and at a close range can be seen to have a dark centre to the white patch. The storm petrel habitually follows ships; Leach's never does this, and has a highly distinctive darting or dancing flight that identifies it even when it is too far away to see the shape of its tail. The third petrel which might be seen, either in the Western Approaches or off the south-western coast of Ireland, is Wilson's petrel, intermediate between the other two in size, but with a square tail like the storm petrel and its feet projecting beyond it. It follows ships, so you may see it close enough to detect the yellow webs to its feet which will settle its identity.

Other birds likely to be seen well out at sea include the fulmar (p. 139), the kittiwake (p. 139), the most marine of our gulls, the diving auks (p. 149) and the gannet (p. 154), which is much larger than any of them.

Diving Birds, 1   *Broad blunt bill*

DUCKS

type: the Tufted Duck

TUFTED DUCK, DRAKE	black and white, white back, distinct crest
TUFTED DUCK, DUCK	brown, short crest, sometimes small white face-patch
COMMON POCHARD, DRAKE	chestnut and grey
COMMON POCHARD, DUCK	brown
SCAUP, DRAKE	black and grey, grey back
SCAUP, DUCK	brown, large white face-patch
RED-CRESTED POCHARD, DRAKE	red bill, rufous head, crest
RED-CRESTED POCHARD, DUCK	pale cheek, crest
GOLDENEYE	angular head, white wing-patches
GOLDENEYE, DRAKE	black and white, black head with white spot
GOLDENEYE, DUCK	grey-brown, chocolate-brown head
COMMON SCOTER, DRAKE	all black, orange patch on bill
COMMON SCOTER, DUCK	dark brown, pale cheek
VELVET SCOTER	larger, white wing-patches
VELVET SCOTER, DRAKE	one pale patch on face, bright orange sides to bill
VELVET SCOTER, DUCK	two pale patches on face
LONG-TAILED DUCK	short bill
LONG-TAILED DUCK, DRAKE	black and white, long tail
LONG-TAILED DUCK, DUCK	brown, white face, pointed tail
EIDER	line of bill continuous with forehead
EIDER, DRAKE	Mainly white, black crown and flanks
EIDER, DUCK	brown

Much the most familiar of our diving ducks, especially on fresh water, are the **Tufted Duck** and the **Common Pochard**, which are both common on reservoirs and on lakes in town parks in winter. Their drakes are very distinct and the ducks too are quite easily told apart. The drake tufted duck is black with white flanks and belly, and a long crest or tuft hanging from the back of its head. It can only be confused with the larger, and on fresh water much scarcer, drake **Scaup**, whose plumage is similar but with a grey back and no crest. The drake pochard is also larger than a tufted and has a similar plumage pattern to the drake scaup, but with bright chestnut instead of the scaup's black (actually very dark green) on the head and neck. When I was first learning my birds, I always used to confuse the drake pochard with the drake wigeon, but they really have nothing in common except for the chestnut head and neck, and the wigeon is easily distinguished by its buff forehead and peaked crown. Moreover, if you watch a pochard for a few minutes, it will usually dive, while a wigeon, being a surface feeder, will not.

The females of these three diving ducks are all rather dull brown and whitish birds, but the size differences remain. The duck tufted has a much shorter and often rather obscure crest and sometimes a small white patch or line at the base of the bill. The duck scaup has no crest at all, but a much larger and more conspicuous white patch round the base of the bill. The duck pochard has neither crest nor white patch, but is just dull and brown. Even her eyes are brown, where her drake's are red and those of the tufted and scaup yellow. The duck pochard indeed is one of the dullest looking British birds. When they fly, tufteds and scaups of both sexes, but not pochards, show a white bar on each wing. Both tufted ducks and pochards breed more or less throughout the British Isles, though rather patchily in the south, where they are very much commoner in the winter half of the year. The scaup is exclusively a winter visitor to our coasts, and uncommon inland.

In recent years another pochard has been increasing as a winter visitor, especially in the eastern counties. This is the **Red-crested Pochard**, which has also been increasing on the Continent, but as it is often kept in captivity in Britain and the young birds allowed to go free, it is hard to tell whether the birds seen on our reservoirs are genuine wild winter visitors or escapes. The red-crested is appreciably larger than the common pochard, and very distinct from it in plumage. The drake has a bright rufous head and red bill (the common pochard's bill is grey), but the duck's head is dark with a pale cheek, recalling the duck common scoter; both sexes have a tufted crest.

Because of its bright yellow eye, goldeneye is one of the old wildfowlers' names for the tufted duck, but the true **Goldeneye** is a larger and quite different looking duck, though also having a yellow eye. It is most readily told by the curious angular shape of its head, often described in the books as buffle-shaped, though I have never been able to discover what a buffle is; it is not in the *Concise Oxford Dictionary*. The drake goldeneye looks almost white, except for his black (actually very dark green) head, with a big white spot at the base of the bill, and dark mantle. The ducks and immatures are mainly grey-brown with chocolate-brown heads. All goldeneye show a conspicuous white patch on each wing when they fly. Though primarily sea ducks, they are not uncommon in winter on some reservoirs and lakes inland, especially in the London area.

The **Common Scoter** is one of our easier ducks to identify, for its drake's plumage is unrelieved black, though the regrettable tendency for other ducks also to look all-black against the light must be borne in mind. On a close view you can see that the drake's black bill has both an orange patch on the upper mandible and a knob at the base. The duck has little more to distinguish her; she is dark brown with pale cheeks. Neither shows any white on the wing in flight. Common scoters are frequent in flocks off our coasts at almost all times of year, though commonest in the winter. They breed with us, however, only on a few freshwater lochs in the north of Scotland, and on one large Irish lough. They are rare inland elsewhere, occurring most often on migration in April.

Among the larger flocks of common scoters in the winter, there are sometimes bigger birds that show a conspicuous white patch on the wing as they fly and a less obvious one at rest. These will be **Velvet Scoters,** which also differ from common scoters in the drake having one and the duck two whitish patches on the face; in the orange sides and smaller knob of the drake's bill; and in their reddish legs. Velvet scoters are very rare inland, occurring most regularly on the east coast of Great Britain and the eastern side of the Irish Sea.

The **Long-tailed Duck** is another sea-going diving duck that only exceptionally comes inland in Britain. The east coast and northern isles of Scotland and the northern coasts of Ireland are the best places to seek it, between October and March. The long-tail is very variable in plumage, especially between summer and autumn, but only the winter plumage is at all commonly seen in Britain. The drake in his black and white winter garb, with the long tail that has earned his name of sea pheasant, is a fine sight, but the duck is a dull brown affair, chiefly notable for her short bill and white face, with a darker crown and a dark patch at the side of the neck. Her tail is pointed, but nowhere near as long as her mate's.

The **Eider** is the largest British diving duck, indeed our largest duck of any kind except for the shelduck, and is a great favourite wherever it occurs. It is resident, and breeds widely round our northern coasts, south to Coquet Island in Northumberland and Walney Island in Lancashire, and from Down to Donegal in Ireland. In winter eiders show an increasing tendency to wander southward, and a non-breeding flock frequents the Burry estuary in South Wales throughout the year. The most famous eider colony, of course, is the one on the Farne Islands off the coast of Northumberland, where their former association with the saint has given them the name of St. Cuthbert's ducks. Inland eiders are very rare indeed. Drake eiders in full fig are unmistakable, all white above except for some black on the head, tail and flanks, but in the various eclipse and immature plumages they can be very confusing mixtures of black, white and brown if you do not see the shape of their bill, unique among British ducks in continuing the line of the forehead without any change of angle. The shape of the bill is also the best way of telling the ducks, which otherwise look rather like bulky female mallard without the blue speculum. At most times of year the ducks are easily recognised by the company they keep, but in summer the two sexes hive off into bachelor and nursery parties.

Another diving duck is now liable to turn up at reservoirs on the west side of England. This is the ruddy duck from North America, which has escaped from the Wildfowl Trust collection on the Severn estuary. It is a small dumpy diving duck, with the curious habit of cocking its tail up like a wren. Drakes in spring and summer are rusty-red, with conspicuous white cheeks, black cap and bright blue bill; in autumn and winter they are duller, with the rusty-red parts grey-brown. Ducks are grey-brown, with paler brown cheeks crossed by a dark bar.

Diving Birds, 2 *Narrow, pointed bills; medium-sized birds with dumpy to somewhat elongated build*

1. THE SMALLER GREBES

type: the Dabchick

DABCHICK, SUMMER	chestnut cheeks and throat, white face spot
DABCHICK, WINTER	plain brown
BLACK-NECKED GREBE	tip-tilted bill
BLACK-NECKED GREBE, SUMMER	black neck, ear tufts point downwards
BLACK-NECKED GREBE, WINTER	blackish and white, no capped effect
SLAVONIAN GREBE, SUMMER	chestnut neck, ear tufts point upwards
SLAVONIAN GREBE, WINTER	blackish and white, capped effect
SMEW, DRAKE	white and black, black crest
SMEW, DUCK	chestnut head and nape, white cheeks

Our only common and widespread small grebe is the **Dabchick** or little grebe, which is indeed our smallest breeding bird of fresh water, apart from the red-necked phalarope. It is a dumpy small bird that is constantly diving, especially when conscious that it is being watched, and has a whinnying alarm note that is often heard in the spring half of the year. In winter the dabchick is plain brown, paler beneath, but in summer its cheeks and throat are chestnut and there is a white spot near the base of the bill. Juveniles have a striped and mottled appearance, like other young grebes. Dabchicks usually breed on ponds and small lakes, or quiet bays in larger ones, but in winter they also resort to small rivers and to estuaries on the coast, where they need to be distinguished from two other smallish grebes, the black-necked and the Slavonian.

Both these are rare breeding birds in Scotland, but regular in autumn and winter on the coast, especially in estuaries and in the south and east. The **Black-necked Grebe** is the more frequent of the two on fresh water in the south, especially on spring and autumn passage. The **Slavonian Grebe** nests regularly on several lochs in the northern Highlands, but the black-necked is erratic in its choice of breeding places, colonies appearing and

147

dying out after a few years. To-day it probably nests only in Scotland, but during the present century it has also bred from time to time in England and Wales, and in Ireland too, where a colony of some 250 pairs once established itself for a few years but is now extinct.

In their handsome breeding dress the two are quite distinct, both from each other and from the dabchick. The black-necked, slightly larger than the dabchick, has its whole head, neck and breast black, its flanks chestnut, and a fine pair of downward-pointing golden-chestnut ear tufts. The Slavonian, a little larger still, about the size of a moorhen, has its head black, its neck, breast and flanks chestnut, and its golden-chestnut ear tufts pointing upwards. The difference between the two birds' ear tufts is well expressed by their American vernacular names, eared grebe for the black-necked and horned grebe for the Slavonian. The black-necked always looks a more crested or tuft-headed bird, and the Slavonian more flat-headed.

In their more familiar winter plumage, these fineries have all vanished; both birds are blackish above and white below, and must be told apart by the shape of the bill and the pattern of black and white on the face. The black-necked always has its bill slightly tip-tilted upwards and in winter has the black on its crown gradually merging into the white below the eye. The Slavonian, on the other hand, has a straight bill and its black crown contrasts sharply with its white cheeks at eye level. The juvenile plumage of the coot (p. 135), another diver, is superficially similar to this, but is unlikely to be seen after very early autumn, or on the sea. The dabchick, on the other hand is brown and white rather than black and white, and has both much less white on the face and a straight bill.

A bird that beginners often mistake at first for a grebe is the female or immature Smew, the smallest of our three saw-billed ducks (p. 154), which like the two larger ones has a narrow unducklike bill. Like the grebes, the smew is a great diver, and it is often some minutes before you can catch it on the surface long enough to make sure of its identity. The smew is larger than any of the three smaller grebes, about the size of a coot or tufted duck, and the ducks and immatures are most readily identified by the contrast between their chestnut-brown head and nape and their pure white cheeks. The handsome drakes look totally different, being almost completely white with a black patch round the eye and various narrow black lines elsewhere. Smew are winter visitors only, mainly from December to March, to coastal waters, especially in the south and east, and a few inland lakes and reservoirs, especially around London.

2. THE AUKS

type: the Guillemot

GUILLEMOT	often brown above, awl-shaped bill
RAZORBILL	always black above, flattened bill
PUFFIN	smaller, round white face, broad multi-coloured bill
BLACK GUILLEMOT	white wing-patch, red legs
BLACK GUILLEMOT, SUMMER	mainly black
BLACK GUILLEMOT, WINTER	barred black and white
LITTLE AUK	very small, tiny bill

Our auks are exclusively cliff-nesting marine species, except when blown inland by storms. The two commonest and most likely to be confused are the **Guillemot**, which has a pointed awl-shaped bill, and the **Razorbill**, whose bill is flattened in the vertical plane, shaped like the old-fashioned cut-throat razor, and striped with vertical white lines. Both are somewhat elongated in shape, dark above and white below, and have their cheeks and throat dark in summer and white in winter. Razorbills and Scottish guillemots are almost black on their dark parts, but guillemots from the rest of the British Isles are only dark brown. Additional distinctions are that the razorbill has a white line back from the bill to the eye, while the guillemot has a black one back from the eye to the nape. The so-called bridled form of the guillemot, which has a white ring round the eye, has this black line white.

On a good view, no other British bird can well be confused with the **Puffin**, which has a curiously Oriental appearance with its round white face and broad flat bill coloured with bands of blue-grey, red and yellow.

Smaller and dumpier than the guillemot, it has the same basic dark above and white below plumage, but even at a distance can be separated by its faster, more whirring flight. The monstrous bill is smaller, but still disproportionately large, in winter, and much smaller and brownish in young birds, but in winter most puffins are far out at sea. Puffins' legs are red in summer and yellow in winter.

These three common auks all breed in large colonies on sea cliffs and marine islands, mainly in the north and west of the British Isles, and not at all on the south and east coast between the Farne Islands and the Isle of Wight. They spend the winter at sea, not many coming far enough inshore to be seen by land-bound bird watchers. The **Black Guillemot,** our other breeding auk, has much smaller colonies, more sparsely distributed around the coasts of Scotland, Ireland and the Isle of Man, and stays inshore in winter instead of going off to sea.

The black guillemot in breeding plumage is our only black sea-bird with a large white wing-patch (apart from the much larger and quite differently shaped velvet scoter), while in winter it is the only one with its upperparts barred black and white. It is larger and more elongated than the puffin, but smaller than the guillemot and razorbill. Its legs are red.

The **Little Auk** is our smallest diving bird of any kind, but is uncommon off our coasts and much more likely to be seen as a storm-blown waif inland. It is so small and dumpy, scarcely as big as a starling, that it can hardly be mistaken for anything except a young puffin or razorbill, neither of which have the distinctive bills of their parents. The little auk's bill, however, is tiny and much smaller than either.

Diving Birds, 3 *Narrow, pointed bills; large elongated birds*

LARGER GREBES, DIVERS, CORMORANTS, GANNET AND LARGER SAW-BILLS

types: the Cormorant and the Gannet

GREAT CRESTED GREBE, SUMMER	double horned crest, rufous tippets
GREAT CRESTED GREBE, WINTER	white eyestripe, capped effect
RED-NECKED GREBE, SUMMER	chestnut neck and breast, white cheeks
RED-NECKED GREBE, WINTER	yellow on bill, no eyestripe or capped effect
RED-THROATED DIVER, SUMMER	red throat, grey head
RED-THROATED DIVER, WINTER	tip-tilted bill
BLACK-THROATED DIVER, SUMMER	black throat with vertical barring, grey head
BLACK-THROATED DIVER, WINTER	straight bill
GREAT NORTHERN DIVER, SUMMER	black head and throat, with plain and barred rings
GREAT NORTHERN DIVER, WINTER	heavy bill
CORMORANT	white patch on face
CORMORANT, SUMMER	white patch on thigh

SHAG	all dark
SHAG, SUMMER	recurved crest
GANNET	white with black wing-tips
GOOSANDER	white wing-patch, red bill, loose mane
GOOSANDER, DRAKE	dark head, white flanks and under-parts
GOOSANDER, DUCK	rufous head, white chin
RED-BREASTED MERGANSER	white wing-patch, red bill, stiff mane
RED-BREASTED MERGANSER, DRAKE	dark head, rufous breast, grey flanks and underparts
RED-BREASTED MERGANSER, DUCK	rufous head

All the birds in this group are great divers, and the main difficulty in separating them from each other arises from the fact that they are so often under water when you want them to be on the surface. They are all somewhat cigar-shaped, both on the water and in their not very graceful flight.

The smallest of those which breed with us, and much the commonest on fresh water in the south, is the **Great Crested Grebe,** which is about the same size as the common pochard, though much more elongated in shape. In breeding plumage it is striking and quite unmistakable, with its double-horned crest and rufous side-tippets, both unique features among British birds. In one of its curious courtship ceremonies it uses these adornments to great effect as it nods its head from side to side. In winter, however, the great crested grebe is much plainer looking, no longer crested and just dark above and white below, with white cheeks and eyestripe; indeed, it is surprising how white a winter great crested can look on the water. When it flies, which is not often, it shows a pale wing-bar. Young birds in their first striped plumage can be rather puzzling, especially if you chance upon them away from their parents, which they usually pursue with shrill food-demanding cries. The great crested grebe now breeds on most of the larger lakes and reservoirs of England and Wales and more sparsely elsewhere. This is another of the major triumphs of British bird protection, for during the nineteenth century it was nearly exterminated, thanks to a more than usually asinine fashion for women's hats, combined with the Victorians' penchant for decorating their homes with birds in glass cases.

In winter many great crested grebes go down to the sea, especially to estuaries, where their smaller size, wing-bars in flight and straight bills help to distinguish them from the red-throated diver. They also need to be separated from the smaller **Red-necked Grebe,** an uncommon winter visitor, mainly to inshore waters on the east coast. The red-necked is intermediate in size between the dumpier Slavonian and the more elongated great crested. In winter it differs from both in having yellow on its bill and in having the black of the crown gradually shading into the white of the face below the eye (like the much smaller black-necked grebe) instead of being sharply demarcated at eye level. From the great crested it also differs in having no narrow white stripe above the eye. In summer plumage, rarely seen in Britain, all these difficulties disappear, for its neck and breast turn a handsome chestnut, while its cheeks remain white, separating it at once from the white-necked great crested and the black-cheeked Slavonian.

The three divers found commonly in British waters present the same problem of winter similarities that are wiped away as soon as they don their breeding dress. In winter they are all plain birds, dark above and white on the face and below; they sit low in the water and look ungainly when they fly, with their long necks slightly depressed. They are best told apart by size and bill shape. The **Red-throated Diver** is the smallest, about the size of a mallard, and the most easily identified, for its bill is even more markedly tip-tilted upwards than the black-necked grebe's. The separation of the **Black-throated Diver** and the **Great Northern Diver** in winter is, however, an exercise for the student about to major in bird watching, for they are much of a size, the great northern somewhat larger and nearly as big as a shag. The great northern usually looks somewhat less uniform and more speckled on its upperparts, and has a much stouter, heavier bill, which makes a steeper angle with the forehead.

In spring and summer, on the other hand, the red-throated and black-throated both identify themselves with the features that give them their names, both also having grey heads, while the great northern has a black head and both plain and barred rings on its neck. The barring on the black-throated's neck is vertical, on either side of its black throat patch. The upperparts of the great northern are also chequered black and white all over, instead of only in patches as in the black-throated. Great northerns in summer plumage are surprisingly frequent off the coast of Scotland in autumn, and a few are seen during the summer too; breeding has often been suspected but never proved. Black-throated divers, on the other hand, breed on many of the larger lochs in the Highlands and the Outer Hebrides, and the red-throated is more widespread on smaller lochs and lochans in the Highlands and islands and in one district of north-western Ireland. In winter all three are frequent off the coasts of the British Isles, the red-throated being the commonest and the black-throated the least frequent.

Nine times out of ten, when you sight a cigar-shaped bird in the sea and it dives before you can identify it, on coming up again it proves to be a cormorant or a shag. The quickest way of telling them from divers is to look at the angle at which they hold their bills, which is level if it is a diver and upwards if it is a cormorant or shag. (This is quite different from the tip-tilting of the red-throated diver's bill, which is due to the shape of the lower mandible.) **Cormorants** are the commonest large dark diving birds on the south and east coasts, and **Shags** in the north and west. Cormorants are larger and can be told by their heavier flight, white patch on the face and in spring and summer also by the white patch on their thighs, easily seen in flight. Old cormorants are liable to develop whitish heads, never found in shags at any age. Indeed, adult shags have no white about them at all, their dark greenish plumage being relieved only by a patch of bare yellow skin at the base of the bill. Besides their quicker flight, they can also be told in summer by their recurved crests. Immatures of both species, however, have whitish underparts, often a good deal whiter in the cormorant than the shag, but size and speed of flight are better ways of distinguishing them. Cormorants breed on rocky coasts pretty well all round the British Isles, and also frequent low-lying shores in winter; in some districts they also visit fresh water fairly often. Shags, on the other hand, come inland only when blown by storms, and prefer rocky shores throughout the year, not breeding and rarely appearing in the east and south between Northumberland and the Isle of Wight.

The brown immature **Gannet,** though larger than the cormorant and more likely to be seen diving from the air than from the water, is cigar-shaped and potentially confusing; indeed, I have more than once mistaken some in a head-on view for grey geese. Immature gannets in their second and third years can also be puzzling, for their plumage is a varying admixture of juvenile brown with adult white. Adult gannets, however, with their white plumage and black wing-tips, can hardly be mistaken for anything else, especially if seen performing their magnificent air-to-sea plummeting dive, by which you can tell them at great distances. They are larger than both cormorants and great black-backed gulls, though this does not prevent them from being treated with indignity by great skuas. The gannet is a highly colonial sea-bird, nesting in gannetries of up to 17,000 pairs on a dozen islands off our northern and western coasts. The most accessible for the ordinary bird watcher are the Bass Rock in the Firth of Forth, Ailsa Craig in the Firth of Clyde and Grassholm off the coast of Pembrokeshire. Gannets are often seen well out to sea off all coasts, especially in winter, but inland only as storm-blown wanderers.

Two more birds, both large saw-billed ducks, can be classed as cigar-shaped diving birds, the **Goosander** and the **Red-breasted Merganser,** both above mallard size and distinguishable from grebes and divers by their white wing-patches, which are especially prominent in flight. The goosander is the larger of the two, but size is not much help in separating the ducks and immatures, which in both species have rufous heads and red bills, but are best told apart by the tuftier mane and more sharply defined white chin of the goosander. The merganser's mane stands on end like a boy's hair that has not been smarmed down with grease, but the goosander's hangs down loosely, like uncut, shaggy locks. The two drakes are easier, for though both have black (actually dark bottle-green) heads and necks, the mane differences are even more accentuated than in the ducks and the rest of their plumage is quite different. The goosander looks black and white, for it has white flanks and whitish breast, with underparts often tinged pink, while the merganser has white only as a ring round the lower neck and in a line along the flanks, its breast being rufous and its under-parts grey. Immature drakes look like the ducks.

Goosanders breed widely on rivers and lochs in the Highlands, more locally in the Lowlands and the extreme north of England. Mergansers breed on rivers and lochs, including sea lochs, in most coastal counties of Scotland, except south of Aberdeen in the east, and in Ireland, and are also spreading into Cumberland. Both come south in the winter, goosanders mainly to fresh water, especially the big reservoirs around London, and mergansers to salt water, mainly estuaries. The smew, our third species of saw-bill, was discussed earlier (p. 148).

Diving Birds, 4   *Diving from air; grey and white, black-capped; narrow pointed bills*

THE TERNS

type: the Common Tern

COMMON TERN	vermilion bill, dark tip
ARCTIC TERN	bill all carmine; short legs
LITTLE TERN	yellow bill, black tip; white forehead
SANDWICH TERN	large; black bill, yellow tip; slight crest
ROSEATE TERN	black bill, red base; pinkish breast
BLACK TERN, SUMMER	black and grey
BLACK TERN, WINTER	all-black bill, less deeply forked tail

Our five sea terns look like small, graceful gulls, with longer wings, deeply forked tails and black caps (on the crown only, not hoods like the black-headed gull). They are all summer visitors, breeding on sand dunes, shingle banks and rocky marine islands. On spring and autumn migration common and Arctic terns may, like the black tern, appear on fresh water, but the three other sea terns are uncommon or rare inland. Terns can be recognised by their dipping flight, as they plunge into the sea to catch the small fish and sand-eels which they eat. Their juveniles all have brown-speckled plumages.

All our sea terns have the same plumage pattern, white with French grey upperparts and black cap, so that the main distinctions between them must be sought in size and bill colour. The **Common Tern,** rather smaller than a black-headed gull, is the most frequently seen, but often it is too far off to be distinguished from the very similar **Arctic Tern,** which is the commoner breeding species in the north of Scotland. In plumage the two are almost identical, but the common tern has its bill and legs vermilion (red tinged with yellow) as against the Arctic's carmine (red tinged with blue). The bill of the common has a dark tip, but the Arctic's is all red. The Arctic's legs are very short, so that if the two are obliging enough to perch side by side, the common stands much higher and the Arctic almost seems to crouch. The two species are in fact so alike that in bird-watching slang an indeterminate bird is known as a "comic tern." Even quite experienced bird watchers often have to give up as hopeless a comic tern that is too far off to see its bill colour, though there are refinements, for those who are thoroughly familiar with both species, such as the whiter appearance of the common tern's breast in contrast with its upperparts, and the fact that, seen against the sun, all the Arctic's wing quills appear translucent, whereas only the first four of the common's quills do so.

The next most frequent tern in most districts is the **Little Tern,** which is much smaller than any of the other sea terns, about as big as a song thrush. Apart from its small size, it is also easily told by its yellow legs and black-tipped yellow bill, and even in the breeding season has a white forehead. Other terns have white foreheads only in winter plumage.

The **Sandwich Tern,** the largest of the five (common gull-size), is the earliest migrant, often arriving at the end of March. It has a black bill with a yellow tip, black legs and feet with yellow soles and a slight crest. Many acquire their white winter foreheads before they leave their breeding colonies.

The **Roseate Tern** is much more local than the others and has red legs and a black bill with a red base. Though it also has a pinkish tinge on its breast and longer tail streamers than the others, these features are often hard to judge and are of less value than the colour of the bill.

Terns at a distance can often also be identified by their call notes, but unfortunately there seems to be no really watertight difference between the voices of the common and Arctic. The Sandwich's *kirrick* is distinctive, however, and the harsh *aach* note of the roseate, quite unlike any other tern call, is an excellent way of picking the bird out of a swirling mass of other terns.

The common tern breeds round the greater part of the British and Irish coasts, and also by freshwater lochs in Scotland and Ireland. The little tern is also widespread, but very local or absent from the coasts of South Wales, Ireland and northern Scotland. The Arctic tern breeds from Ireland, Anglesey and the Farne Islands northwards, and like the common is not infrequent by fresh water in Scotland and Ireland. The Sandwich tern is much more local, breeding in often large colonies in East Anglia, the Farne Islands, north-west England and rather more widely in Scotland and Ireland. The roseate tern is more local still, having its headquarters on either side of the Irish Sea, with a few colonies elsewhere in Scotland and

Ireland, and occasional pairs breeding in common terneries in other parts of England.

The **Black Tern,** the only marsh tern at all frequently seen in Britain, used to breed in eastern England, but is now only a passage migrant in spring and autumn. A predominantly freshwater tern, it is unmistakable in spring, when its plumage is largely black, with grey on the back and underwing and white under the tail. In the autumn, however, it is black and white like the sea terns, sharing their white foreheads, and then the best distinctions are its wavering flight, dipping constantly down to the water but never diving in, and its all-black bill, less deeply forked tail and more sharply-defined white shoulder-patch. In this plumage also it needs to be carefully distinguished from the much rarer white-winged black tern, which is easy enough in spring with its white forewing, rump and tail, but in autumn can only with difficulty be told from the black tern; it lacks the latter's dark spot on either side of the breast.

PART THREE: WHERE TO LOOK

BIRD HABITATS .

This section is intended to be used in conjunction with the following one (p.167), which details a selection of actual localities recommended for bird watching, classified by habitat. Here the typical birds of the principal habitats are briefly described.

Land Habitats

BUILT-UP AREAS   Plate 9

Completely built-up areas, such as city centres and industrial sites, are unpromising for the bird watcher, though anything may fly over. I have seen a peregrine over the Houses of Parliament, rooks over London Bridge and a heron over Camden Town. Only the house sparrow and the feral pigeon are at home without any waste ground, bare soil or turf to forage on, though there may be swifts feeding in the air above. Swifts also nest in the roofs of old open-eaved houses and house martins build under the eaves in the main streets of small market towns. Starlings fly into the centres of many large cities to roost on trees and buildings, mainly in the winter. Black-headed gulls, the modern city scavengers, and carrion crows, a hangover from the Middle Ages, are constantly cruising overhead, and the gulls often come to the windows of tall office blocks to be fed. Both jackdaws and kestrels may nest on town buildings, and many cathedrals have their resident flock of jackdaws. The black redstart, a newcomer, likes to feed on bombed, building and other waste sites and to nest in nearby buildings, and so does the pied wagtail, which has also nested in bombed basements in the City of London.

TOWN PARKS AND SQUARES   Plates 10, 11

As soon as sizeable clumps of trees and stretches of grass appear, the number of birds at once increases. Most of the built-up area birds will also stray into the parks and squares, where they join the breeding tits (great, blue and sometimes coal), robins, hedgesparrows, wrens, greenfinches, chaffinches, starlings, blackbirds, song and mistle thrushes, tawny owls and woodpigeons. The only regular summer visitor to town parks is the spotted flycatcher, though many chiffchaffs and willow warblers pass through on migration. Some larger and well-timbered town parks run to jays, stock doves, pied woodpeckers and, if there are plenty of berried shrubs, even waxwings. Playing fields on the outskirts of towns attract feeding gulls, starlings and thrushes, including both fieldfares and redwings in winter. For the water birds of town parks, see page 166.

GARDENS AND ORCHARDS   Plates 12, 13

Nearly all the birds of town parks and squares also frequent gardens and orchards, and of course the larger the continuous area (for birds take no account of garden fences), the more varied the bird population is likely to be. In larger and more countrified gardens you may also hope to see such primarily woodland and farmland birds as marsh and even long-tailed tits, treecreepers, linnets, bullfinches, common redstarts, nuthatches, tree sparrows, barred woodpeckers, swallows, turtle doves, cuckoos and even pheasants, which soon learn that gardens are shot-free sanctuaries. Old orchards are favoured by little owls and goldfinches, and in the extreme south-east still by wrynecks. Most of our woodland warblers will nest in larger gardens, and in some areas they are joined by cirl buntings, redpolls and hawfinches. Hoopoes, when they do appear, love to forage on a lawn. Even an isolated garden conifer (pine, larch, spruce or fir) will attract goldcrests and tits. Rookeries are often built in clumps of trees in churchyards and the gardens of rectories and other large country houses, which tend to be undisturbed because people dislike fusillades of shots near their homes and churches. Collared doves frequent gardens near chicken runs.

FARMLAND   Plates 14, 15

The greater part of the countryside of England and Wales, and much of Scotland and Ireland too, consists of farmland, under either grass (pasture and hay meadow) or the plough (arable), criss-crossed by hedgerows of varying thickness and studded with oaks, elms and ashes. The hedgerow birds are mostly those of the parks and gardens, especially blackbird, song thrush and chaffinch, with the addition of a few shyer ones, such as the yellowhammer, the common whitethroat and, in parts of the south and west, the cirl bunting, which are not often seen in gardens. The hedgerow trees bring in a few more, notably carrion crow, magpie, little owl, kestrel and green woodpecker.

In the open fields, on the other hand, many more birds feed than breed. The few that nest include the corn bunting, skylark, lapwing and quail, but in winter huge flocks of many species feed on the fields: rooks, jackdaws, starlings, skylarks, thrushes of various kinds, lapwings, golden plover, woodpigeons, stock doves, gulls, partridges and pheasants. In the stackyards and on the stubbles are flocks of finches, buntings and sparrows, preyed on by the sparrowhawk. In some districts grey geese feed on the farmland, while stone curlews forage in the wide arable fields below the southern downs and red grouse come down to the northern stubbles in hard weather. In many northern and western districts oystercatchers, redshanks and curlews breed in the riverside meadows and corncrakes among the standing hay. Swallows and house martins use the farm buildings for their nests, and so do house sparrows, starlings, pied wagtails and barn owls.

DOWNLAND   Plates 16, 17

The wide rolling downlands of southern and eastern England, from the wolds of Yorkshire and Lincolnshire south to the Cotswolds and the downs of Sussex and Wessex, now as much arable as grass, have their own special bird community: skylark, corn bunting, wheatear, meadow pipit, cuckoo, quail, partridges, lapwing, stone curlew where there are no bushes; linnet, stonechat, tree pipit, woodlark and yellowhammer where there are. If there are trees as well, as on Salisbury Plain, the kestrel and hobby may be added. Flocks of starlings, mistle thrushes, and goldfinches resort to the downs after the breeding season, while the escarpment of the downs is always a good place to look for a hovering kestrel and may also produce a migrating harrier or short-eared owl. Since the downs ceased to be grazed by sheep, and more especially since the myxomatosis epidemic carried off the rabbits that were keeping the bushes in check, many areas of downland have become increasingly covered with scrub and so now share the birds of the areas of scattered trees (p. 162).

LOWLAND MOORS AND OPEN HEATHS   Plates 18, 19

The difference between a moor and a heath, in popular parlance, depends on where you live. Though botanists may have finer distinctions, for bird watchers the heaths of the south and east are the moors of the north and west. On the southern heaths, besides the ubiquitous blackbird, willow warbler and wren, and the widespread linnet, common whitethroat, wheatear, hedgesparrow, meadow pipit, tree pipit and skylark, there are grasshopper warblers, stonechats (mainly near the sea), whinchats, woodlarks, red-backed shrikes, nightjars, hobbies and cuckoos. The Breckland heaths of East Anglia specialise in the crossbill, stone curlew and ringed plover, and the Greensand heaths from Surrey to Dorset in the Dartford warbler. In winter siskins and redpolls come to feed on the birches, and great grey shrikes may use the thorn bushes for their look-outs.

Farther north many kinds of wader, lapwing, golden plover, common snipe, dunlin, curlew and greenshank, nest on the low moors that stretch down to the sea, along with mallard, teal and other kinds of duck, and various gulls. The twite is a small bird of the northern moors, not found breeding in the south, by way of compensation for the absence in the north of the woodlark, red-backed shrike, hobby and other southern specialities. In the extreme north, from Caithness to Shetland, the Arctic skua nests

25. CONIFEROUS WOODLAND: *a,* Crossbill; *b,* Crested Tit; *c,* Coal Tit; *d,* Goldcrest

a　*b*

26 & 27. DECIDUOUS WOODLAND: *a*, Sparrowhawk; *b*, Jay; *c*, Green Woodpecker; *d*, Great Spotted Woodpecker; *e*, Pied Flycatcher; *f*, Treecreeper

a

28 & 29. SCRUB, PARKLAND AND SCATTERED TREES: *a*, Redstart; *b*, Turtle Dove; *c*, Blackcap; *d*, Nightingale; *e*, Lesser Whitethroat

a

36 & 37.   SEACLIFFS: *a*, Kittiwake; *b*, Shags; *c*, Puffin; *d*, Razorbills

b c
d e
f g

34 & 35. SEA SHORES AND ESTUARIE
a, Avocet; b, Black-headed Gull;
Shelduck; d, Oystercatcher; e, Lit
Terns; f, Ringed Plover; g, Dunlin

d e

32 & 33. MARSHES, FENS, BOGS AND SWAMPS: *a*, Redshank, *b*, Water Rail; *c*, Common
Snipe; *d*, Bittern (with an eel); *e*, Marsh Harrier; *f*, Bearded Tit; *g*, Reed Warbler

f g

30 & 31. FRESHWATER MARGINS: *a*, Heron; *b*, Sand Martins; *c*, Kingfisher; *d*, Sedge Warbler; *e*, Yellow Wagtail

38 & 39. LOWLAND FRESHWATER: *a*, Mute Swans; *b*, Tufted Ducks; *c*, Wigeon; *d*, Coot; *e*, Great Crested Grebe

40. THE OPEN SEA: *a*, Guillemot; *b*, Fulmar; *c*, Lesser Black-backed Gull
d, Great Black-backed Gull

on the low moorland flows, while Orkney has the hen harrier and short-eared owl, Shetland the whimbrel, and both the great skua.

INLAND CLIFFS, QUARRIES, SAND AND GRAVEL PITS Plates 20, 21

Birds that breed on inland cliffs and crags include the raven, carrion and hooded crows, jackdaw, kestrel, peregrine, common buzzard, stock dove and feral pigeon, even occasionally the barn owl. In some parts of Wales the chough nests in quarries and disused mineshafts inland. Sand and gravel pits also have their specialised breeding birds, notably the sand martin, which burrows in their sides and the little ringed plover, which nests on the bare gravel. When the bee-eaters bred in Britain in 1955, it was in a Sussex sand-pit.

UPLAND MOORS AND ROUGH GRAZINGS Plates 22, 23

Many of the birds of the lowland heaths also go up on to the heather moors and grassy hills that cover so much of the north and west of both Great Britain and Ireland, but the three really typical birds of these uplands are the skylark, the meadow pipit and, where there is heather, the red grouse. Wheatears, wrens and blackbirds are all common, while both twite and ring ouzel are hill birds never seen in the south except on migration (ring ouzel) or in winter flocks, usually by the sea (twite). After the breeding season, flocks of starlings and mistle thrushes take to the northern hills, as they do to the southern downs, while in winter both snow and Lapland buntings may be found feeding high up on some hills, especially in the Pennines. Most of the waders that breed on the lower northern moors also breed on the higher ones, especially the lapwing, curlew and golden plover; gulleries too can be quite high up on moors. The moorland birds of prey are the merlin, kestrel and peregrine, with the hen harrier and golden eagle in the Highlands, the kite in mid-Wales, and the short-eared owl liable to come in wherever there is a plague of voles. Carrion or hooded crows are everywhere, and in many places ravens also. Black grouse prefer the edge of moorland and woodland to the open moor. Swifts often feed high in the air above the hills.

For the birds of the MOUNTAIN TOPS, see page 87. Plate 24

WOODLAND Plates 25, 26, 27

Most of our garden birds were originally woodland ones, and nearly all those mentioned in the section on p. 159 will go at least a little distance into a wood. Among the birds most often seen in extensive tracts of woodland are the woodpeckers, blackcap, garden warbler, marsh, great and blue tits, common redstart, robin, blackbird, wren, jay, woodcock, pheasant, tawny owl and long-eared owl. In winter parties of all five common tits forage through the woodlands, often accompanied by nuthatches, treecreepers and goldcrests, and in late summer and early autumn by chiffchaffs and willow warblers. Certain oakwoods on the west side of England and Wales, notably the Forest of Dean, can usually be relied on to produce breeding pied flycatchers, wood warblers and common redstarts. Starlings often nest in holes quite far into woods. The sparrowhawk and common buzzard are the breeding birds of prey of extensive woodlands, and in the south the occasional goshawk and honey buzzard might also be looked for. If the woods are coniferous, with pine, spruce or larch trees, goldcrests and coal tits are especially likely to occur, and in parts of the Highlands will be joined by the crested tit, crossbill, siskin and capercaillie.

SCRUB, PARKLAND AND AREAS WITH SCATTERED TREES
Plates 28, 29

Clearings in woods, edges of woods, young plantations, sites of felled woodland, well-timbered parks and commons and overgrown scrub and hedgerows all provide varied conditions that appeal to a great many small land birds, especially those which are common in town parks and gardens. Some heathland and downland birds, such as the nightjar, woodlark and tree pipit, and of course many woodland birds, also like these habitats. Birds that are at least as likely to be found among scattered trees and scrub as anywhere else include most of the warblers and woodpeckers, the spotted flycatcher, willow tit, hawfinch, long-tailed tit, yellowhammer, nightingale, red-backed shrike, mistle thrush, turtle dove, long-eared owl and magpie. The grasshopper warbler is especially partial to sites of felled woodland, the bullfinch to overgrown hedgerows, the cirl bunting to elms at the foot of the downs, the black grouse to the edge of woodland and moorland, and short-eared owls and hen and Montagu's harriers to young plantations. Several hole-nesting birds, including the tree sparrow, common redstart, stock dove and little owl, like scattered old trees in a park or along a river or stream. Clumps of conifers always attract goldcrests, coal tits and crossbills and, where they are scattered over downland, hobbies. In beech-mast years, clumps of beeches attract winter flocks of chaffinches and bramblings. Rookeries are more often built in isolated spinneys or clumps of trees than in large woods, though herons seem to prefer the protection of a wood.

Waterside Habitats

FRESHWATER MARGINS
Plates 30, 31

Several kinds of land bird frequent the margins of fresh water, rivers, streams, lakes, ponds and flooded gravel pits. Dippers, grey wagtails and common sandpipers all nest by upland streams, and grey wagtails also increasingly in the lowlands. Sand martins and kingfishers nest in holes in the banks, and reed buntings and reed and sedge warblers in the thick marginal vegetation, where in winter wrens and blue tits may feed. Goldfinches, redpolls and siskins feed in alders along south country riversides, while hooded and carrion crows, wagtails and meadow pipits often feed at the water's edge. Many kinds of wader turn up by freshwater margins on migration, especially snipe, lapwings and common, green and wood sandpipers; nor are dunlin and ringed plover rare inland on passage. Herons, mallard, teal and moorhens all frequently feed at the water's edge, while teal are fond of hiding by day in the thick surround of sedges and reeds that often affords nesting cover to moorhens, coots, water rails and mute swans. Little ringed plovers often nest quite close to the water at flooded gravel pits.

MARSHES, FENS, BOGS AND SWAMPS   Plates 32, 33

The term "marsh" is a very loose one, covering anything from waterlogged swamps to grass fields that used to be swamps before they were drained. Bogs and fens, on the other hand, are strictly defined by ecologists; they are respectively plant communities on wet acid and wet alkaline peat. Marshes, bogs and fens have very specialised bird communities too. Damp valley grassland, for instance, of the sort that is covered with rushes and often flooded in winter, often has nesting whinchats, yellow wagtails, lapwings, snipe, redshanks, curlews, and in the north oystercatchers. Wetter marshes and open bogs and fens encourage grasshopper warblers, several kinds of duck, moorhens, water rails and (now very rare) spotted crakes. Gulls too, especially black-headed gulls, often choose bogs for their gulleries.

Reed-beds (see p. 82) are often the precursors of fens in the plant succession, and have their own special bird in the reed warbler; marsh warblers on the other hand prefer osier beds. The extensive reed-beds of East Anglia are the stronghold of the bearded tit, bittern and marsh harrier. Swallows, martins, starlings and wagtails often roost in reed-beds, and blue tits feed there in winter.

SEWAGE FARMS

Sewage farms, at least the old-fashioned kind with plenty of shallow pools rich in the invertebrate animals that waders love, are a very specialised kind of freshwater margin or marsh. They are the favoured haunts both of waders and of bird watchers (indeed, a lady bird watcher was once heard to inquire what were sewage farms really for!), and among their regular visitors are snipe, lapwings, common and green sandpipers, greenshanks, ruffs, common redshanks, dunlin and ringed plover, with less frequent little stints, little ringed plovers, curlew sandpipers and wood sandpipers. But on a sewage farm in May or September literally almost any northern hemisphere wader may turn up. Many other less exciting birds are sewage farm regulars, among them the martins, swallow, swift, linnet, greenfinch, house sparrow, sedge warbler, meadow pipit, yellow and pied wagtails, starling, moorhen, mallard, teal, carrion crow, kestrel, heron and gulls.

SEA SHORES AND ESTUARIES   Plates 34, 35

There are three main kinds of sea shore, rocky, sandy and muddy; estuaries are generally muddy. The five common gulls frequent all of them, but the other inhabitants vary. Rocky shores are the barrenest of the three in bird life; they are usually backed by cliffs and share some nesting species with them (see p. 165), together with a few more, such as eiders, terns and oystercatchers. In winter they have fewer birds still, apart from the gulls, mainly rock pipits, with some turnstones and perhaps purple sandpipers on the weed-covered rocks and maybe an odd kingfisher or black redstart. The sanderling is one of the few birds that prefer sandy shores to all others, but dunlin, ringed plover and a few other waders also feed there, while pied wagtails, snow buntings and shore larks may forage along sandy beaches.

Muddy shores and estuaries are much the most productive for the bird watcher, especially in the winter half of the year. Few estuaries are without scattered pairs of shelduck, and both grey and black geese and various kinds of seagoing duck are freely seen ashore on mud-banks or along the tideline. The great majority of waders that frequent salt-water shores at all prefer them to be muddy. Indeed, the more experienced bird watcher considers himself to be distinctly aggrieved if he goes down to the shore and sees no more than five species of wader. This basic minimum consists of the curlew, common redshank, lapwing, dunlin and ringed plover; others that he might reasonably hope to add to his winter total include knot, turnstone, the two godwits and the grey and golden plovers, with whimbrel and perhaps greenshank as well at migration times. A spotted redshank too would make it definitely a good day. Less exciting birds that feed on muddy shores are rooks, crows, jackdaws, starlings and herons, while peregrines, merlins and sparrowhawks hunt over the mudflats as well as along the sea-walls and over the saltings. For the sea-wall and saltmarsh as winter habitats, see page 88.

Docks and harbours are a specialised urban sea-shore habitat. Gulls, especially herring gulls, are their staple inhabitants, with the house sparrow and feral pigeon among land birds, and an increasing number of mute swans, which live by scavenging wherever refuse barges are unloaded.

SAND DUNES AND SHINGLE

The wilder sea shores, if not backed by cliffs, may have extensive tracts of sand dunes or shingle behind them. Terneries and sometimes gulleries are often found on both, while ringed plovers and even in one or two spots perhaps still Kentish plovers, breed indifferently on sandy and shingly tracts and beaches. The land birds of sand dunes are often the same as those of heaths, and may include skylarks, meadow pipits, cuckoos, wheatears and partridges.

SEA CLIFFS
Plates 36, 37

Steep sea cliffs with plenty of ledges are the favoured nesting sites of many sea-birds. Of the gulls, the principal cliff-breeder almost all round the British Isles is the herring gull, which almost everywhere is now liable to be joined by the gull-like but quite unrelated fulmar. In the north and west especially there are likely to be both great and lesser black-backs as well. Kittiwakes nest in tight and noisy colonies, also mainly in the north and west, where again scattered groups of common gulls may be found. Where there are kittiwakes, and often where there are not, you are likely to find guillemots, nesting in very tight-packed colonies on narrow ledges, and razorbills scattered about in isolated pairs, usually higher up than the guillemots. Black guillemots are more independent still, in loose colonies away from other auks, while gannets nest exclusively on the cliffs and ledges of a handful of marine islands. Cormorants and shags are wide-spread, the cormorants more in the south and east, the shags only in the north and west. Puffins and Manx shearwaters nest in burrows on cliff-tops or marine islands rather than in the cliffs themselves, while storm and Leach's petrels use holes in old walls or piles of boulders on such islands.

Several kinds of land bird like to nest on cliffs, among them three or four kinds of crow, the raven, carrion crow, jackdaw and chough, and birds of prey, notably the peregrine, kestrel and common buzzard. Rock doves, feral pigeons and in the far north of Scotland starlings, are also birds of the cliffs. The smallest cliff specialist among British birds is the rock pipit.

Water Habitats

FRESH WATER
Plates 38, 39

Lakes, ponds and reservoirs are the principal freshwater habitats available for birds, and all our surface-feeding ducks, together with common pochard, tufted duck, and in winter goldeneye, goosander and smew among the diving ducks, frequent them. Also present are likely to be mute swans, perhaps Canada geese, great crested grebes, dabchicks and coots and the five common gulls, the two smaller ones, black-headed and common, being the commonest. In winter there may be whooper swans in the north, Bewick's swans in the Fens and both in Ireland, while black-necked grebes are not uncommon on autumn passage on certain reservoirs. Moorhens generally prefer smaller, sometimes very small, ponds with vegetation around them, while the introduced mandarin duck likes lakes that are surrounded by woodland. Not many water birds are found actually on our rivers and streams, but among them are the two smaller gulls, mallard, moorhen and sometimes the dabchick.

Our four breeding grebes are the only birds which actually nest on the water, their nests consisting of floating piles of aquatic vegetation anchored to a reed or bulrush stem or a submerged stone. A group of waterfowl that are mainly seagoing in winter breed on freshwater lochs in Scotland, and one or two of them also in Ireland; they include the black-necked and Slavonian grebes, red-throated and black-throated divers and common scoter.

Lakes and ponds in town parks are likely to be frequented by at least mute swans, mallard, pochard, tufted duck, moorhen and coot, with two or three kinds of gull, most likely black-headed and common. If there are Canada geese and other more exotic waterfowl, they are likely to be pinioned.

Swallows, martins and swifts regularly feed over fresh water of all kinds, and so does the black tern on migration. The osprey is our only bird of prey that habitually feeds by plunging to the water.

THE SEA   Plate 40

The birds most often seen just offshore, both on open coasts and in estuaries, are the five commoner gulls: black-headed, common, herring, great and lesser black-backs. In spring and summer terns, gannets, auks, skuas, kittiwakes and fulmars are mostly seen near their breeding colonies, but in winter gannets, guillemots and razorbills often appear off other coasts, the gannets visible far out at sea, while terns and skuas pass along these coasts on spring and autumn migration. In winter all our grebes and divers and a good many kinds of duck frequent inshore waters, the ducks including common and velvet scoters, scaup, goldeneye, long-tailed duck and red-breasted merganser among the divers, and mallard, pintail and wigeon among the surface feeders. Eiders frequent the sea at all seasons, and so do common scoters, for many non-breeders summer off our coasts. Swans, grey geese, black geese and shelducks are all seen at times on the sea or in estuarine waters, though the brent is the only goose that is predominantly marine in its habits. Cormorants quite often fly by on all coasts, shags only in the north and west.

Well out at sea, or occasionally seen from promontories, are the really oceanic birds, the petrels, shearwaters, fulmar, and in winter also gannets, kittiwakes, skuas and auks. Sea voyages in September, especially in western seas, such as from Penzance to Scilly or across the Minch are often very rewarding in the scarcer petrels and shearwaters. Though the five commoner gulls, especially herring gulls, will follow ships, they do not usually stay far from the shore.

TOPOGRAPHICAL GUIDE

The aim of this section is to give some guidance as to where to go to watch birds. Coupled with the previous section on habitats, it should enable beginners and strangers to any district both to go to places likely to be rewarding in bird life, and to have some idea of what they are likely to see there. The list of localities is inevitably highly selective, for there are many more places where an interesting variety of birds can be seen, and no two bird watchers, even knowing a district well, would agree on precisely the places to be included. However, I have tried to include all the best places, except where this would draw undesirable attention to rare breeding species. I cannot, of course, guarantee that any reader who visits a locality listed here will have a good day's bird watching, but I think he will have a reasonable chance if he goes at the right time of year for the birds likely to be seen there. Nor can I enter into correspondence with readers about where rare birds are likely to be found. Many rare birds still breed in Britain only because their precise nesting places are not widely known; the kite is the outstanding example. Nobody does such a bird any good by attempting to break its secret. A rare breeding bird cannot be shared by a multitude, except vicariously on film or television, or where, as with the Speyside ospreys and the wild geese of the Severn, the watchers can be organised to watch from a hide at a safe distance.

Access. Readers intending to travel from a distance to visit any locality listed here are warned to **make inquiries about access beforehand.** Most open moorland or heathland, especially in Scotland, is open freely, but by no means all, especially in those parts of the north of England where birds are for shooting, not watching. Woodlands are impossible to predict, but on the coast it is usually possible to walk along the shore, if not on the sea-wall or cliff-top. The great majority of footpaths marked on the one-inch Ordnance Survey maps are public ones, but you can never be absolutely sure. Woods and open country in the possession of the National Trust (marked on the one-inch O.S. maps) are very often open to the public. With farmland everywhere, discretion is necessary, and if the farmer is cross with harmless you, remember that he may have good reason to dislike wandering members of the public, especially near large towns.

Very few sewage farms can be visited without a permit from the local authority; the borough engineer is often the person to write to in the first place. The majority of reservoirs also have restricted access. Around London permits are issued by the Metropolitan Water Board; elsewhere you should write to the local water authority, obtaining its address, if need be, from the local public library. For nature reserves and bird sanctuaries owned or run by public bodies and societies, I have given the situation as regards permits as far as I have been able to check it in 1962, using the following abbreviations:

P   Permit needed

PF   Permit needed away from footpaths

NP   No permit needed

Habitats. To make full use of the lists under these headings, check back to the corresponding headings in the previous section. Woodlands are so numerous that I have had to exercise especially severe selection; also with moorlands in the north and west. In some districts where inland waters are numerous, only the larger and more productive ones have been listed. To locate many inland waters, especially gravel pits, it is essential to use the latest edition of the one-inch Ordnance Survey maps. Even the first post-war series does not show many of the most important gravel pits, and some big new reservoirs have been constructed since the war.

In a very rough attempt to assess the quality of bird-watching haunts, a number, considered by the author to be the best (*in 1962*: gravel pits and sewage farms especially vary rapidly in bird-watching quality) have been starred, as a purely personal selection.

Special Birds. Under this heading birds of special interest in each county are shown, including heronries containing at least ten nests at the last national census in 1954, gull roosts with more than 1000 gulls at the national survey in the same year, and the more important black-headed gulleries, in England and Wales, censused in 1958. Sea-bird colonies on cliffs are given (in the Habitat section for convenience) when they contain at least two of the five following species: razorbill, guillemot, puffin, kittiwake, fulmar.

Reserves and Sanctuaries. All the major bird sanctuaries owned by public bodies are listed by counties, with all nature reserves where birds are the primary or a significant interest.

Societies, etc. Under this heading for each county are listed all bird watching or ornithological societies or clubs, local natural history societies with ornithological sections, bird observatories, ringing stations, field centres and ornithological research institutions. Many other local natural history societies, too numerous to mention, also have some interest in birds. Most local societies have no permanent address, but the name and addresses of their secretaries can be had by inquiry either from the Intelligence Unit, Council for Nature, 41 Queen's Gate, London, s.w.7, or at your local public library. The British Trust for Ornithology (2 King Edward Street, Oxford) can supply addresses for bird observatories and ringing stations. A few local societies, which have permanent addresses, are listed in the Appendix at the end (p. 244).

Literature. Under each county an attempt has been made to show not only the annual bird report for the whole county but also the latest book on the birds of the whole county, or at least a check-list. Where no annual report, county bird book or check-list is available, any other recent publications bearing on the county's birds are given. Most of the bird societies mentioned also have annual reports. Other books and papers, especially where published since 1950, are also given if they seem especially important or readable. The choice of books and papers in this latter category is again inevitably highly selective and does not purport to be comprehensive.

England

BEDFORDSHIRE

Habitats

WOODLAND: Bluebell Wood, Whipsnade Zoo; Deadmansey Wood, Whipsnade; Flitwick Moor (willow tit); King's Wood, Heath and Reach; The Lodge, Sandy; Odell Great Wood.

MARSHES: Flitwick Moor (water rail).

SEWAGE FARMS: *Bedford, Dunstable.

GRAVEL PITS: Arlesey, Felmersham, Henlow, Houghton Regis, Leighton Buzzard, Wyboston.

LAKES, RESERVOIRS: Battlesden, Eversholt, Luton Hoo, Southill, Stewartby, Tingrith, Woburn Park.

Special Birds

Long-eared owl: frequent in pinewoods on the Greensand, which runs in an east-west strip from Sandy to Woburn.

Heronries: Bromham Park, Southill Lake.

Lady Amherst's pheasant: feral in several woods within ten miles of Woburn.

Black-headed gullery: Stewartby Clay Pit.

Reserves and Sanctuaries

Bluebell Wood, Whipsnade Zoo (Zoological Society of London).
Grounds of The Lodge, Sandy (Royal Society for the Protection of Birds).

Societies, etc.

Bedfordshire and Huntingdonshire Naturalists' Trust.
Bedfordshire Natural History Society and Field Club.

Literature

Annual bird report in *Bedfordshire Naturalist* (Beds. N.H.S.).
County bird list by H. A. S. Key in that journal for 1946.
The Birds of the Letchworth Region, by A. R. Jenkins (1958).

BERKSHIRE

Habitats

WOODLAND: Windsor Forest (nightjar), *Windsor Great Park (hawfinch, woodcock).

HEATHLAND: Burghfield Common (nightjar), Snelsmore Common.

DOWNLAND: Fair Mile, Cholsey.

MARSHES: Kennet valley, esp. Ruscombe.

SEWAGE FARMS: Abingdon, *Old Windsor (Ham Island), Reading (Manor Farm).

GRAVEL PITS: *Aldermaston, Appleford, Burghfield, Farmoor, Marsh Benham, Radley, Summerleaze (near Maidenhead), Sutton Courtenay, *Theale, Woodley.

LAKES, RESERVOIRS: Bearwood, Bulmershe, Buscot, Englefield Park, Hurst (Haines Hill), Rapley Farm (near Bagshot), Silwood Park, Virginia Water, Whiteknights Park (Reading), Windsor Great Park (*Great Meadow Pond).

Special Birds

Willow tit: breeds Westrop Wood, Cold Ash.

Heronries: Buscot Park, Coley Park (Reading), Wytham Wood.

Canada goose: breeds in Buscot Park, Windsor Great Park and on various waters in mid-Berks centred on Cranemoor Lake, Englefield Park.

Mandarin duck: breeds in Windsor Great Park and by Virginia Water; sometimes wanders to surrounding waters.

Stone curlew: breeds Berkshire downs.

Reserves and Sanctuaries

Ham Island, Old Windsor (Middle Thames N.H.S.; P).

High Standing Hill Forest Nature Reserve, Windsor Forest (Nature Conservancy; P).

Societies, etc.

Berkshire, Buckinghamshire and Oxfordshire Naturalists' Trust.

Middle Thames Natural History Society (Windsor and Maidenhead areas).

Newbury District Ornithological Club.

Oxford Ornithological Society.

Reading Ornithological Club.

Literature

Annual bird report for whole county published by Oxford Orn. Soc., for parts of county by the other societies.

County bird list, *The Birds of Berkshire* by W. B. Alexander (1952).

Birds of the Middle Thames, by A. C. Fraser (1954).

BUCKINGHAMSHIRE

Habitats

WOODLAND: *Black Park (woodlark, redstart, nightjar); Burnham Beeches (redstart); Church Wood, Hedgerley; Dancers End, near Tring; Salcey Forest.

HEATHLAND AND SCRUB: Coombe Hill; Littleworth Common (nightjar), Stoke Poges Common (nightjar).

SEWAGE FARMS: Slough.

GRAVEL PITS: Emberton, Great Linford, Milton Keynes, Newport Pagnell, Stanton Low, Wraysbury.

LAKES, RESERVOIRS: Boarstall Decoy, *Foxcote Res., Shardeloes, Weston Turville Res.

Special Birds

Heronries: Ankerwyke, Chearsley Furze, Hambleden (Oaken Grove), Taplow Court, Tyringham Park, Wraysbury.

Reserves and Sanctuaries

Burnham Beeches (City of London Corporation; NP).

Church Wood, Hedgerley (Royal Society for Protection of Birds, NP; key with Middle Thames N.H.S.).

Coombe Hill (National Trust).

Dancers End, near Tring (Society for the Promotion of Nature Reserves; NP).

Wilkinson Bird Sanctuary, Eton (Eton College; P).

Societies, etc.

Berkshire, Buckinghamshire and Oxfordshire Naturalists' Trust.

Buckinghamshire Archæological Society, Natural History Section (mainly Aylesbury area).

Middle Thames Natural History Society (Slough and High Wycombe areas).

Literature

Annual bird report in *Middle Thames Naturalist* (M.T.N.H.S.).

County list by K. Price in *Records of Buckinghamshire* (Bucks, Arch. Soc. 1947).

Birds of the Middle Thames, by A. C. Fraser (1954).

Birds in an Eton Garden, by H. M. Bland (1935).

CAMBRIDGESHIRE

Habitats

WOODLAND: Chippenham Fen, Gamlingay Wood.

MARSHES: Fulbourn Fen, *Nene Washes, *Ouse Washes, Wicken Fen (grasshopper warbler).

SEWAGE FARMS: *Cambridge.

GRAVEL PITS: Fen Drayton, Hauxton, Landbeach, Milton, Waterbeach, Wimblington.

Special Birds

Long-eared Owl: breeds at Wicken Fen and several isolated fen woods.

Heronries: Chettisham, Guyhirn.

Bewick's swan: regular on Nene and Ouse Washes, the latter its main haunt in England.

Pink-footed goose: Fens.

Pintail: Ouse Washes are most important winter haunt in eastern England.

Little ringed plover: breeds at several gravel pits.

Dotterel: still one fairly regular migration halt, at Melbourn, and less regular ones on chalk in S.E.

Stone curlew: breeds on the chalk.

Gull roosts: Cambridge sewage farm, Ouse Washes.

Black-headed gullery: Ely sugar beet factory.

Quail: breeds on the chalk.

Red-legged partridge: common

Reserves and Sanctuaries
Chippenham Fen (National Trust; P).
Hayley Wood (Cambridgeshire Naturalists' Trust).
Wicken Fen (National Trust; NP).

Societies, etc.
Cambridgeshire and Isle of Ely Naturalists' Trust.
Cambridge Bird Club.
Madingley Ornithological Field Station, Cambridge University.

Literature
Cambridge Bird Report annually (Cambridge B.C.).
The Birds of Cambridgeshire, by David Lack (1934).
Adventurer's Fen, by E. A. R. Ennion (1942), is about Wicken Fen.
The Birds of the Letchworth Region, by A. R. Jenkins (1958).

CHESHIRE

Habitats
WOODLAND: Alderley Edge; Bollin valley, including Cotterill Clough; Burton Wood, Wirral; Delamere Forest (nightjar); Eastwood Sanctuary, Stalybridge; Harrock Wood, Thurstaston, Wirral; Pettypool Wood.

MOORLAND: Longdendale; Lyme Park.

MARSHES: Abbotts Moss, near Winsford; Burton Marsh, Wirral.

LAKES, RESERVOIRS: Bosley Res., Budworth Mere, Combermere, Crewe Hall Pool, Marbury Mere, Northwich Flashes, Pettypool, Pick Mere, Rede's Mere, *Rostherne Mere, Shotton Pools, *Tatton Mere, Winsford Flashes, Witton Flashes, Huntington Res.

ESTUARIES: Dee, esp. *Hilbre Islands; Mersey.

COASTAL MARSHES: Dee (Burton, Denhall), *Mersey (Frodsham, Ince).

MIGRATION WATCH POINTS: Hilbre Islands.

Special Birds
Rook: Rookery in electric pylons, Moore near Runcorn.

Heronries: Combermere Abbey, Eaton Hall, Huxley, Tabley Mere (now largest in Britain, 143 nests).

Grey geese: Dee estuary, esp. Parkgate.

Canada goose: breeds at Combermere and Tabley.

Shelduck: breeds inland, Delamere Forest.

Waders: immense flocks of knots, redshanks, dunlins, oystercatchers and other birds that feed in Liverpool Bay congregate on Hilbre Islands at high tide.

Ternery: Burton Marsh.

Gull roosts: Mersey estuary, Ince to Hale; Rostherne Mere, Witton Flashes.

Black-headed gulleries: Oakmere, Delamere Forest; Combermere; Baddiley Mere; Dee estuary.

Reserves and Sanctuaries

Burton Wood, Wirral (National Trust; NP).

Cotterill Clough, Bollin valley (Society for the Promotion of Nature Reserves).

Eastwood Bird Sanctuary, Cheetham Park, Stalybridge (Royal Society for the Protection of Birds; P).

Harrock Wood, Wirral (National Trust; NP).

Hilbre Islands (Hoylake Urban District Council).

Marbury Reed-bed (S.P.N.R.).

Rostherne Mere (Nature Conservancy; P).

Weston Marsh, near Runcorn (Merseyside Naturalists' Association).

Societies, etc.

Cheshire Conservation Trust.

Liverpool Naturalists' Field Club.

Liverpool Ornithologists' Club.

Manchester Ornithological Society (runs Rostherne Mere Bird Observatory; P).

Merseyside Naturalists' Association.

Literature

Annual bird reports from Lancashire and Cheshire Fauna Committee. Records also published by three above societies.

The Birds of Cheshire, by T. Hedley Bell (1962), with Supplement (1967).

Birds of the Wirral Peninsula, by R. J. Raines (1961).

The late A. W. Boyd's *A Country Parish* (1951) dealt with the birds around his home at Great Budworth.

CORNWALL

Habitats

WOODLAND: Glynn valley oakwoods, between Liskeard and Bodmin (wood warbler).

MOORLAND: Bodmin Moor, Goonhilly Downs (Lizard).

MARSHES: Maer Marsh, Bude; *Marazion Marsh.

LAKES, RESERVOIRS: Crowan Res.; Dozmary Pool, Bodmin Moor; Loe Pool, Helston; Tamar Lake, near Bude.

ESTUARIES: *Camel, Fal, *Hayle, St. Germans River, St. John's Lake, *Tamar.

CLIFF SEA-BIRD COLONIES: Scilly Is.: Annet (storm petrels, Manx shearwaters), Gorregan (auks, kittiwakes), Mincarlo (puffins), Rosevear (storm petrels); Carn-les-Boel and Morvah, Penwith; on N. coast puffins are at Lye Rock, near Trevone, the Rumps (Polzeath) and west of Newquay, and guillemots and razorbills are scattered all along, and esp. at Hellsmouth, near Godrevy Point.

MIGRATION WATCH POINTS: Marazion Marsh; *St. Agnes, Scilly Is.; St. Ives Island.

Special Birds

Raven: widely distributed.

Chough: now almost extinct, N. coast.

Heronries: Camel River, St. Winnow, Warren (R. Tamar).

Common buzzard: widely distributed.

Avocet: winters regularly on Tamar estuary.

White-fronted goose: Walmsley Sanctuary, Camel estuary.

Roseate tern: breeds in Scillies.

Gull roost: Tamar Lake.

Reserves and Sanctuaries

Scilly Isles (uninhabited; P. for Annet).

Tamar Lake (statutory bird sanctuary).

Trethias Island, Treyarnon Bay (Cornwall Bird Watching and Preservation Society).

Walmsley Sanctuary, Tregorden, Camel estuary (C.B.W.P.S.).

Societies, etc.

Cornwall Bird Watching and Preservation Society.

Cornwall Naturalists' Trust.

St. Agnes Bird Observatory, Scilly Isles.

Literature

Annual bird report published by C.B.W.P.S.

Bird Life in Cornwall, by B. H. Ryves (1948).

Birds of the Cornish Coast, by R. D. Penhallurick (1969).

Marsh and Shore-bird Watching on the Cornish Coast, by H. M. Quick (1948).

CUMBERLAND

Habitats

WOODLAND: Barron Wood; Gelt Woods; Glencoin Wood (pied flycatcher); The Border National Forest Park (Kershope, Spadeadam); Hardknott National Forest Park; Scale Wood, Crummock (pied flycatcher).

MOORLAND: Gilsland-Bewcastle Moors (black grouse, short-eared owl), Lazonby Fell; Northern Pennines.

GRAVEL PITS: Oulton.

LAKES, RESERVOIRS: Bassenthwaite, Buttermere, Crummock Water, Derwentwater, Devoke Water, Ennerdale Water, Loweswater, Siddick Pond, Talkin Tarn, Thirlmere, Thurstonfield Lough, Tindale, Ullswater, Wastwater; Whins Pond, Edenhall.

ESTUARIES: *Solway Firth (Esk and Eden), Moricambe (Wampool and Waver), *Ravenglass (Esk, Mite and Irt), Duddon.

COASTAL MARSHES: Burgh, Calvo, Newton, *Rockcliffe, Skinburness.

DUNES: *Drigg Point, Ravenglass (terneries, black-headed gullery); Grune Point, Skinburness.

CLIFF SEA-BIRD COLONIES: *St. Bees Head (puffin, guillemot, razorbill, fulmar, kittiwake).

MIGRATION WATCH POINTS: Grune Point, Skinburness.

Special Birds

Siskin: until recently the only English county where they bred.
Pied flycatcher: breeds generally in the Lakes area.
Heronry: Muncaster Castle.
Whooper swan: winters on large lakes, Whins Pond and R. Eden.
Grey and Barnacle geese: coastal marshes, esp. Rockcliffe and Burgh; the pink-foot is the principal wintering goose on the Solway.
Goosander: common in winter on the Lakes, Whins Pond and R. Eden.
Red-breasted merganser: colonising coastal districts as breeder.
Gull roosts: Ullswater.
Black guillemot: a few pairs breed at St. Bees Head.

Reserves and Sanctuaries

Drigg Dunes (Cumberland County Council; P).

Societies, etc.

Carlisle Natural History Society.
Grune Point Ringing Station.
Lake District Naturalists' Trust.
Penrith Natural History Society.
Solway Bird Watchers' Society.

Literature
The Birds of Lakeland, edited by Ernest Blezard (1943) was Vol. VI of the *Transactions* of the Carlisle N.H.S., and has been brought up to date in subsequent issues of the *Transactions*.
Current records published in *The Field Naturalist* and *The Changing Scene*, journals of a consortium of Lake District natural history societies.

DERBYSHIRE

Habitats
MOORLAND: the Peak moorlands are the southernmost breeding places in England for several moorland birds, e.g. golden plover.
SEWAGE FARMS: Egginton.
GRAVEL PITS: Egginton, Willington.
LAKES, RESERVOIRS: Barbrook Res., Combs Res., Derwent Res., Ladybower Res., Longdendale Res., Ogston, Osmaston Manor, Toddbrook Res.

Special Birds
Pied flycatcher: breeds locally in north of county.
Dipper: breeds on Rivers Derwent, Dove, Goyt and Wye.
Heronries: Calke Park, Catton Hall.
Canada goose: winter flock at Kedleston and Osmaston Parks.
Black-headed gullery: Willington gravel pit.

Societies, etc.
Derbyshire Naturalists' Trust.
Derbyshire Ornithological Society.

Literature
Annual bird report published by D.O.S.
Most recent list of birds in *Victoria County History* (1905).

DEVON

Habitats
WOODLAND: Black Tor Copse, Dartmoor; Chapel Wood, Spreacombe; Stoke Woods and Huxham Brake (nightingales); Watersmeet, near Lynmouth; Wistmans Wood, Dartmoor; Yarner Wood.
HEATHLAND, SCRUB: Harpford, Lympstone, Venn Ottery and Woodbury Commons, E. Devon; Dowlands Cliffs and Landslips, Axmouth.
MOORLAND: Brendon Common, Exmoor; *Dartmoor (ring ouzel, merlin, common sandpiper, red and black grouse).
LAKES, RESERVOIRS: Arlington Court, near Barnstaple; Beesands Ley; Burrator Res.; Creedy Pond, near Crediton; Fernworthy Res.; Hennock Res., near Bovey Tracey; Lopwell Res., R. Tavy; Orcheston Ponds, near Holbeton; Shobrooke Park, near Crediton; *Slapton Ley;

Tamar Lake, near Bude; Wistlandpound Res., Exmoor; Kitley Pond, near Yealmpton.

ESTUARIES: Avon, Axe, Dart, Erme, *Exe, *Kingsbridge, Plym, *Tamar, Tavy, *Taw, Teign, *Torridge, Yealm and Wembury Bay.

DUNES: Braunton Burrows, Dawlish Warren.

CLIFF SEA-BIRD COLONIES: *Berry Head (kittiwake, razorbill, guillemot, fulmar), *Lundy (do., plus puffin), Martinhoe (fulmar, guillemot, razorbill).

MIGRATION WATCH POINTS: Lundy, Start Point.

Special Birds

Siskin: now breeds in Devon.

Pied flycatcher: breeds Yarner Wood.

Whinchat: plentiful on Dartmoor.

Nightingale: western limit in Britain lies in E. Devon; main stronghold, Chudleigh Knighton—Kingsteignton area.

Common buzzard: plentiful.

Heronries: Arlington Court, Halwell House, Killerton, Powderham Park, Sharpham House, Stedcombe Manor, Tracey near Honiton.

Brent goose: small flock regularly in Exe estuary.

Canada goose: breeds Shobrooke Park and other E. Devon waters.

Avocet: winters in Tamar estuary.

Gull roosts: Tamar Lake, Exe and Teign estuaries.

Reserves and Sanctuaries

Axmouth-Lyme Regis (including Dowlands Landslip) (Nature Conservancy; P).

Berry Head (Brixham Urban District Council; NP).

Black Tor Copse Forest Nature Reserve (Duchy of Cornwall).

Braunton Burrows (NP).

Chapel Wood, Spreacombe (RSPB; P).

Exe estuary and Dawlish Warren (statutory bird sanctuary).

Slapton Ley (Herbert Whitley Trust; NP).

Wembury Bird Sanctuary (Devon B.W. and P.S.; NP).

Wistmans Wood (Duchy of Cornwall).

Yarner Wood (Nature Conservancy; P).

Societies, etc.

Devon Bird Watching and Preservation Society.

Devon Naturalists' Trust.

Lundy Field Society (runs Lundy Bird Observatory).

Slapton Cabin (Devon B.W.P.S.).

Slapton Ley Field Centre (Field Studies Council).

Torquay N.H.S., Ornithological Section.

Literature

Annual bird report issued by Devon B.W.P.S., also quarterly journal *Devon Birds.*

The Birds of Devon, by Robert Moore (1969).

The Birds of South-East Devon, by L. R. W. Loyd (1929).

Bird Life in Devon, by W. Walmsley White (1931).

Lundy, Isle of Puffins, by Richard Perry (1940).

Ilfracombe Flora and Fauna, by Mervin G. Palmer (1946).

A List of the Birds of Lundy, by Peter Davis (1954).

DORSET

Habitats

HEATHLAND: *Purbeck and Poole Harbour (Studland to Arne); north of Wareham; Holt and adjacent heaths.

DOWNLAND: Cranborne Chase.

MARSHES: Lodmoor and *Radipole Lake, Weymouth.

LAKES, RESERVOIRS: Little Sea, Studland; *East and West Fleets, behind Chesil Bank; Milton Abbas; Sherborne; Sutton Bingham Res. nr. Yeovil.

ESTUARIES, ETC.: *Poole Harbour, Portland Harbour, Studland Bay (grebes).

SHINGLE: Chesil Bank (terneries).

CLIFF SEA-BIRD COLONIES: Durlston Head; Portland Bill, West Cliff.

MIGRATION WATCH POINTS: *Portland Bill.

Special Birds

Raven: breeds along cliffs west of Swanage.

Dartford warbler: as frequent on the Dorset heaths as anywhere in England.

Heronry: Poole Harbour.

Mute swan: the Abbotsbury swannery is the only place in the British Isles where swans nest colonially.

Balearic shearwater: seen regularly off Portland Bill in late summer and early autumn.

Black-tailed godwit: winters regularly in Poole Harbour.

Purple sandpiper: winters regularly at Portland Bill.

Gull roost: Poole Harbour.

Reserves and Sanctuaries

Abbotsbury Swannery (Ilchester estate; entrance fee).

Arne (Nature Conservancy; P).

Brownsea Island (National Trust and Dorset Naturalists' Trust)

Hartland Moor (Nature Conservancy; P; danger from unexploded bombs).

Morden Bog (Nature Conservancy; P).

Radipole Lake (Weymouth Corporation).
Studland Heath (Nature Conservancy; NP)

Societies, etc.
Dorset Field Ornithology Group.
Dorset N.H. and Arch. Soc.
Dorset Naturalists' Trust.
Portland Bird Observatory and Field Centre.
South Dorset Bird Watching Soc.

Literature
Annual bird reports in *Proceedings* of Dorset N.H.A.S.
Latest county list, by Rev. F. L. Blathwayt, in same *Proceedings* for 1940.

DURHAM

Habitats
WOODLAND: Castle Eden Dene, Wynyard Park.
SEWAGE FARM: Darlington.
ESTUARIES: Jarrow Slake, *Tees.
COASTAL MARSHES: Cowpen Marsh (Teesmouth).
LAKES, RESERVOIRS: Crookfoot Res.; Dorman's Pool, Teesmouth;
    Hurworth Burn Res.; Tanfield Ponds, Stanley.
CLIFF SEA-BIRD COLONIES: *Marsden Rock (kittiwakes, cormorants).
MIGRATION WATCH POINTS: Heugh Battery, Hartlepool; Souter
    Point.

Special Birds
Pied flycatcher: breeds in woodlands in western dales.
Purple sandpiper: winters, Hartlepool.
Gull roost: Tees estuary.
Black-headed gulleries: five small, mostly on moors.

Reserves and Sanctuaries
Castle Eden Dene (Durham County Council; PF).

Societies, etc.
N.H.S. of Northumberland, Durham and Newcastle-upon-Tyne.
Northumberland and Durham Naturalists' Trust.
Teesmouth Bird Club.

Literature
Annual bird reports in *Transactions* of county N.H.S.
Latest list of birds, by G. W. Temperley, in same *Transactions* for 1951.
Birds of Teesside, by P. J. Stead (in press).

ESSEX

Habitats
WOODLAND: Belfairs Great Wood, Hadleigh; Blakes Wood, Danbury; Bull Wood, Hockley; *Epping Forest (hawfinch, redstart, red-backed shrike, nightjar); Hainault Forest; Hales Wood and Saffron Walden; Hatfield Forest; Ongar Park and Gaynes Park Woods; Shipwrights Wood, Benfleet.

HEATH, SCRUB AND PARKLAND: Danbury and Lingwood Commons; South Weald Park; Thorndon Park (nightjar); Woodham Walter Common.

MARSHES: small areas in valleys of Chelmer, Lea, Stort, Stour and Roman Rivers.

SEWAGE FARMS: Bishop's Stortford, Romford.

GRAVEL PITS: Fishers Green; Ham River, South Ockendon; Nazeing; Sewardstone.

LAKES, RESERVOIRS: *Abberton Res.; Gosfield Park, Halstead; *Hanningfield Res.; Hollow Pond, Snaresbrook; *Lea Valley Res. (King George V, William Girling, Walthamstow); Navestock Park; Berwick Ponds, Rainham; Wanstead Basin.

ESTUARIES: *Blackwater, Colne, Crouch, *Hamford Water, Mersea Island, *Stour, Thames.

COASTAL MARSHES: *Blackwater (Bradwell, Mersea, Ramsey, Tollesbury); Colne (Fingringhoe, Langenhoe); Crouch (Bridgemarsh, *Dengie); Roach (Paglesham); Thames (Aveley, Leigh, Rainham, Ripple Level, West Thurrock).

MIGRATION WATCH POINTS: Bradwell-on-Sea, Colne Point, The Naze, Southend Pier.

Special Birds
Nightingale: Epping Forest is now the best area to hear a nightingale within 20 miles of London.

Heronries: Hylands Park, Little Parndon, Skippers Island, Tollesbury, Walthamstow Res.

Mute swan: large non-breeding flock in Stour estuary, Manningtree.

Greylag goose: feral flock on Horsey Is., Hamford Water.

Brent goose: large flocks between Wakering Stairs and Blackwater estuary.

Red-crested pochard: more often seen wild on Abberton Res. than anywhere else in Britain.

Collared dove: breeds Clacton, Walton-on-Naze.

Golden plover: wintering flocks, Fairlop airfield and Chelmer valley near Chelmsford, among other places.

Gull roosts: King George V Res., William Girling Res.

Black-headed gulleries: Cob Islands, Tollesbury; Horsey Is.; Pewit Is. Little Oakley; Rat Is., R. Colne; Tillingham Marshes.

Red-legged partridge: common.

Reserves and Sanctuaries
Belfairs Great Wood (Southend-on-Sea Corporation).
Bull Wood, Hockley (Rochford R.D.C.).
Epping Forest (City of London Corporation).
Fingringhoe Wick (Essex Naturalists' Trust).
The Glen, Thundersley (Benfleet U.D.C.).
Hainault Forest (London C.C.).
Hatfield Forest (National Trust).
Hadleigh Marshes (Essex C.C. and Benfleet U.D.C.).
Hales Wood (Nature Conservancy; P).
Shipwrights Wood (Benfleet U.D.C.).

Societies, etc.
Abberton Reservoir Duck Ringing Station.
Bradwell Bird Observatory.
Colchester and District N.H.S., Orn. Section.
Essex Naturalists' Trust.
London N.H.S., Orn. Section.
Essex Bird Watching and Preservation Soc.
High Beach Field Study Centre (Walthamstow B.C.).
Romford Ringing Station.
St. Osyth Bird Watching and Protection Soc.
South Essex N.H.S., Orn. Section.

Literature
Essex Bird Report published annually by Essex B.W.P.S.
London Bird Report (London N.H.S.) covers area within 20 miles of London.
The Birds of Essex, by W. E. Glegg (1929).
The Birds of the London Area since 1900, by the London N.H.S. (1957) covers area within 20 miles of London.
A Guide to the Birds of Essex, by R. Hudson and G. A. Pyman (1968).

GLOUCESTERSHIRE

Habitats
WOODLAND: *Forest of Dean (hawfinch, redstart, nightjar, woodcock).
MARSHES: Elmore.
GRAVEL PITS: Fairford, *Frampton, Lechlade, South Cerney.
LAKES, RESERVOIRS: Coombe Canal; Dowdeswell Res.; Hewletts Res., Cheltenham.
ESTUARIES: *Severn, esp. at Severn Beach and Guscar Rocks, opposite Sheperdine.
COASTAL MARSHES: *Dumbles, Slimbridge.

Special Birds
Cirl bunting: local in the Severn vale.
Pied flycatcher: common in Forest of Dean.

Marsh warbler: breeds in osier beds in Severn vale.

Dipper: breeds on a few streams in the Cotswolds.

Common buzzard: a few pairs breed, chiefly in the Forest of Dean and along the Cotswold escarpment.

Heronries: Cambridge, Elmore.

White-fronted goose: regular wintering flock at the New Grounds, Slimbridge.

Pink-footed goose: small flock at New Grounds, Oct.-Dec.

Gull roost: Severn estuary, Frampton to Purton.

Herring gull: small breeding colony on Wye cliffs opposite Chepstow.

Corncrake: a few pairs still breed near Tewkesbury.

Reserves and Sanctuaries

The New Grounds, Slimbridge (Wildfowl Trust; P).

Societies, etc.

Bristol Nat. Soc., Orn. Section.

Dursley and District Bird Watching and Preservation Soc.

Gloucestershire Trust for Nature Conservation.

Nailsworth Bird Recorders Club.

North Gloucestershire Nat. Soc.

Wildfowl Trust (has duck decoy, wildfowl collection and research laboratory at the New Grounds, Slimbridge).

Literature

Annual bird reports on North Glos. published by North Glos. N.S. and on South Glos. by Bristol N.S.

Latest book on birds of whole county is Mellersh's, *A Treatise on the Birds of Gloucestershire* (1902), but see list for Bristol district by H. H. Davis in Bristol N.S. *Proceedings* for 1947, and chapter on wild life by Sir William Taylor in the *National Forest Park Guide* for the Dean Forest and Wye valley (1956).

HAMPSHIRE

Habitats

WOODLAND: *New Forest (hawfinch, crossbill, woodcock); Pigeon Copse, Liss; Selborne Hanger (Gilbert White associations), Woolton Hill, near Newbury.

HEATH, SCRUB: Ludshott Common and Waggoners' Wells; *New Forest (woodlark, red-backed shrike, stonechat, nightjar, hobby); Selborne Common (Gilbert White associations); Silchester Common (nightjar), Woolmer Forest; Heckfield Heath (nightjar).

DOWNLAND: Old Winchester Hill, *Quarley Hill area.

MARSHES: Chilbolton Common (grasshopper warbler).

SEWAGE FARMS: Basingstoke.

LAKES, RESERVOIRS: Alresford Pond; Arle Bury; Avington; Dogmersfield; Fawley Res.; Fleet Pond; Frensham Great Pond; Hatchet

Pond, Beaulieu; Marsh Court, Stockbridge; Sowley Pond, near Lymington; Stratfieldsaye; Winnall, Winchester; Woolmer Pond.

ESTUARIES: *Christchurch Harbour; Solent, *Keyhaven to Needs Oar Point; Beaulieu River; Southampton Water, esp. Dibden Bay, Titchfield Haven; *Langstone Harbour; Chichester Harbour.

COASTAL MARSHES: Keyhaven, Stanpit.

MIGRATION WATCH POINTS: Christchurch Harbour and Hengistbury Head, Langstone Harbour, Titchfield Haven.

Special Birds

Dartford warbler: New Forest.

Great grey shrike: increasing in winter in New Forest.

Common buzzard: frequent in the New Forest.

Heronries: Alice Holt Forest, Godshill, Hayling Island, Hinton Admiral, Sowley Pond, Wickham.

Brent goose: Langstone Harbour.

Black-tailed godwit: winters in Langstone Harbour and Titchfield Haven.

Stone curlew: Quarley Hill is noted late summer gathering ground.

Gull roost: Southampton Water.

Black-headed gulleries: eight between Lepe and Keyhaven.

Lady Amherst's pheasant: Exbury area of New Forest.

Reserves and Sanctuaries

Catherington Down (Hants, C.C. and Hants. and I.O.W. Naturalists' Trust). Farlington Marshes (Hants. and I.O.W. Naturalists' Trust).

Forest Nature Reserves in the New Forest: Bramshaw, Mark Ash, Matley and Denny (Nature Conservancy and Forestry Commission; PF).

Old Winchester Hill (Nature Conservancy; NP: danger from unexploded bombs).

Pennington Marshes (Hants. and I.O.W. Naturalists' Trust).

Pigeon Copse (RSPB; P).

Selborne Common (National Trust).

Sinah Common Wildfowl Refuge (Langstone and District Wildfowlers).

Stanpit Marsh (Christchurch Corporation and Hants. and I.O.W. N.T.).

Waggoners' Wells and Ludshott Common (National Trust).

Woolton Hill (National Trust).

Societies, etc.

Christchurch Harbour Ornithological Group.

Hampshire Field Club and Arch. Soc., Orn. Section.

Hampshire and Isle of Wight Naturalists' Trust.

Newbury District Ornithological Club.

New Forest Ornithologists' Club.

Literature

Annual bird report in *Proceedings* of Hants. Field Club.

Latest book on county's birds, *The Birds of Hampshire and the Isle of*

Wight, by J. E. Kelsall and P. W. Munn (1905), but new one in preparation by E. Cohen; see also chapter by E. Cohen on birds in *The New
Forest,* by J. Berlin and others (1960).

Gilbert White's great classic, *The Natural History of Selborne* (1788) is
still a useful introduction to the natural history of this north-east
Hampshire parish.

HEREFORDSHIRE

Habitats

WOODLAND: Bringewood Chase, near Ludlow; Brockhill, Cother and
Burnt Woods, near Great Malvern; the Chase, Ross-on-Wye; Haugh
Wood, Woolhope.

MOORLAND: Black Mountains (ring ouzel, red grouse), Malvern Hills.

MARSHES: Byton Moor, Wigmore Moor.

LAKES, RIVERS: Berrington Pool; Eastnor; Shobdon Decoy Pool;
R. Wye, esp. at Turners Boat.

Special Birds

Nightingale: not normally found west of R. Wye or Hereford city.
Pied flycatcher: breeds in woodlands in N.W.
Heronry: Berrington.

Societies, etc.

Herefordshire and Radnorshire Nature Trust.
Herefordshire Ornithological Club.

Literature

Annual bird report published by H.O.C.

Most recent bird list *Herefordshire Birds,* by H. A. Gilbert and C. W.
Walker (2nd ed., 1954); see also J. G. Harrison, *Handbook of Birds of
the Malvern District* (1941).

HERTFORDSHIRE

Habitats

WOODLAND: Ashridge estate, inc. Frithsden Beeches; *Broxbourne,
Cowheath and Wormley Woods (wood and grasshopper warblers, nightjar, woodcock); Cuffley Great Wood (redstart).

SCRUBLAND: Berkhamsted Common (nightjar), Bricket Wood Scrubs.

DOWNLAND: Therfield Heath.

MARSHES: Oughtonhead Common, near Hitchin (grasshopper warbler,
water rail).

SEWAGE FARMS: Hitchin, Royston, *Rye Meads, Wormley.

GRAVEL PITS: Broxbourne, Cheshunt, Colne valley (Hamper Mill to
West Hyde), King's Langley, Old Parkbury.

LAKES, RESERVOIRS: Aldenham (Elstree) Res., Bonningtons, Brocket

Hall Park, Gilston Park, *Hilfield Park Res., Hunsdon, Knebworth, Moor Mill, Panshanger, Radwell, *Tring Res. (three together with Wilstone as an outlier), Whitwell cress-beds, Woodhall Park.

Special Birds
Willow tit: commoner than marsh tit around Harpenden and in upper Lea valley.
Bearded tit: regular at Tring Res. in winter since 1959.
Little ringed plover: breeds at some gravel pits.
Golden plover: regular winter flock, Radlett airfield.
Stone curlew: still on downs between Baldock and Royston.
Black tern: regular on migration, Tring Res.
Gull roosts: Hilfield Park Res., Wilstone Res.

Reserves and Sanctuaries
Ashridge estate (National Trust).
Tring Reservoirs (Nature Conservancy; PF).

Societies, etc.
Hertfordshire N.H.S.
London N.H.S., Orn. Section.
Rye Meads Ringing Station, Lea valley.

Literature
Annual bird reports in *Transactions* of Herts. N.H.S., and for area within 20 miles of London in *London Bird Report* (London N.H.S.).
A History of the Birds of Hertfordshire, by B. L. Sage (1959).
The Birds of the Letchworth Region, by A. R. Jenkins (1958).
The Birds of the London Area since 1900, by the London N.H.S. (1957) covers the area within 20 miles of London.

HUNTINGDONSHIRE

Habitats
WOODLAND: Bevills Wood, Grafham West Wood, Holme Fen, Monks' Wood (grasshopper warbler), Rampton Wood, Salome Wood, Woodwalton Fen (grasshopper warbler).
GRAVEL PITS: Fenstanton, Hemingford Grey, St. Ives, Little Paxton, Stibbington, Wansford.
LAKES, RESERVOIRS: Buckden, Bury Fen (floods), Diddington Res., Fletton Brick Pits, Great Staughton, Kimbolton.

Special Birds
Heronry: Hemingford Park.

Reserves and Sanctuaries
Holme Fen (Nature Conservancy; P).

Monks' Wood (Nature Conservancy; P).

Woodwalton Fen (Society for the Promotion of Nature Reserves and Nature Conservancy; P).

Societies, etc.
Bedfordshire and Huntingdonshire Naturalists' Trust.
Huntingdonshire Flora and Fauna Soc.

Literature
Annual bird report in annual report of Hunts. F.F.S.
Latest county list in *Victoria County History of Huntingdonshire* (1926).

ISLE OF WIGHT

Habitats
WOODLAND: Firestone Copse, Wootton; Parkhurst Forest; Town and Walter's Copses, Newtown.

HEATHLAND: Barton Woods, Clamerkin Woods, Hamstead, Headon Warren (nightjar); Parkhurst Forest.

DOWNLAND: Tennyson Down, Downland ridge from Freshwater to Carisbrooke, St. Catherine's Down; St. Boniface Down.

ESTUARIES: Brading Harbour, Medina, *Newtown Harbour, Wootton Creek, Yar.

CLIFF SEA-BIRD COLONIES: High Down, Main Bench, *Scratchells Bay.

MIGRATION WATCH POINTS: The Needles; St. Catherine's Point.

Special Birds
Raven: easternmost ravens on south coast breed on High Down cliffs.

Black-headed gullery: Newtown.

Great black-back: easternmost breeding on south coast, High Down cliffs.

Reserves and Sanctuaries
Osborne House grounds (Ministry of Works).
Town Copse, Newtown (National Trust).

Societies, etc.
Hampshire and Isle of Wight Naturalists' Trust.
Isle of Wight N.H.S.
St. Catherine's Point Ringing Station.

Literature
Annual reports on birds in *Proceedings* of both Hampshire Field Club and Isle of Wight N.H.S.

Latest county bird list in *A Guide to the Natural History of the Isle of Wight* by Frank Morey (1909). See also Kelsall and Munn (1905) under Hampshire.

KENT

Habitats

WOODLAND: Bedgebury Pinetum; Blean and other woods N. of
Canterbury (redstart); Chislehurst Common; Crockham, Ide and
Toys Hills, and other woods between Westerham and Sevenoaks (wood
warbler); Ham Street Woods; Hayes and Keston Commons; Joyden's
Wood, Bexley; Mereworth Woods; *Northward Hill, High Halstow;
Red Wood, Luddesdown; Stockbury Hill Wood.

PARKLAND: Eastwell Park, Knole Park (redstart), Mote Park.

SEWAGE FARMS: Elmers End, Beckenham.

GRAVEL, ETC. PITS: Aylesford; Burham; Darenth; Dunton Green;
Faversham; Hoppen Pits, Dungeness; Leybourne; Lower Hope Pools,
Cliffe; Murston; New Romney Ponds; Northfleet; Ruxley, Foots
Cray; Stone; Sundridge; Westbere; Yalding.

LAKES: Bayham Abbey; Bedgebury; Danson Park, Bexley; Eastwell
Park, Hever; Kelsey Park, Beckenham; Leeds; Leigh; Lullingstone;
Mote Park, Penshurst; Tonbridge.

ESTUARIES: *Thames, *Medway, *Swale (inc. Windmill Creek and esp.
*Shellness), Pegwell Bay; Stour.

COASTAL MARSHES: Erith to Stone; Swanscombe; Shorne to Grain,
esp. *Cliffe, *Egypt and St. Mary's Bays, Yantlet Creek; Sheppey
(Elmley to Shellness); Murston to Whitstable; Reculver to Birchington;
Stodmarsh to Pegwell Bay; Romney and Walland.

DUNES: Sandwich Golf Links.

SHINGLE: *Dungeness; Reculver; Shellness, Stour; Shellness, Swale.

MIGRATION WATCH POINTS: Dungeness, Sandwich Bay.

Special Birds

Black redstart: breeds in several coastal towns.

Nightingale: fairly plentiful in the Weald, e.g. at Sevenoaks Weald.

Wryneck: now rare, but commoner than in any other county, esp. near
Hythe, Canterbury, Maidstone and the Medway towns.

Long-eared owl: roost at Northward Hill.

Heronries: Chilham, High Halstow (second largest in British Isles, 129
nests), Lympne Castle.

White-fronted goose: winter flocks on Thames, Medway, Swale, Romney
and Walland marshes.

Brent goose: small winter flocks on Medway and Swale marshes.

Shelduck: breeds inland in several places including at Northward Hill
and in Cuxton-Snodland area.

Velvet Scoter: often in common scoter flocks off Dungeness.

Cormorant: inland roosts at Hever and Stodmarsh.

Fulmar: present but not yet breeding on cliffs between Ramsgate and
Dover.

Collared Dove: breeds in several localities in north and east Kent.

Stone curlew: a few pairs nest on the Dungeness shingle.

Avocet: a few winter on the Swale.

Gull roost: Littlestone-on-Sea.

Black-headed gulleries: Medway and Swale estuaries.

Common gull: a few pairs at Dungeness are the only breeding colony south of the Tweed.

Herring gull: 150-200 pairs have bred on buildings in Dover, and a few pairs on the shingle at Dungeness.

Lesser black-back: odd pairs breed among herring gulls in S.E. Kent.

Reserves and Sanctuaries

Blean Woods (Nature Conservancy; P).

Dungeness (RSPB;   P).

Greenwich Park (Ministry of Works).

Ham Street Woods (Nature Conservancy; P).

High Halstow (RSPB and Nature Conservancy; PF).

Leybourne Castle Lakes (K.N.T.).

Red Wood, Luddesdown (K.N.T.).

Ruxley gravel pits (K.N.T.; P).

Shellness (K.N.T.).

Stockbury Hill Wood (K.N.T.).

Wildfowl reserves at Dunton Green, Faversham, Westbere and Sundridge (Kent Wildfowlers' Association).

Wye and Crundale Downs (Nature Conservancy; PF).

Societies, etc.

Canterbury and District Bird Watchers' Association.

Dungeness Bird Observatory.

Kent Naturalists' Trust.

Kent Ornithological Society.

London N.H.S. Orn. Section.

St. Paul's Cray Ornithological Society.

Sandwich Bay Ringing Station.

Thanet Field Club.

Literature

Kent Bird Report published annually by Kent Orn. Soc.; see also *London Bird Report* (London N.H.S.).

The Birds of Kent, 2 vols., by J. M. Harrison (1953).

Birds of the North Kent Marshes, by E. H. Gillham and R. C. Homes (1950).

Report on the Breeding Birds of the Medway Islands, June 3-5, 1955, by E. H. Gillham and others (1955).

The Birds of the London Area since 1900, by the London N.H.S. (1957) covers the area within 20 miles of London.

LANCASHIRE

Habitats
WOODLAND: Roudsea Wood.

MOORLAND: Bowland Forest, East Lancs. Pennines.

MARSHES: *Leighton Moss.

SEWAGE FARMS: Too numerous to mention, but most of them repay observation.

LAKES, RESERVOIRS: *Astley and Pennington Flashes, Leigh; Blelham Tarn; Coniston Water; Esthwaite Water; *Hesketh Park, Southport; Knowsley Park; numerous reservoirs, esp. in Pennines, but most are rather unrewarding.

ESTUARIES: Duddon, *Leven, Lune, Wyre, Ribble, Alt, Mersey.

DUNES: Ainsdale, Freshfield and Formby (nightjar); Sandscale and Roanhead Barrow; Walney Island.

Special Birds
Twite: nests locally on eastern moors.

Pied flycatcher: local in Lakes area.

Heronries: localities omitted in deference to local wishes.

Bittern: habitually present Leighton Moss.

Whooper swan: regular at Leighton Moss, the Bolton reservoirs and Foulridge near Colne.

Pink-footed goose: Ribble marshes and Martin Mere, Southport.

Greylag goose: Silverdale area, Lune valley.

Canada goose: breeds Knowsley Park; regular winter flock in Lune valley.

Gull roosts: several coastal roosts; inland roosts include Esthwaite Water, Guide Res., Blackburn, and Heaton Park and Audenshaw, Manchester; interesting winter concentrations at rubbish tips, etc., in all parts of county.

Black-headed gulleries: eleven, mostly rather small.

Black grouse: Grizedale Forest.

Reserves and Sanctuaries
Esthwaite North Fen (Nature Conservancy; NP).

Holden Clough, Oldham (Oldham Microscopical Society and Field Club).

Roudsea Wood (Nature Conservancy; PF).

Rusland Moss (Nature Conservancy; P).

Southport Sanctuary Wildfowl Refuge (Martin Mere) (Nature Conservancy).

Societies, etc.
Brantwood Conference and Holiday Centre for Naturalists (Council for Nature).

East Lancashire Ornithologists' Club.

Lake District Naturalists' Trust.
Lancaster and District Bird Watching Society.
Lancashire Naturalists' Trust.
Manchester Ornithological Society.
Merseyside Naturalists' Association.

Literature
Annual bird report published by Lancashire and Cheshire Fauna
Committee; see also annual reports of above societies.
Quarterly notes in *The Field Naturalist* (see under Cumberland).
The Birds of Lancashire, by C. Oakes (1953); see also *The Birds of Lakeland*
(under Cumberland).

LEICESTERSHIRE AND RUTLAND

Habitats
WOODLAND: Burbage and Aston Fir Woods, Hinckley; *Charnwood
Forest, esp. Gisborne's Gorse, Out Woods, Stoneywell Wood and
Swithland Wood; Leighfield Forest, esp. Alleston Wood, Barkby Holt,
Loddington Reddish and Ingby Wood; Piper and Oakley Woods, near
Loughborough (hawfinch, nightjar, woodcock).
MOORLAND: *Bradgate Park, *Charnwood Forest, esp. Beacon Hill,
Warren Hills and Charnwood Lodge.
MARSHES: Narborough Bog, Grantham Canal.
SEWAGE FARMS: Loughborough.
GRAVEL, ETC., PITS: Hemington, Ratcliffe, Wanlip.
LAKES, RESERVOIRS: Belvoir Fish Ponds, Burley Fish Ponds, *Cropston
Res., *Eye Brook Res., Groby Pool, *Stanford Res., *Swithland Res.
MIGRATION WATCH POINT: Croft Hill.

Special Birds
Heronries: Stapleford Park.
Canada goose: breeds Cropston Res., Stapleford Park.
Gull roosts: Cropston Res., Eye Brook Res., Swithland Res., Hilton
gravel pits.

Reserves and Sanctuaries
Bradgate Park and Swithland Wood.
Charnwood Lodge (Leicestershire Trust).
Great Fenny Wood (Leicestershire Trust).
Various canal reserves (Leicestershire Trust).

Societies, etc.
Leicestershire and Rutland Ornithological Society.
Leicestershire Trust for Nature Conservation.
Loughborough Naturalists' Club.
Rutland Natural History Society.

Literature
Annual bird report published by L.R.O.S.
Most recent list of county birds in *Victoria County History of Leicestershire* (1907); see also RSPB pamphlet by A. E. Jolley (1947).
Notes on the Birds of Rutland, by C. R. Haines (1907).

LINCOLNSHIRE

Habitats
WOODLAND: Brocklesby Woods, Friskney Decoy Wood; Isle of Axholme woodlands.
HEATHLAND, SCRUB: Linwood Warren; Scotton Common (nightjar); Stapleford Moor; Twigmoor Warren (nighjar).
MARSHES: Marshy fields in most river valleys.
SEWAGE FARMS: Grantham, Lincoln, Wisbech.
GRAVEL PITS: Bardney, Burton, Langtoft, Lincoln (L.M.S. and L.N.E.R. Pits), Sea Bank Clay Pits, Sleaford, Tallington.
LAKES, RESERVOIRS: Brocklesby, Culverthorpe, Denton Res., Fillingham, Harlaxton, Lambert Hill Pond, Laughton, Revesby Res., Syston, Woolton.
ESTUARIES: Humber, Wash.
COASTAL MARSHES: Read's Island, Tetney Fitties, *The Wash.
DUNES: *Gibraltar Point and Skegness, Saltfleetby and Theddlethorpe.
MIGRATION WATCH POINTS: *Gibraltar Point, North Cotes, Tetney.

Special Birds
Twite: regular in winter on the Wash saltmarshes.
Willow tit: Isle of Axholme.
Short-eared owl: often breeds around the Wash.
Heronries: Coningsby (Troy Wood), Doddington, Evedon Wood, Legbourne Wood, Muckton Wood, Wharton Wood, Willoughby Wood.
Bittern: often heard booming, Barrow Haven and Barton-on-Humber.
Pink-footed goose: feeds on northern wolds, roosting on Read's Island; feeds on Croft Marsh and East Fen, roosting on Wainfleet Sand, Wash; feeds in Holbeach area, roosting on Long Sand.
Brent goose: large flock winters in Wash.
Canada goose: breeds Grimthorpe Park.
Gull roosts: The Wash, Tetney High Sands (Humber estuary).
Black-headed gulleries: several on the coast; inland on Laughton and Scotton Commons and Grantham sewage farm.

Reserves and Sanctuaries
Friskney Decoy Wood (Lincolnshire Naturalists' Trust; P).
Gibraltar Point and Skegness (Lindsey County Council, Skegness U.D.C., L.N.T.; NP).
Humber Wildfowl Refuge (Read's Island) (Nature Conservancy; P).
Isle of Axholme woodlands (L.N.T.; P).

Lincolnshire Gate Scrubs (L.N.T.; P).
Linwood Warren (L.N.T.; P).
Saltfleetby-Theddlethorpe Dunes (L.N.T.; NP when R.A.F. not bombing).
Scotton Common (L.N.T.; P).
Sea Bank Clay Pits, near Chapel Point (L.N.T.; P).
Stapleford Moor (Forestry Commission and L.N.T.; P).

Societies, etc.
Gibraltar Point Bird Observatory.
Lincolnshire Naturalists' Trust.
Lincolnshire Naturalists' Union.

Literature
Annual bird report in *Transactions* of L.N.U. and notes on the Wash and
    fen area in *Cambridge Bird Report*.
The Birds of Lincolnshire, by A. E. Smith and R. K. Cornwallis (1955).

LONDON (*see* Middlesex, Surrey)

MIDDLESEX

Habitats
WOODLAND: *Copse Wood, Park Wood and Mad Bess Wood, Ruislip;
    Ken Wood, Hampstead; Perivale Wood; Scratch Wood.
HEATHLAND, SCRUB: Hampstead Heath; Poor's Field, Ruislip (willow
    tit, red-backed shrike).
SEWAGE FARMS: *Perry Oaks, near London Airport; Ponders End.
GRAVEL PITS: Ashford, Bedfont, Charlton, Feltham, Poyle, Shepperton,
    Stanwellmoor.
LAKES, RESERVOIRS: Brent Res. (Welsh Harp), Hendon; Clissold
    Park, Stoke Newington; Groveland Park, Southgate; *Hampton
    Res.; Inner London Parks (Regent's Park, Round Pond, St. James's
    Park, *Serpentine and Long Water); *Kempton Res., Hanworth;
    *King George VI Res., Staines; *Lea valley reservoirs, half in Essex,
    q.v.; Osterley Park; *Queen Mary Res., Littleton; Ruislip; Staines
    Res.; Stoke Newington Res. N.B. Brent and Ruislip are canal reservoirs,
    needing no permit; the rest belong to the Metropolitan Water Board,
    and all except Staines (which is crossed by a public causeway) require a
    permit.
ESTUARIES: *Thames, esp. at Hammersmith, Chiswick, Strand-on-
    Green and Syon Marsh.

Special Birds
Black redstart: breeds on bombed sites in City, now being rapidly built
    up; esp. near Cripplegate Church.
Heronry: Kempton Park.
Goldeneye: regular at Staines Res.

Goosander: regular at Staines Res.
Smew: regular at Brent Res.
Ruff: winters regularly at Perry Oaks sewage farm.
Little ringed plover: breeds at several gravel pits.
Golden plover: regular winter flock on London Airport.
Black-headed gullery: Perry Oaks sewage farm.
Gull roosts: King George V Res., Queen Mary Res., Staines Res.

Reserves and Sanctuaries
Inner London Parks (Ministry of Works).
Perivale Wood (Selborne Society; P).
Ruislip Res. (Ruislip-Northwood U.D.C.; P).

Societies, etc.
London Natural History Society, Ornithological Section.

Literature
Annual bird report in *London Bird Report* (London N.H.S.).
Biennial reports from Committee on Bird Sanctuaries in Royal Parks
  (England).
A History of the Birds of Middlesex, by W. E. Glegg (1935).
The Birds of the London Area since 1900, by the London N.H.S. (1957).
London's Birds, by R. S. R. Fitter (1949).
The Birds of Inner London, 1900-1950, by S. Cramp and W. G. Teagle
  (1952). *British Birds*, 45: 433-56.
W. H. Hudson's *Birds in London* (1898) was reprinted in 1969.

NORFOLK

Habitats
WOODLAND: Blickling Woods; Blo Norton Wood, near Diss; Bulfer
  Grove, near Fakenham; Felbrigg Great Wood; Northrepps Hall
  Woods; Thursford woodlands; Westwick Woods.
HEATHLAND: Breckland, esp. *East Wretham and Weeting Heaths;
  Dersingham Heath; Roydon Common, near King's Lynn; Kelling and
  Salthouse Heaths (nightjar).
MARSHES: Broads, esp. around Barton, *Hickling and Sutton Broads
  and *Horsey Mere; Roydon and South Lopham Fens, near Diss;
  Welney Washes.
SEWAGE FARMS: Cantley, Wisbech.
GRAVEL PITS: Costessy, Snettisham, Welney.
LAKES, RESERVOIRS: Breckland, esp. Fowlmere, Langmere, Ringmere,
  Thompson Water; Broads, esp. Barton, Filby, Heigham Sound,
  *Hickling, Horsey Mere, Ormesby, *Ranworth, Rollesby, Sutton,
  Wroxham; Bayfield, Blickling, Broad Fen, Gunton, Holkham, Scoulton
  Mere.
ESTUARIES: *The Wash, Brancaster Harbour, Wells Harbour, *Blakeney
  Harbour, *Breydon Water.

COASTAL MARSHES: all along north coast from Holme to Salthouse, but esp. *Cley and Salthouse.

DUNES: *Scolt Head Island, *Blakeney Point, Winterton, Yarmouth Denes.

OFFSHORE SANDBANKS: *Scroby Sands, off Great Yarmouth.

MIGRATION WATCH POINTS: Hunstanton, Scolt Head Is.; *Blakeney Point, Walsey Hills and *East Bank (between Cley and Salthouse).

Special Birds

Crossbill: breeds in Breckland.

Snow bunting: regular in winter on north and east coasts.

Lapland bunting: fairly regular in winter on north coast.

Shore lark: regular in winter between Scolt Head and Salthouse.

Bearded tit: breeds in Broads area and on Cley Marshes.

Spoonbill: fairly regular on migration at Breydon Water and Cley.

Heronries: Buckingham Carrs, Denver Sluice, Earsham, Holkham Park, Islington, Kimberley Park, Mautby Hall, Melton Constable, Snettisham, Wickhampton.

Bittern: breeds Broads and Cley Marshes.

Greylag goose: feral flocks from Woodbastwick and Rackheath visit Breydon Water, Broads and north coast.

Canada goose: breeds in Broads, Breckland and Holkham Park.

Brent goose: Blakeney Harbour, Scolt Head Is., the Wash.

Egyptian goose: feral breeding colony in Holkham Park, often seen on nearby marshes.

Shelduck: breeds inland, Wisbech sewage farm.

Gadwall: breeds (originally introduced) in Breckland; has recently spread to the Broads and Cley Marshes.

Garganey: breeds regularly, the Broads and Cley Marshes.

Eider: winter flocks at Heacham and Hunstanton; summering increasingly along north coast.

Fulmar: breeds on cliffs near Sheringham.

Collared dove: original British breeding colony still exists near Cromer.

Stone curlew: breeds fairly commonly in Breckland.

Ringed plover: breeds sparsely inland in Breckland.

Knot: up to 50,000 winter in the Wash; a flock of *c.* 30,000 feeds off Snettisham and roosts at Thornham.

Purple sandpiper: regular on South Hunstanton mussel beds in winter and on front at high tide.

Terneries: Blakeney Point, Scolt Head Island, Scroby Sands.

Gull roosts: Breydon Water, Blakeney Harbour, Hickling Broad, Thompson Water, Wroxham Broad, the Wash.

Black-headed gulleries: 14, mainly on N. coast, but large ones inland at Cantley and Wissington sugar beet factories and Alderfen Broad.

Golden pheasant: frequent in Breckland.

Red-legged partridge: common.

Reserves and Sanctuaries
Breckland
East Wretham Heath (Norfolk Naturalists' Trust; NP).
Weeting Heath (N.N.T. and Nature Conservancy; P).

Broads
Alderfen Broad (N.N.T.; P).
Barton Broad and Barton Turf Marshes (N.N.T.).
Bure Marshes (Ranworth, Cockshoot and Decoy Broads) (Nature
    Conservancy and N.N.T.; P).
Hickling Broad (Nature Conservancy and N.N.T.; P).
Horsey Mere (National Trust; PF).
Martham Marshes (N.N.T.).
Surlingham Broad and Bargate Fen (N.N.T.).

Coast
Blakeney Point (National Trust; NP).
Cley and Arnold's Marshes (N.N.T. and National Trust; PF).
Scolt Head Island (Nature Conservancy, N.N.T. and National Trust;
    NP).
Winterton Dunes (Nature Conservancy; PF).

Elsewhere
Blickling Woods (National Trust).
Blo Norton Wood (N.N.T.).
Bulfer Grove (N.N.T.).
Thursford woodlands (N.N.T.).

Societies, etc.
Norfolk Naturalists' Trust
Norfolk and Norwich Naturalists' Society
Norfolk Wildlife Park (Ornamental Pheasant Trust), Great Witchingham
    (collection of pheasants, waterfowl, etc.).

Literature
The Norfolk Bird and Mammal Report published annually by Norfolk and
    Norwich Nat. Soc.; and notes on the Wash and Fen areas in *Cambridge
    Bird Report*.
A History of the Birds of Norfolk, by B. B. Riviere (1930).
A Check List of the Birds of Cley, by R. A. Richardson (1961).
In Breckland Wilds, by W. G. Clarke (1925).
Broadland Birds, by E. L. Turner (1924).
Bird Watching on Scolt Head, by Miss E. L. Turner (1928).
See also chapter on birds by E. Duffey in *Scolt Head Island* by J. A.
    Steers (1960), and annual report of C.B.O.

NORTHAMPTONSHIRE

Habitats

WOODLAND: Badby Wood, Bedford Purlieus, Bucknell Wood, Castor Hanglands, Harlestone Firs, Salcey Forest, Whittlewood Forest, Yardley Chase.

HEATHLAND: Ailsworth Heath, Harlestone Heath.

MARSHES: Titchmarsh Water Meadows.

SEWAGE FARMS: *Northampton (Ecton).

GRAVEL PITS: Billing, Clifford Hill, Ditchford, Earls Barton, Oundle, Thrapston.

LAKES, RESERVOIRS: Blatherwycke, *Cransley Res., Deene, Daventry Res., *Hollowell Res., Naseby Res., *Pitsford Res., *Raventhorpe Res., Sywell Res., Stanford Res., *Thorpe Malsor Res., Westhorpe Res.

Special Birds

Heronries: Aldwincle, Althorp Park, Milton Park.

Canada goose: breeds on Abington, Blatherwycke, Burghley and Deene lakes.

Gull roost: Hollowell Res., Pitsford Res.

Reserves and Sanctuaries

Borough Fen Decoy (Wildfowl Trust).

Castor Hanglands (Nature Conservancy; P, except for Ailsworth Heath).

Eastcote Sanctuary (private).

Societies, etc.

Kettering and District Naturalists' Society and Field Club, Orn. Sect.

Northamptonshire Natural History Society and Field Club, Orn. Sect.

Peakirk Wildfowl Grounds, near Peterborough (Wildfowl Trust).

Literature

Annual bird report in *Journal* of the Northants N.H.S.

Latest bird list for whole county in *Victoria County History of Northamptonshire* (1902); see also *The First Fifty Years,* by Kettering and District Naturalists' Society (1956).

NORTHUMBERLAND

Habitats

WOODLAND: Allen Banks, Haydon Bridge; the Border National Forest Park; Dipton Woods, Hexhamshire; Hulne Park, Alnwick.

PARKLAND: Chillingham Park.

MOORLAND: Cheviots, Northumberland National Park, Tosson Hill.

MARSHES: Holborn Moss, Coom Rigg Moss.

LAKES, RESERVOIRS: Bolam, *Capheaton, Catcleugh Res., *Coltcrag

Res., *Fontburn Res., *Gosforth Park, *Hallington Res., Holywell Ponds (Seaton Delaval), Killingworth Pond, Northumberland loughs (Broomlee, Crag, Greenlee, Grindon, Halleypike), Rothbury lakes, Seaton Burn ponds, Whittle Dene Res.

ESTUARIES: Tweed, *Goswick Sands to Fenham Flats, *Budle Bay, Alnmouth Bay.

DUNES: *Holy Island, Ross Links.

CLIFF SEA-BIRD COLONIES: *Farne Islands, Dunstanburgh, Cullernose Point.

MIGRATION WATCH POINTS: Bamburgh, Farne Islands, Holy Island, St. Mary's Island, Seaton Sluice.

Special Birds

Pied flycatcher: breeds in wooded dales.

Heronries: Chillingham Park; Lee Hall, Bellingham.

Eider: breeds Holy Is., Farne Is., Coquet Is.; winters also at Seaton Sluice.

Purple sandpiper: winters regularly on coast south to St. Mary's Island.

Gull roost: Goswick Sands.

Kittiwake: breeds on a warehouse at North Shields as well as on the Farnes and at Dunstanburgh.

Reserves and Sanctuaries

Chillingham Park (Tankerville estate).

Coom Rigg Moss (Nature Conservancy; P).

Farne Islands (National Trust).

Gosforth Park Bird Sanctuary (Northumberland and Durham N.H.S.).

Societies, etc. Farne Islands Study Centre.

Monks' House Bird Observatory (closed in 1960, but reopened on private and part-time basis in 1961).

Natural History Society of Northumberland, Durham and Newcastle upon Tyne.

Northumberland and Durham Naturalists' Trust.

Tyneside Bird Club.

World Bird Research Station, Glanton.

Literature

Annual bird report published by Northumberland and Durham N.H.S.

The Birds of Northumberland, by G. Bolam (1932).

The Farne Islands, by Grace Watt (1951).

A Naturalist on Lindisfarne, by Richard Perry (1946).

The House on the Shore, by E. A. R. Ennion (1959).

Abel Chapman's books, *Bird Life of the Borders* (1889) and *The Borders and Beyond* (1924) are also both still well worth reading.

NOTTINGHAMSHIRE

Habitats
WOODLAND: Sherwood Forest (Dukeries) (woodcock).
PARKLAND: Dukeries (Clumber, Rufford, Thoresby and Welbeck Parks).
MARSHES: Oxton Bogs, Wilford Lane Marsh.
SEWAGE FARMS: Nottingham.
GRAVEL PITS: Attenborough, Besthorpe, Blaxton, Finningley, Gun-
thorpe, Holme Pierrepont, Hoveringham, Netherfield, Retford.
LAKES, RESERVOIRS: Annesley, Babworth, Clumber Park, Mansfield
Res., Moor Green, Newstead Abbey, Rufford Park, Salterford Dam,
*Thoresby Park, *Welbeck Park, Wollaton.

Special Birds
Willow tit: locally fairly common.
Heronries: Osberton, Rolleston.
Canada goose: breeds in Dukeries and at Kingston-upon-Soar.
Shelduck: breeds in small numbers in Trent valley.
Collared dove: breeds in Newark.
Common tern: small numbers breed in Trent valley.
Gull roosts: Netherfield gravel pit, Nottingham sewage farm.
Black-headed gulleries: nine, mostly small, except at Blaxton and Fin-
ningley gravel pits, Nottingham sewage farm and Besthorpe gravel
pit.

Societies, etc.
Collingham and District Bird Watching Group.
Trent Valley Bird Watchers.

Literature
Annual bird report published by Trent Valley Bird Watchers.
The Birds of Nottinghamshire, by Trent Valley Bird Watchers (1961).

OXFORDSHIRE

Habitats
WOODLAND: Waterperry Wood, *Wychwood Forest (redstart, wood-
cock).
PARKLAND, SCRUB: Blenheim Park, Beacon Hill, Watlington Hill.
DOWNLAND: Chiltern escarpment from Beacon Hill to Swyncombe
Down.
MARSHES: Cherwell valley, Somerton area; Otmoor; Port Meadow,
Oxford; Windrush valley floor, Burford to Witney (whinchat).
GRAVEL PITS: Cassington, Dorchester, Sonning Eye, Standlake, Stanton
Harcourt.

LAKES, RESERVOIRS: *Blenheim Park, Clattercote Res.

Special Birds
Cirl bunting: along Icknield Way, esp. north of A.40.
House martin: largest colony in Britain on Clifton Hampden Bridge over R. Thames.
Heronry: Nuneham Courtenay.
Stone curlew: still along Chiltern escarpment.
Gull roost: Port Meadow.
Quail: frequent at foot of Chiltern escarpment south of Watlington, esp. near Ewelme.

Reserves and Sanctuaries
Aston Rowant (Nature Conservancy; PF).
Beacon Hill Forest Nature Reserve (Forestry Commission and Nature Conservancy; P).
Waterperry Forest Nature Reserve (ditto).
Watlington Hill (National Trust).
Wychwood Forest (Nature Conservancy; P).

Societies, etc.
Banbury Ornithological Society (runs Wykham Park Observatory).
Berkshire, Buckinghamshire and Oxfordshire Naturalists' Trust.
Edward Grey Institute for Field Ornithology, Department of Zoological Field Studies, Oxford University.
Oxford Ornithological Society.
Reading Ornithological Club.

Literature
Annual bird report published by Oxford Ornithological Society.
The Birds of Oxfordshire, by W. B. Alexander (1947).
The Birds of Blenheim Park, by Margaret M. Pickles (1960).

RUTLAND (*see* Leicestershire)

SHROPSHIRE

Habitats
WOODLAND: Wenlock Edge, Wyre Forest.
HEATHLAND: Whixall Moss.
MOORLAND: Brown Clee Hill, Clee Hill, Longmynd, Stiperstones.
SEWAGE FARMS: Shrewsbury.
LAKES, RESERVOIRS: Berrington Pool, Bomere Pool, *Ellesmere meres (Blake, Cole, Crose, Newton, White), Hawk Lake, Baschurch meres, Sambrook Pool (Hinstock), Shavington, Sundorne Pool, Trench Pool (Hadley), Venus Pool, Walcot Park.

Special Birds

Raven: frequent in hills.

Pied flycatcher: breeds locally in woodlands.

House martin: colony of about 140 nests on Atcham Bridge, near Shrewsbury.

Common buzzard: frequent in hills.

Heronries: Attingham Park, Halston.

Canada goose: breeds on Ellesmere meres and in most parks.

Cormorant: roost on White Mere.

Gull roosts: Ellesmere.

Black-headed gulleries: three small.

Red grouse: Longmynd, Stiperstones.

Societies, etc.

Preston Montford Field Centre (Field Studies Council).

Shropshire Ornithological Society.

Shropshire Trust for Nature Conservation.

Literature

Annual bird report published by Shropshire Ornithological Society.

No county bird list since *The Fauna of Shropshire*, by H. E. Forrest (1899).

SOMERSET

Habitats

WOODLAND: Leigh Woods, Avon Gorge: Rodney Stoke Wood; Holford and Shervage Woods, Quantocks; Horner and Cloutsham Woods, Exmoor.

HEATHLAND: Brean Down, Shapwick Heath.

MOORLAND: Brendon Hills; *Exmoor, esp. Dunkery Beacon, Selworthy Beacon, Winsford Hill; Mendip Hills; Quantock Hills.

SEWAGE FARMS: Saltford.

GRAVEL PITS: Minehead clay pits.

LAKES, RESERVOIRS: *Barrow Gurney Res., *Blagdon Res., Chard Res., *Cheddar Res., *Chew Valley Lake, *Durleigh Res., *Sutton Bingham Res.

ESTUARIES: Bridgwater Bay, *Parrett, Sand Bay.

COASTAL MARSHES: *Porlock, Minehead, *Steart.

DUNES: Berrow.

CLIFF SEA-BIRD COLONIES: Steep Holm (gulls and cormorants).

Special Birds

Cirl bunting: breeds fairly widely in lowland areas.

Willow tit: Shapwick Heath.

Pied flycatcher: a few pairs breed on Exmoor.

Marsh warbler: Central peat moors.

Ring ouzel: a few pairs breed on Exmoor.

Heronries: Brockley Park, Halswell Wood, Midelney Manor, Otterhampton, Pixton Park, Somerton Wood, Swell Wood, Uphill.
Merlin: breeds here and there on Exmoor.
Common buzzard: breeds on Mendip as well as farther west.
White-fronted goose: marshes around Parrett mouth.
Shelduck: late summer moulting ground in Bridgwater Bay.
Gadwall: breeds, Chew Valley Lake.
Gull roosts: Avon estuary, Steep Holm.
Water rail: regular in Sand Bay in winter.
Black grouse: a few pairs breed on Exmoor.
Red grouse: a few pairs breed on Exmoor.

Reserves and Sanctuaries
Bridgwater Bay (Nature Conservancy; P required for Steart Island).
Rodney Stoke (Nature Conservancy; PF).
Shapwick Heath (Nature Conservancy; P).
Steep Holm (Steep Holm Trust).

Societies, etc.
Bristol Naturalists' Society, Ornithological Section.
Mid-Somerset Naturalists' Society.
Somersetshire Archæological and Natural History Society, Orn. Sect.
Steep Holm Gull Ringing Station.

Literature
Annual bird reports published for whole county by Somerset N.H.S., and for north of county by Bristol N.S.
No county list since Rev. M. A. Mathew (1893), but see H. H. Davis's (1947) Bristol list under Gloucestershire.
The Breeding Birds of Somerset and their Eggs, by Stanley Lewis (1955).
The writings of the late E. W. Hendy deal with the Exmoor end of Somerset, viz. *The Lure of Bird-Watching* (1928), *Wild Exmoor through the Year* (1930) and *Somerset Birds and some other folk* (1943). See also *Bird Haunts in Southern England,* by G. K. Yeates (1947), for Exmoor and Sedgemoor. A new county check-list is being prepared by Miss E. M. Palmer and Mr. D. K. Ballance.

STAFFORDSHIRE

Habitats
WOODLAND: Bagot's Wood (nightjar); Forest Banks (woodcock) Hawksmoor Wood, near Cheadle; Hopwas Wood, near Tamworth; Hurt's Wood, Dovedale.
HEATHLAND: Enville Heath (nightjar).
MOORLAND: Cannock Chase, the Roaches.
SEWAGE FARMS: Whittington.
LAKES, RESERVOIRS: *Aqualate Mere, *Belvide Res., *Blithfield Res., Branston, Cannock Chase Res., Chillington, *Gailey Pool, Maer, Rudyard Res., Tong, Trentham Park.

Special Birds
Dipper: R. Dove and many other N. Staffs. streams.
Heronries: Aqualate Mere, Bagot's Wood.
Canada goose: breeds Branston and Gailey Res.
Gull roost: Belvide Res., Blithfield Res.
Black grouse: Warslow and R. Dane areas.

Reserves and Sanctuaries
Hawksmoor Wood (National Trust).
Wren's Nest (Nature Conservancy and Dudley Corporation; NP).

Societies, etc.
West Midland Bird Club.
West Midland Trust for Nature Conservation.

Literature
The West Midland Bird Report, annually from W. Mid. B.C.
The Birds of Staffordshire, by J. Lord and A. R. M. Blake (1962).

SUFFOLK

Habitats
WOODLAND: Staverton Forest and Butley Thicks.
HEATHLAND: Breckland, esp. Horn, Weather and Thetford Heaths; Coastal, esp. Thorpeness North Warren and *Westleton Heath.
GRAVEL PITS: Benacre Ness.
LAKES, RESERVOIRS: Benacre Broad, Easton Broad, Fritton Decoy, Livermere, Oulton Broad.
ESTUARIES: *Breydon Water, Lake Lothing, Blyth, *Alde/Ore, Butley River, *Deben (Sluice House to Great Point, and Kirton to Falkenham), Orwell, Stour.
COASTAL MARSHES: Benacre Broad, Southwold to Dunwich (Reydon, Corporation, Westwood, Dingle), *Minsmere Level, *Havergate Island.
SHINGLE: Benacre Ness, Orfordness.
MIGRATION WATCH POINTS: Lowestoft, Walberswick.

Special Birds
Hawfinch: at least as common as in any other county.
Crossbill: breeds in Breckland.
Bearded tit: breeds coastal marshes, esp. Minsmere.
Long-eared owl: Herringfleet area.
Short-eared owl: coast, breeds Havergate Island.
Marsh and Montagu's harriers: coastal marshes, esp. Minsmere.
Spoonbill: fairly regular on migration, Breydon Water.
Heronries: Henham, Livermere, Methersgate Hall, North Cove, Snape.
Bittern: breeds coastal marshes, esp. Minsmere.

Canada goose: breeds Breckland.
Shelduck: breeds inland, Butley Thicks.
Gadwall: breeds coastal marshes.
Stone curlew: breeds Breckland and coastal heaths.
Ringed plover: breeds inland, Breckland heaths.
Avocet: Havergate Island and Minsmere are the only breeding places in British Isles.
Sandwich tern: Havergate Island; North Weir Point, Orfordness.
Gull roost: R. Orwell, Breydon Water.
Black-headed gull: large gullery on Havergate Island; three smaller ones, two on coast, one at Bury St. Edmunds.
Kittiwake: nests on South Pier Pavilion, Lowestoft.
Golden pheasant: frequent in Breckland.
Red-legged partridge: common.

Reserves and Sanctuaries
Cavenham Heath (Breckland) (Nature Conservancy; P for part only).
Havergate Island (Royal Society for the Protection of Birds; P).
Horn and Weather Heaths (Royal Society for the Protection of Birds; P).
Minsmere (RSPB; P).
North Warren, Thorpeness (RSPB; NP).
Orfordness-Havergate (RSPB and Nature Conservancy; P for part only).
Thetford Heath (Norfolk Naturalists' Trust and Nature Conservancy; P).
Westleton Heath (Nature Conservancy; PF).

Societies, etc.
Dingle Bird Club.
Flatford Mill Field Centre, East Bergholt (Field Studies Council).
Suffolk Naturalists' Society, Ornithological Section.
Suffolk Naturalists' Trust.
Walberswick Ringing Station (Dingle Bird Club).

Literature
Annual bird report in *Transactions* of Suffolk Nat. Soc.
The Birds of Suffolk, by C. B. Ticehurst (1932).
RSPB pamphlets on Minsmere and Havergate.
In Breckland Wilds, by W. G. Clarke (1925).

SURREY

Habitats
WOODLAND: Barfolds Copse, Haslemere; *Bookham Common; Box Hill and Mickleham Downs; Holmwood Common; Hurt Wood and Leith Hill area; Limpsfield Common; Lower Wood, Claygate; Ranmore Common; Reigate Hill; Selsdon Wood; Wisley and Ockham Commons.
HEATHLAND, SCRUB: *Ashtead and Epsom Commons (grasshopper warbler; red-backed shrike); Banstead, Walton and Headley Heaths;

*Bookham and Effingham Commons; Chobham Common; Esher Common and Oxshott Heath (grasshopper warbler, nightjar); *Frensham, Tilford and Hankley Commons; Hindhead Common; Richmond Park (woodlark, redstart); *Thursley, Ockley and Witley Commons.

SEWAGE FARMS: Beddington, Epsom, Esher, Guildford, Hersham, Molesey, Old Woking.

GRAVEL PITS: Ash Vale, Ham, Walton on Thames.

LAKES, RESERVOIRS: Badshot Lea Pond; *Barn Elms Res., Barnes; Boldermere (Hut Pond), Wisley; *Chelsea and Lambeth Res., Molesey; Enton Ponds, Witley; Fetcham Mill Pond; Frensham Great and Little Ponds; Gatton Park; *Island Barn Res., Molesey; Kew Gardens; Obelisk Pond, Windsor Great Park; Pen Ponds, Richmond Park; Silvermere; Vachery Pond, Cranleigh; Virginia Water; Walton Res.

ESTUARIES: Thames towpath, Putney to Kew Gardens.

Special Birds

Hawfinch: frequent, e.g. Oxshott.
Willow tit: breeds Selsdon Wood.
Dartford warbler: West Surrey heaths.
Stonechat: breeds on West Surrey heaths.
Nightingale: frequent on commons, e.g. Bookham, Effingham.
Heronries: Gatton Park, Richmond Park, Virginia Water.
Canada goose: breeds on several waters around Redhill and Reigate.
Gadwall: regular at Barn Elms Res., and Richmond Park.
Gull roosts: Barn Elms Res., Chelsea and Lambeth Res., Island Barn Res.

Reserves and Sanctuaries

Barfolds Copse, Haslemere (Royal Society for the Protection of Birds; P).
Bookham Common (National Trust).
Box Hill (National Trust).
Lower Wood, Claygate (London N.H.S.; P).
Richmond Park (Ministry of Works).
Selsdon Wood (National Trust).
The Wood, Surbiton (Surbiton Corporation).

Societies, etc.

Beddington Ringing Station (London N.H.S.).
Juniper Hall Field Centre, Mickleham (Field Studies Council).
London Natural History Society, Ornithological Section.
Surbiton and District Bird Watching Society.
Surrey Bird Club.
Surrey Naturalists' Trust.

Literature

Surrey Bird Report published annually by Surrey Bird Club.
London Bird Report (London N.H.S.) covers area within 20 miles of London.

Biennial reports from Committee on Bird Sanctuaries in Royal Parks (England) cover Richmond Park.

No book on birds of whole county since *The Birds of Surrey* by J. A. Bucknill (1900).

The Birds of the London Area since 1900, by the London N.H.S. (1957) covers the area within 20 miles of London.

London's Birds, by R. S. R. Fitter (1949) covers the Surrey part of the County of London.

A History of Richmond Park, by C. L. Collenette (1937).

RSPB pamphlet by Howard Bentham (1954).

SUSSEX

Habitats

WOODLAND: Bowling Alley Wood; Hampden Park, Eastbourne; Kingley Vale; Og's Wood, Polegate; St. Leonards and Tilgate Forests (woodcock).

HEATHLAND: *Ashdown Forest, Crowborough Common (nightjar), Lullington Heath, Wiggonholt Common.

DOWNLAND: Beachy Head to Seaford Head, Mount Caburn, Cissbury Ring.

MARSHES: *Amberley Wild Brooks; Glynde Level; Rother valley, Bodiam to Northiam.

GRAVEL, ETC., PITS: Chichester; *Midrips and Wicks, Broomfield; Nook Beach, Rye Harbour.

LAKES, RESERVOIRS: Burton Park, *Darwell Res., Pett Level Pools, Piddinghoe Pond, Powder Mill Res., Thorney Deep, *Weir Wood Res.

ESTUARIES: *Chichester Harbour, *Pagham Harbour, Adur, Cuckmere Haven, *Rother (Rye Harbour).

COASTAL MARSHES: Thorney, Sidlesham Ferry, *Pett Level, Pevensey Levels.

SHINGLE: The Crumbles, Eastbourne; *Nook Beach, Rye Harbour; *Midrips and Wicks, Dungeness.

MIGRATION WATCH POINTS: Langney Point, Selsey Bill.

Special Birds

Heronries: Eridge Park, Fishbourne, Glynde Place, Leasam Wood, Parham Park.

Canada goose: breeds Petworth Park.

Common scoter: usually in some numbers in sea off Midrips and Rye Harbour in winter.

Velvet scoter: often some with the common scoters.

Black-tailed godwit: winters in Chichester Harbour in some numbers.

Black-headed gullery: Rye Harbour.

Herring gull: four roof-nesting colonies in Hastings.

Reserves and Sanctuaries

Beachy Head (Eastbourne Corporation).

Black Down (National Trust).
Bowling Alley Wood (Royal Society for the Protection of Birds; P).
Cissbury Ring (National Trust).
Cuckmere Valley (Eastbourne College).
Kingley Vale (Nature Conservancy; NP, danger from unexploded bombs).
Lullington Heath (Nature Conservancy; PF).
Og's Wood, Polegate (Eastbourne College).
The Mere, Hampden Park (Eastbourne College).
Shoreham-by-Sea Waterworks Copse and Ringing Station (S.O.S.).

Societies, etc.
Hastings Natural History Society.
Selsey Bill Bird Observatory.
Shoreham Ornithological Society.
Sussex Naturalists' Trust.
Sussex Ornithological Society.
Worthing N.H.S., Orn. Sect.

Literature
Sussex Bird Report now issued annually by Sussex Orn. Soc.; see also
Hastings and East Sussex Naturalist (Hastings N.H.S.).
A History of Sussex Birds, 3 vols., by J. A. Walpole-Bond (1938).
Birds of Eastbourne, by E. C. Arnold (1936).
A Guide to the Birds of Sussex, by G. des Forges and D. D. Harber (1963).

WARWICKSHIRE

Habitats
WOODLAND: Broadmoor Wood; Tile Hill Wood, Coventry; Waverley Wood.
PARKLAND: Edgbaston Park, Ragley Park, Sutton Park.
MARSHES: Alvecote Pools, Coleshill Pool.
SEWAGE FARMS: Boggington, Coleshill, Polesworth.
GRAVEL PITS: Bransdon, Packington.
LAKES, RESERVOIRS: *Alvecote Pools, Bartley Res., Brandon, Chesterton Pool, Claydon Res., Earlswood Lakes, Edgbaston Park, Napton Res., Seeswood Pool, *Shustoke Res., Sutton Park, *Warwick Park, Wormleighton Res.

Special Birds
Heronries: Combe Abbey, Temple Grafton, Warwick Park, Wootton Pool.
Canada goose: Packington Park.

Reserves and Sanctuaries
Alvecote Pools (West Midland Trust; P).
Broadmoor Wood (Birmingham Natural History Society).

Edgbaston Park (Birmingham N.H.S.).
Tile Hill Wood (Coventry Corporation).

Societies, etc.
West Midland Bird Club.
Coventry and District N.H. and Sci. Society, Orn. Sect.
Nuneaton Bird Watchers' Club.
Warwick Natural History Society.
West Midland Trust for Nature Conservation.

Literature
West Midland Bird Report, annually from W. Mid. B.C.; also notes in
  Annual Reports of Warwick N.H.S.
Notes on the Birds of Warwickshire, by C. A. Norris (1948).
The Coventry District: a naturalist's guide, by H. M. Dix and D. R.
  Hughes (1960).

WESTMORLAND

Habitats
WOODLAND: Naddle Low Forest.
HEATHLAND: Meathop Moss.
MOORLAND: Pennines, esp. Cross Fell, Moor House.
LAKES: Brackenber, Elterwater, Grasmere, *Haweswater, Rundale,
  Rydal Water, Seamore, Sunbiggin Tarn, Ullswater, Windermere.
ESTUARIES: Kent.

Special Birds
Pied flycatcher: breeds generally.
Short-eared owl: breeds in the Pennines.
Heronries: Dallam Tower, Smardale Mill.
Whooper swan: winters on Windermere, Elterwater, Rydal and other
  waters.
Gull roosts: Ullswater, Windermere, Kent estuary.
Black-headed gulleries: ten, mostly small, except at Sunbiggin Tarn,
  Halefield and Greenside Tarn.

Reserves and Sanctuaries
Meathop and Catcrag Mosses (Society for the Promotion of Nature
  Reserves).
Moor House (Nature Conservancy; PF).

Societies, etc.
Ambleside Field Society.
Eden Field Club.
Kendal Natural History Society.
Lake District Naturalists' Trust.

Literature
As for Cumberland (p. 176).
Birds of Westmorland and the Northern Pennines, by J. O. Wilson (1933).

WILTSHIRE

Habitats
WOODLAND: Great Ridge Wood, Grovely Wood, *Savernake Forest, Stourhead Park.
DOWNLAND: Marlborough Downs, Salisbury Plain.
SEWAGE FARMS: Rodbourne, Salisbury.
LAKES, RESERVOIRS: Bowood, Braydon Pond, Clarendon Park, Coate Water, Fonthill, Longleat, Petersfinger Pits, Ramsbury Manor, Shear Water, Stourhead, Tockenham Res., Westbury Pond, Wilton Water.

Special Birds
Dipper: breeds in south and west Wiltshire.
Common buzzard: well distributed over whole county.
Heronries: Bowood Park, Great Bradford Wood, Hurdcott Park.
Stone curlew: frequent on Salisbury Plain.
Quail: breeds most years, Salisbury Plain.

Reserves and Sanctuaries
Fyfield Down (Nature Conservancy; PF).

Societies, etc.
Salisbury N. H. S.
Wiltshire Archæological and Natural History Society.
Wiltshire Trust for Nature Conservation.

Literature
Annual bird report in *Magazine* of county Society.
Wiltshire Birds, by L. G. Peirson (1959).
Bird Haunts in Southern England, by G. K. Yeates (1947) covers Salisbury Plain.

WORCESTERSHIRE

Habitats
WOODLAND: Grovely Dingle; Randan Woods, near Bromsgrove; Wyre Forest (woodcock).
HEATHLAND: Abberley Hill, Bredon Hill, Castlemorton Common, Clent Hills, Hartlebury Common, Kempsey Common, Malvern Hills.
LAKES, RESERVOIRS: Bartley Res., Bittell Res., Cofton, Croome Park, Hewell Park, Pirton, Spetchley, Westwood Park.

Special Birds
Cirl bunting: breeds Malvern Hills.
Marsh warbler: breeds in Avon and Teme valleys.
Dipper: breeds on R. Teme and other western streams.
Heronries: Croome Park, Westwood Park.
Gull roost: Bittell Res.
Corncrake: still breeds locally in extreme south of county.

Reserves and Sanctuaries
Grovely Dingle (National Trust; PF).
Wren's Nest (Nature Conservancy and Dudley Corporation; NP).

Societies, etc.
West Midland Bird Club.
West Midland Trust for Nature Conservation.

Literature
West Midland Bird Report published annually by W. Mid. B.C.
The Birds of Worcestershire, by A. J. Harthan (1961).
Handbook of Birds of the Malvern District, by J. G. Harrison (1941).

YORKSHIRE

Habitats
WOODLAND: Askham Bog; Colt Park, Ribblehead; Crimsworth Dean and High Greenwood Wood, near Hebden Bridge; Grass Wood, Grassington (woodcock); Moorlands, near York.
HEATHLAND: Hatfield Moors, Skipwith Common.
MOORLAND: Cronkley Fell, Marsden Moor, Stainmoor.
SEWAGE FARMS: Ben Rhydding, Ilkley, Knaresborough.
GRAVEL PITS: Blaxton.
LAKES, RESERVOIRS: Ardsley Res., Barden Moor Res., Blackmoorfoot Res. (Huddersfield), Bretton Park, Bubworth Ings, Castle Howard, Chelker, *Eccup Res., *Fairburn Ings, Farnley, Fewston Res., Glasshouses Dam, *Gouthwaite Res., Harewood Park, Hornby, *Hornsea Mere, Ilton Res., *Langsett Res., *Leighton Res., *Lindley Res., *Lockwood Beck Res., Malham Tarn, Marsh Ghyll, Nostell Dam, Ripley, Roundhill Res., Sawley, Scaling Dam, *Stocks-in-Bowland Res., Studley Park, *Swillington Ings, *Swinsty Res., Swinton Park, Wentworth Woodhouse, White Holme, Whitemoor Res., Wintersett Res.
ESTUARIES: *Tees, *Humber (Broomfleet, Whitton).
SHINGLE: Spurn Head.
CLIFF SEA-BIRD COLONIES: *Bempton Cliffs, Flamborough Head.
MIGRATION WATCH POINTS: Redcar and Teesmouth, Hornsea Mere, *Spurn Head.

Special Birds

Pied flycatcher: breeds in the western dales and in two areas, east (North York Moors) and west (Pennines) of the Vale of Mowbray.

Swallow and Sand martin: huge autumn roost at Fairburn Ings, estimated to hold 250,000 birds.

Heronries: Gargrave, Harewood Park, Healaugh, Hornsea Mere, Moreby Park, Scampton Park.

Pink-footed goose: large numbers feed on the East Yorkshire wolds and roost in the Humber Wildfowl Refuge, Read's Island.

Canada goose: breeds at many waters; winter flocks at Gouthwaite Res., and Nostell Dam.

Gannet: a few pairs breed at Bempton.

Gull roosts: Ardsley Res., Barden Moor Res., Eccup Res., Hornsea Mere, Stocks Res., Wintersett Res.

Black-headed gulleries: over two dozen, mainly in the Pennines, the largest at Woo Gill Tarns near Pateley Bridge and Summer Lodge Tarn near Gunnerside.

Reserves and Sanctuaries

Askham Bog (Yorkshire Naturalists' Trust; P).

Colt Park (Nature Conservancy; P).

Fairburn Ings (West Riding County Council; P).

Grass Wood (Y.N.T.).

Humber Wildfowl Refuge (Nature Conservancy; P).

Moorlands (Y.N.T.).

Spurn Promontory (Y.N.T.).

Societies, etc.

Doncaster and District Ornithological Society.

Hutton Buscel Field Centre (British Junior Naturalists' Association).

Knaresborough Ringing Station.

Leeds and District Bird Watchers' Club.

Malham Tarn Field Centre (Field Studies Council).

Spurn Head Bird Observatory.

Yorkshire Naturalists' Trust.

Yorkshire Naturalists' Union, Ornithology Section.

Literature

Annual bird reports from the Y.N.U. in *The Naturalist*.

Yorkshire Birds, by R. Chislett (1952).

Birds of the Spurn Peninsula, Vol. I, by R. Chislett and G. H. Ainsworth (1958).

" The status of wild birds in Leeds," by A. H. B. Lee in *The Naturalist*, No. 867; 1958.

Wales

ANGLESEY

Habitats
WOODLAND: The Dingle, Llangefni; Penrhos Wood.
MARSHES: Malldraeth (grasshopper warbler).
LAKES: Beaumaris, Coron, Dinam, Llygerian, Llywenan, Maelog, Malldraeth Pool, Pen-lon, Penrhyn, Trafwll.
ESTUARIES: Aberffraw, *Malldraeth, Holyhead, Menai Strait.
DUNES: Aberffraw, Newborough Warren.
CLIFF SEA-BIRD COLONIES: *Holyhead Island, esp. South Stack; Porth-wen; Puffin Island and coast west from Penmon Point.

Special Birds
Terneries: Aberffraw; Newborough Warren (but no longer on Llanddwyn Island); the Skerries, off Carmel Head, but no longer roseates.
Black-headed gullery: Llyn Llewenan.

Reserves and Sanctuaries
Newborough Warren—Ynys Llanddwyn (Nature Conservancy; PF).

Societies, etc.
Cambrian Ornithological Society.

Literature
No notes in annual report of C.O.S. or county bird list since *A Handbook to the Vertebrate Fauna of North Wales*, by H. E. Forrest (1919), but see Chapter 5 of C. E. Raven's *In Praise of Birds* (1950), and the pamphlet by H. H. Carter and others on their expedition to Puffin Island in 1959, and paper by P. E. S. Whalley in *North Western Naturalist*, Dec. 1954.

BRECONSHIRE

Habitats
WOODLAND: Cwm Clydach; Nant Irfon, Abergwesyn; Penmoelallt.
MOORLAND: Black Mountains; Brecon Beacons, inc. Craig Cerrig Gleisiad and Craig-y-Cilau; Mynydd Epynt.
LAKES, RESERVOIRS: Llangorse Lake, *Talybont Res.

Special Birds
Pied flycatcher: breeds in woodlands north of Brecon Beacons.
Heronries: Pen-y-Wern; Beulah.
Black-headed gulleries: two small ones near Brecon.

Reserves and Sanctuaries
Craig Cerrig Gleisiad (Nature Conservancy; P).
Craig-y-Cilau (Nature Conservancy; P for caves).
Cwm Clydach (Nature Conservancy; NP).
Nant Irfon (Nature Conservancy; PF).
Penmoelallt (Forestry Commission and Nature Conservancy; usually NP).
Talybont Reservoir.

Societies, etc.
Brecknock Society.

Literature
No annual bird report.
" The Birds of Brecknock," by G. C. S. Ingram and H. Morrey Salmon,
in *Brycheiniog* (journal of the Brecknock Society), 1957.
For historical interest: *Bird Life in Wild Wales,* by J. Walpole-Bond
(1904).

CAERNARVONSHIRE

Habitats
WOODLAND: Aber valley woodlands, Coed Dolgarrog, Coed Gorswen,
Coed Tremadoc, Cwm Glas (Crafnant); Snowdonia National Forest
Park (Beddgelert and Gwydyr Forests).
MOORLAND: Snowdonia, inc. Cwm Idwal.
LAKES: the numerous lakes of Snowdonia are not very rich in bird life,
but may have wild swans in winter.
ESTUARIES: *Conway, *Foryd Bay, Glaslyn, Menai Strait, *Ogwen.
COASTAL MARSHES: Conway.
DUNES: Abersoch.
CLIFF SEA-BIRD COLONIES: *Bardsey; Great and Little Orme's Heads;
St. Tudwals Islands.
MIGRATION WATCH POINT: *Bardsey.

Special Birds
Chough: breeds on Bardsey and scattered over the north of the county.
Pied flycatcher: breeds in the wooded valleys of Snowdonia and the
Conway river system.
Heronries: Penrhyn Park, Vaynol Park.
Grey geese (greylags, white-fronts): Conway estuary, Foryd Bay.
Manx shearwater: breeds Bardsey.
Black-headed gulleries: small ones near Capel Curig and Moel Siabod.
Black grouse: recently introduced in Gwydyr Forest.

Reserves and Sanctuaries
Coed Dolgarrog (Nature Conservancy; PF).
Coed Gorswen (Nature Conservancy; PF).

Coed Tremadoc (Nature Conservancy; PF).
Cwm Glas, Crafnant (Nature Conservancy; P for part).
Cwm Idwal (Nature Conservancy; NP for small parties).
Snowdon (Nature Conservancy).

Societies, etc.
Bardsey Bird and Field Observatory.
Cambrian Ornithological Society.

Literature
Annual reports of Bardsey Bird Observatory and Cambrian O.S.
No county bird list since *A Handbook to the Vertebrate Fauna of North Wales*, by H. E. Forrest (1919).
Snowdonia, a New Naturalist volume (1949); birds by Bruce Campbell; see also much less up-to-date chapter on birds by K. Orton in *The Mountains of Snowdonia*, by H. R. C. Carr and G. A. Lister (1948).

CARDIGANSHIRE

Habitats
WOODLAND: Devil's Bridge (Coed Rheidol).
MOORLAND: Plynlimon region, Mynydd Bach.
MARSHES: Borth Bog, *Tregaron Bog (Cors Tregaron).
ESTUARIES: Dovey, Teifi.

Special Birds
Pied flycatcher: widespread in woodlands, except in S.W.
Kite: the S.E. of the county adjoins the traditional kite country.
Heronries: Llanfair Woods, Llanllyr.
White-fronted goose: Dovey estuary; Tregaron Bog (Greenland race).
Purple sandpiper: regular at Aberystwyth in winter.
Black-headed gulleries: five, the largest near Strata Florida.
Black grouse: now fairly widespread in hills.

Reserves and Sanctuaries
Cardigan Island (West Wales Naturalists' Trust).
Coed Rheidol (Nature Conservancy; PF).
Cors Tregaron (Nature Conservancy; PF).

Societies, etc.
West Wales Naturalists' Trust, Cardiganshire Branch.

Literature
Bird notes appear quarterly in *Nature in Wales*, journal of the W.W.N.T.
No county bird list, but G. C. S. Ingram, H. M. Salmon and W. M. Condry are preparing one; see also "An annotated list of some birds seen in the Aberystwyth district, 1946-56," by W. S. Peach and P. M.

Miles, in *Nature in Wales* for 1961, also chapter on birds by W. M. Condry in *Forestry Commission Guide* on Cambrian Forests (1959).

CARMARTHENSHIRE

Habitats
WOODLAND: Allt Rhyd-y-Groes.
MOORLAND: Black Mountain.
LAKES, RESERVOIRS: Llanelly Res., Llyn Pencarreg; Talley Pools; Witchett Pool, Laugharne Burrows.
ESTUARIES: Taf, Towy, Gwendraeth, *Burry.
DUNES: Laugharne and Pendine Burrows, Towyn Burrows.

Special Birds
Pied flycatcher: breeds in woodlands in N. and N.E.
Kite: the northern part of the county includes the traditional kite country.
Heronries: Aberglasney, Craigddu.
Eider: winters in Burry estuary.
Black-tailed godwit: winters in Towy estuary.

Reserves and Sanctuaries
Allt Rhyd-y-Groes (Nature Conservancy; P).

Societies, etc.
West Wales Naturalists' Trust.

Literature
Bird notes appear quarterly in *Nature in Wales*, journal of the W.W.N.T.
The Birds of Carmarthenshire, by G. C. S. Ingram and H. Morrey Salmon (1954).

DENBIGHSHIRE

Habitats
MOORLAND: Berwyn Mountains, Denbigh Moors, Snowdonia, Upper Conway valley.
RESERVOIRS: Alwen Res.
ESTUARIES, SEASHORES: Rhos-on-Sea, Llandulas.

Special Birds
Pied flycatcher: breeds in woodlands, mainly in Conway and Dee river systems.
Heronry: Brynmorwylld Wood, Llanrhaiadr.
Grey geese (greylags, white-fronts): Clwyd valley.
Fulmar: nests inland near Abergele.

Black-headed gulleries: two small ones.

Societies, etc.
Cambrian Ornithological Society.

Literature
Annual reports of Cambrian O.S.
No county list since *A Handbook to the Vertebrate Fauna of North Wales* by H. E. Forrest (1919).

FLINTSHIRE

Habitats
HEATHLAND: Fenn's Moss.
LAKES: Llyn Helyg, Hanmer Mere.
ESTUARIES: *Dee.
DUNES: Prestatyn, Point of Air.

Special Birds
Black-headed gullery: Llyn Helyg.

Societies, etc.
Cambrian Ornithological Society.
Flintshire Ornithological Society.

Literature
Annual reports of Flintshire O.S. and Cambrian O.S.
No county bird list since *A Handbook to the Vertebrate Fauna of North Wales*, by H. E. Forrest (1919).

GLAMORGAN

Habitats
WOODLAND: Vale of Neath woodlands.
LAKES, RESERVOIRS: Kenfig Pool, *Llanishen Res., Oxwich Ponds, Roath Park.
ESTUARIES: *Burry, Ely, Ogmore.
COASTAL MARSHES: *Burry estuary (Llanmadoc to Loughor).
DUNES: Llangenith and Whiteford Burrows, Gower; Margam and Kenfig Burrows.
CLIFF SEA-BIRD COLONIES: Flatholm (gulls only), Worms Head.
MIGRATION WATCH POINTS: Lavernock Point, Nash Point.

Special Birds
Heronries: Hensol Castle, Penrice Castle.

Brent goose: a few in Burry estuary.
Eider: non-breeding at Whiteford, Gower, all the year.
Black-headed gullery: Oxwich marsh.

Reserves and Sanctuaries
Broad Pool, Gower (Glamorgan Naturalists' Trust).
Gower Coast (Nature Conservancy; NP).

Societies, etc.
Cardiff Naturalists' Society.
Glamorgan Naturalists' Trust.
Gower Ornithological Society.

Literature
Annual bird reports in *Transactions* of Cardiff N.S.
" Birds of Glamorgan," by G. C. S. Ingram and H. Morrey Salmon in
   Glamorgan County History, Vol. I (1936).
" The birds of Swansea borough," by A. F. James and J. A. Webb, in
   Proceedings of Swansea Scientific and Field Naturalists' Society, 1945.
Chapter on wild life by Colin Matheson in *Forestry Commission Guide* to
   Glamorgan Forests (1961).

MERIONETH

Habitats
WOODLAND: Coed Camlyn, Coed Cymerau, Coed Ganllyd, Coed-y-
   Rhygen.
MOORLAND: Berwyn Mountains, Cader Idris, the Rhinogs.
LAKES, RESERVOIRS: Bala Lake, Tal-y-llyn Res., Trawsfynydd Res.
ESTUARIES: Artro, *Dovey, *Dwyryd (Traeth Bach), Dysynni (Broad
   Water), Mawddach.
DUNES: Morfa Dyffryn and Mochras, Morfa Harlech.

Special Birds
Pied flycatcher: breeds generally in woodlands.
Nightjar: Merioneth is now the only county in Wales where the nightjar
   breeds at all commonly.
Cormorant: nesting colony in the Bird Rock, Craig yr Aderyrn, near
   Towyn, is the only inland breeding colony in England and Wales.
Black-headed gulleries: four, the largest on Morfa Harlech.

Reserves and Sanctuaries
Cader Idris (Nature Conservancy; P for parts).
Coed Camlyn (Nature Conservancy; P).
Coed Cymerau (Nature Conservancy; PF)
Coed Ganllyd (National Trust and Nature Conservancy; NP).

Coed-y-Rhygen (Nature Conservancy; P).
Morfa Dyffryn (Nature Conservancy; PF).
Morfa Harlech (Nature Conservancy; P above high-water mark).
The Rhinogs (Nature Conservancy; NP).

Societies, etc.
West Wales Naturalists' Trust, Merioneth Branch.

Literature
Bird notes appear quarterly in *Nature in Wales*, journal of the W.W.N.T.
No county list since *A Handbook to the Vertebrate Fauna of North Wales*,
by H. E. Forrest (1919), but see chapter on birds by W. M. Condry in
Forestry Commission Guide to Cambrian Forests (1959).

MONMOUTHSHIRE

Habitats
WOODLAND: Forest of Dean National Forest Park, inc. Blackcliff and
Wyndcliff.
MOORLAND: Black Mountains.
RESERVOIRS: Wentwood Res.
ESTUARIES: Severn.

Special Birds
Heronries: Piercefield Park; near Pwllhead Wood.
Great black-back: breeds on the Denny, small island in Severn estuary,
off Redwick.

Reserves and Sanctuaries
Blackcliff and Wyndcliff Forest Reserve (Forestry Commission and Nature
Conservancy: PF).

Societies, etc.
Cardiff Naturalists' Society.
Newport Naturalists' Society.

Literature
Annual bird reports in *Transactions* of Cardiff N.S.
" The Birds of Monmouthshire," by G. C. S. Ingram and H. Morrey
Salmon, in same journal, 1939.
Chapter on wild life by Sir William Taylor in *National Forest Park Guide*
for Dean Forest and Wye Valley (1956).

MONTGOMERYSHIRE

Habitats
MOORLAND: Berwyn Mountains, Plynlimon.

MARSHES: Severn valley near Welshpool.
LAKES: Lake Vrynwy.

Special Birds
Pied flycatcher: breeds generally in woodlands.
Heronries: Bryngwyn Hall, Leighton Park.
White-fronted goose: wintering flock in Severn valley.
Canada goose: breeds Powis and Leighton Parks.
Black-headed gulleries: four, the largest at ponds north of Llangadfan and Llyn-y-Tawr near Caersws.
Black grouse: Llwycharth area.

Societies, etc.
Montgomeryshire Field Society.

Literature
Annual report of Montgomeryshire F.S.
No county list since *A Handbook to the Vertebrate Fauna of North Wales*, by H. E. Forrest (1919), but see "An annotated list of birds observed in east Montgomeryshire," by P. G. R. Barbier, in *Nature in Wales*, 1958, also " Notes on domestic and wild animals in Montgomeryshire," by Colin Matheson (*Coll. Hist. and Arch., Mont.*, 1933), and chapter on birds by W. M. Condry in *Forestry Commission Guide* to Cambrian Forests (1959).

PEMBROKESHIRE

Habitats
WOODLAND: Benton Wood, Lawrenny Park.
MOORLAND: Prescelly Mountains; *Dowrog and Tretio Commons, St. David's.
LAKES, RESERVOIRS: Bosherston Pools, Dale Pools, Dowrog Pool, *Orielton Decoy, Rosebush Res., Trefeiddan Pool.
ESTUARIES AND SEASHORES: Fishguard Harbour, Nevern, Newgale Sands, Teifi, Angle Bay, Gann (Dale), Milford Haven.
DUNES: Freshwater West.
CLIFF SEA-BIRD COLONIES: Caldey and St. Margaret's Islands; Dinas Island; Linney Head to St. Govan's Head, esp. Stack Rocks (often inaccessible owing to Army operations); Ramsey and Bishops and Clerks; *Skokholm; *Skomer, the best island in England and Wales for breeding sea-birds).
MIGRATION WATCH POINTS: Ramsey, Skokholm, Skomer.

Special Birds
Chough: breeds on coast and islands, especially St. David's area, Caldey and Skomer.

Heronries: Picton Wood; the small heronry near Solva is the only one on cliffs in England and Wales.

Gannet: Grassholm has the only gannetry in England and Wales, apart from the few pairs on Bempton Cliffs, Yorks.

Manx shearwater, Storm petrel and Puffin: all breed on both Skokholm and Skomer.

Black-headed gulleries: two small ones near St. David's.

Reserves and Sanctuaries
Grassholm (Royal Society for the Protection of Birds; only accessible on a few calm summer days).
Ramsey (private).
St. Margaret's Island (W.W.N.T.).
Skokholm (W.W.N.T.).
Skomer Island (Nature Conservancy; NP).

Societies, etc.
Dale Fort Field Centre (Field Studies Council).
Orielton Field Centre (F.S.C.).
Skokholm Bird Observatory (F.S.C.).
West Wales Naturalists' Trust, Pembrokeshire Branch.

Literature
Bird notes appear quarterly in *Nature in Wales*, journal of the W.W.N.T.
The Birds of Pembrokeshire, by R. M. Lockley (1949).
Island of Skomer, by John Buxton and R. M. Lockley (1950).
See also R. M. Lockley's books on Skokholm, *The Way to an Island* (1941) and *Dream Island Days* (1943).

RADNORSHIRE

Habitats
MOORLAND: Llanbedr Hill, Radnor Forest.
LAKES, RESERVOIRS: Elan Valley Reservoirs, Hindwell Pool, Llan Bwch-llyn, Llanwefr Pool, St. Michael's Pool.

Special Birds
Pied flycatcher: breeds in many woodlands.
Heronries: Abbey Cwmhir, Cefndyrys.
Black-headed gulleries: six, mostly small, the largest at Llanwefr Pool.

Societies, etc.
Herefordshire Ornithological Club.   Herefordshire and Radnorshire Nature Trust.

Literature
Radnorshire notes included in annual report of Herefordshire O.C.

The Birds of Radnorshire, by G. C. S. Ingram and H. Morrey Salmon (1955).

For historical interest: *Bird Life in Wild Wales*, by J. Walpole-Bond (1904).

Scotland

Societies, etc.

Royal Society for the Protection of Birds, Scottish Office.

Scottish Centre for Ornithology and Bird Protection.

Scottish Ornithologists' Club.

Scottish Society for the Protection of Wild Birds.

Literature

Bird notes appear quarterly in *Scottish Birds*, journal of the S.O.C.

The Scottish Naturalist.

The Birds of Scotland, 2 vols., by E. V. Baxter and L. J. Rintoul (1953).

For most parts of Scotland the most recent county list of birds is still provided by J. A. Harvie-Brown's great series, *A Vertebrate Fauna of Scotland* (1887-1906).

Bird Haunts in Northern Britain, by G. K. Yeates (1948).

Wild Venture: a bird watcher in Scotland, by Kenneth Richmond (1958).

The Influence of Man on Animal Life in Scotland by James Ritchie (1920).

Books by Seton Gordon and Dugald Macintyre.

For historical interest: *Sketches of the Wild Sports and Natural History of the Highlands*, by Charles St. John (1846).

See also *The Return of the Osprey*, by P. E. Brown and G. Waterston (1962).

Highlands: Special Birds

The following birds are more or less widespread breeding species in the counties north of the Highland line (viz. Aberdeen, Angus, Argyll, Banff, Caithness, Inverness, Moray, Nairn, Perth, Ross and Cromarty, Sutherland), and virtually nowhere else in Britain; Scottish crossbill, golden eagle, greenshank, dotterel, capercaillie, ptarmigan. The greenshank and dotterel are summer visitors; the rest may be found at all seasons. Several species of duck (gadwall, wigeon, pintail, common scoter, eider, goosander, red-breasted merganser) either breed only in the Highlands or much more commonly there than anywhere else, likewise the red-throated and black-throated divers.

ABERDEENSHIRE (Ab.) AND KINCARDINESHIRE (Kc.)

Habitats

WOODLAND: Ab.: Ancient pinewoods of Ballochbuie, Glentanar and Mar; Crathes.

MOORLAND AND MOUNTAIN: Ab.: *Cairngorms, Mar Forest.
LOCHS: Ab.: *Cotehill, Meikle and Sand Lochs, Collieston; Skene; Strathbeg.
ESTUARIES: Ab.: *Ythan.
DUNES: Ab.: Sands of Forvie (black-headed gullery). Kc.: St. Cyrus.
CLIFF SEA-BIRD COLONIES: Ab.: Bullers of Buchan, Whinnyfold; Fowlsheugh.

Special Birds
See Highlands: Special Birds (p. 220).
Carrion/hooded crow: interbreeding zone crosses the two counties.
Rook: Ab.: the largest rookery in Britain in the wartime census was at Hatton Castle, Turriff (5,000 nests).
Heronries: Ab.: Parkhill, Dyce.
　　　　　　　Kc.: Kingcausie, Maryculter.
Eider: large breeding colony, Ythan estuary.

Reserves and Sanctuaries
Caenlochan (Nature Conservancy; P in late summer and autumn).
Cairngorms (Nature Conservancy; P in parts of Mar in autumn).
Crathes Woods (National Trust for Scotland).
Sands of Forvie (Nature Conservancy; P in breeding season and late summer and autumn).
St. Cyrus (Nature Conservancy; NP).

Societies, etc.
Scottish Ornithologists' Club, Aberdeen Branch.

Literature
The Vertebrate Fauna of Dee, by G. Sim (1903).

ANGUS

Habitats
MOORLAND AND MOUNTAIN: Clova Mountains, inc. Caenlochan Glen (golden eagle, ptarmigan).
LOCHS: Balgavies, Craigton Res., Crombie Mill, Dun's Dish, *Forfar, Kinnordy (large black-headed gullery), Lintrathen, *Rescobie.
ESTUARIES: Montrose Basin; Tay, esp. Invergowrie Bay.
DUNES: Buddon Ness.

Special Birds
See Highlands: Special Birds (p. 220).
Heronry: North Dun Wood, Montrose.

Reserves and Sanctuaries
Caenlochan (Nature Conservancy; P in late summer and autumn).

Societies, etc.
Scottish Ornithologists' Club, Dundee Branch.

Literature
A Fauna of the Tay Basin and Strathmore, by J. A. Harvie-Brown (1906).

ARGYLL

Habitats
WOODLAND: Argyll National Forest Park (west of L. Long and around
L. Goil and L. Eck). Ancient pinewoods of Ardgour, Black Mount and
Glen Orchy; Arriundle Oakwood, Sunart.
MOORLAND AND MOUNTAIN: Ben Lui; Rannoch Moor.

Special Birds
See Highlands: Special Birds (p. 220).
Carrion/hooded crow: interbreeding zone.
Hen-harrier: breeds on Forestry Commission ground.
Heronries: Ardentallan Point, L. Feochan; Largie Castle, Kintyre;
Rudha na Daimh, L. Sunart; Rudha nan Eoin, L. Long; Tayvallich,
L. Sween; Torrisdale Castle, Kintyre.

Reserves and Sanctuaries
Arriundle Oakwood Forest Nature Reserve (Nature Conservancy and
Dept. of Agriculture for Scotland; NP).
Ben Lui (Nature Conservancy; NP).
Benmore Gardens, near Dunoon (Ministry of Works).

Literature
A Vertebrate Fauna of Argyll and the Inner Hebrides, by J. A. Harvie-
Brown and T. E. Buckley (1892).
The Birds of the Firth of Clyde, by the Rev. J. M. McWilliam (1936),
covers South Argyll.
Chapter on birds by E. Hindle in *Argyll National Forest Park Guide* (1954).

AYRSHIRE (Ay.) AND BUTE (Bt.)

Habitats
WOODLANDS: Ay.: Culzean Castle policies; Glen Trool National Forest
Park, S.W. of L. Doon.
Bt.: Brodick Wood, Arran.
MOORLAND AND MOUNTAIN: Bt.: Arran, inc. Glen Diomhan.
LOCHS AND RESERVOIRS: Ay.: Camphill Res.; Craigendunton Res.;
Culzean Pond, Loch o' the Lowes,
New Cumnock; Macaterish (large
black-headed gullery), Martnaharn,
Shankston.

LOCHS AND RESERVOIRS [*contd.*]: Bt.: Dhu, Fad and Quien.
CLIFF SEA-BIRD COLONIES: Ay.: *Ailsa Craig.

Special Birds

Carrion/hooded crow: interbreeding zone.
Heronries: Ay.: Bargany, Girvan; Melburn Castle, Largs.
         Bt.: Brodick Wood, Arran.
Gannetry: Ay.: Ailsa Craig.
Collared dove: Ay.: small breeding colony, Girvan.
Terneries: Ay.: Horse Island, Lady Island.

Reserves and Sanctuaries

Culzean Castle (National Trust for Scotland).
Glen Diomhan, Arran (Nature Conservancy; NP).
Horse Island, off Ardrossan (Royal Society for the Protection of Birds; P).
Lady Isle, off Troon (Scottish Society for the Protection of Wild Birds; P).

Literature

The Birds of the Island of Bute, by the Rev. J. M. McWilliam (1927).
The Birds of Ayrshire, by E. R. Paton and O. G. Pike (1929).
The Birds of the Firth of Clyde, by the Rev. J. M. McWilliam (1936), covers
    both Ayr and Bute.
Chapter on birds by Gavin Maxwell in *Glen Trool National Forest Park
    Guide* (1954).

BANFFSHIRE (Bf.) MORAYSHIRE (My.) AND NAIRNSHIRE (Nn.)

Habitats

WOODLAND: Bf.: Ancient pinewood of Glen Avon.
         My.: Darnaway Forest.
MOORLAND AND MOUNTAIN: Bf.: Cairngorms.
LOCHS: My.: Buckie, Darnaway Forest pools (large black-headed
         gulleries), Lochindorb, *Spynie.
    Nn.: *Cran, Flemington, *Loy.
ESTUARIES: My.: *Findhorn Bay, Lossie, Spey.
DUNES: My.: Culbin Sands.
CLIFF SEA-BIRD COLONIES: Bf.: Troup Head.

Special Birds

See Highlands: Special Birds (p. 220).
Carrion/hooded crow: interbreeding zone in Banff and Moray.
Crested tit: My.: in pinewoods in Spey and Findhorn valleys.
        Nn.: in pinewoods in Strathnairn.
Heronries: Bf.: Ballindalloch.
        My.: Oakenhead, Pitgaveney; Speymouth, Fochabers.

Collared dove: My.: well-established breeding colony at Covesea, more recent one near Forres.

Literature

A Vertebrate Fauna of the Moray Basin, by J. A. Harvie-Brown and T. E. Buckley (1896).

For historical interest, see list of Banffshire birds in *Life of a Scotch Naturalist: Thomas Edward*, by Samuel Smiles (1876).

BERWICKSHIRE

Habitats

WOODLAND: The Hirsel, Coldstream; Paradise Wood, Whiteadder Water.

MOORLAND: Lammermuir.

MARSHES: Bemersyde Moss (large black-headed gullery), *Hule Moss.

LOCHS, RESERVOIRS: Duns Castle, the Hirsel, Primrosehill Pond, Watch Res.

CLIFF SEA-BIRD COLONIES: *St. Abb's Head.

Special Birds

Pied flycatcher: a few pairs breed.
Little owl: a few pairs breed.

Societies, etc.

Berwickshire Naturalists' Club.

Literature

Bird notes annually in *History* of Berwickshire N.C.
A Fauna of the Tweed Area, by A. H. Evans (1911).
The Birds of Berwickshire, 2 vols., by G. Muirhead (1889).
Birds of Northumberland and the Eastern Borders, by G. Bolam (1912).

BUTE (*see* Ayrshire and Bute)

CAITHNESS

Habitats

LOCHS: Heilen, Hempriggs, St. John's, Sarclet, Scarmclate, Watten, Loch of Wester.

MARSHES: Lochar Moss (black-headed gullery).

ESTUARIES: Dunnet Bay, Sinclair's Bay, Wick Bay.

DUNES: Ackergill and Keiss Links.

CLIFF SEA-BIRD COLONIES: Duncansby Head, Dunnet Head, Holbourn Head, Noss Head.

Special Birds
See Highlands: Special Birds (p. 220).
Arctic skua: breeds on moorland flows inland.

Literature
A Vertebrate Fauna of Sutherland, Caithness and West Cromarty, by
   J. A. Harvie-Brown and T. E. Buckley (1887).

CLACKMANNANSHIRE (*see* Stirlingshire and Clackmannanshire)

DUMFRIESSHIRE

Habitats
WOODLAND: The Border National Forest Park; Tynron Juniper Wood.
LOCHS: *Lochmaben Lochs (Castle, Hightae Mill, Kirk, Mill).
ESTUARIES: Esk (Solway), Nith.
COASTAL MARSHES: *Caerlaverock Merse.

Special Birds
Pied flycatcher: breeds in wooded dales.
Heronries: West Skelston, Dunscore; Whitcairn, St. Mungo.
Grey and Barnacle geese: Solway, esp. Caerlaverock.
Canada goose: breeds Kinmount and near Lochmaben.

Reserves and Sanctuaries
Caerlaverock (Nature Conservancy; P for part).
Castle Loch, Lochmaben.
Tynron Juniper Wood (Nature Conservancy; NP).

Societies, etc.
Scottish Ornithologists' Club, Dumfries Branch.

Literature
The Birds of Dumfriesshire, by H. S. Gladstone (1912).

DUNBARTONSHIRE (Db.) AND RENFREWSHIRE (Rf.)

Habitats
WOODLAND: Db.: Torrinch (island in L. Lomond).
LOCHS, RESERVOIRS: Db.: *Lomond, esp. mouth of R. Endrick at
                          Balmaha.
               Rf.: Balgray, Linn, Lyoncross, Ryat and Waulk-
                     mill group of dams; *Castle Semple and
                     Barr (very large black-headed gullery);
                     Dunwan Dam; High Dam, Eaglesham;
                     Lochgoin; Stanley Dam, Paisley.

ESTUARIES: Db.: Clyde. Rf.: Clyde.
MOORLAND: Db.: Kilpatrick Hills (several small black-headed gulleries).

Special Birds
Carrion/hooded crow: interbreeding zone.
Gull roost: Clyde estuary near Dumbarton.

Reserves and Sanctuaries: Loch Lomond (Nature Conservancy).

Literature
The Birds of the Firth of Clyde, by the Rev. J. M. McWilliam (1936), covers
  both counties.
"The breeding birds of Renfrewshire," by J. A. Gibson, in *Glasgow and
  West of Scotland Bird Bulletin*, 1955.

EAST LOTHIAN (*see* Lothians)

FIFE (Ff.) AND KINROSS-SHIRE (Kn.)

Habitats
LOCHS, RESERVOIRS: Ff.: *Cameron Res., Dunfermline Town Loch,
                        *Fitty, Gelly, Kilconquhar, Lindores,
                        *Morton Lochs, Peppermill Dam, Tulli-
                        allan Castle.
                  Kn.: *Leven, the most important loch in Scotland
                        for breeding wildfowl with a large black-
                        headed gullery.
ESTUARIES: Ff.: Eden; Forth, esp. *Longannet Point; Tay.
COASTAL MARSHES: Ff.: Cultness Marsh, Rosyth.
DUNES: Ff.: *Tentsmuir (black-headed gullery).
CLIFF SEA-BIRD COLONIES: Ff.: Inchkeith, Isle of May.
MIGRATION WATCH POINT: Ff.: Fife Ness, Isle of May.

Special Birds
Heronries: Ff.: Kincardine-on-Forth.
Terneries: Ff.: Shelly Point and Tentsmuir Point.

Reserves and Sanctuaries
Isle of May (Nature Conservancy; NP).
Morton Lochs (Nature Conservancy; PF).
Tentsmuir Point (Nature Conservancy; NP).

Societies, etc.
Isle of May Bird Observatory and Field Station.
Scottish Ornithologists' Club, St. Andrews Branch.

Literature
Annual reports of Isle of May Bird Observatory in *Scottish Birds.*

A Vertebrate Fauna of Forth, by L. J. Rintoul and E. V. Baxter (1935), covers all Kinross and the southern part of Fife.

A Fauna of the Tay Basin and Strathmore, by J. A. Harvie-Brown (1906), covers the northern part of Fife.

The Isle of May, by W. J. Eggeling (1960).

"A check-list of the birds of Tentsmuir, Fife," by Jack Grierson, *Scottish Birds*, Summer 1962.

GALLOWAY (Kirkcudbrightshire (Kk.) and Wigtownshire (Wg.)

Habitats

WOODLAND: Kk.: Glen Trool National Forest Park.

MOSSES: Kk.: Kirkconnel Flow, Silver Flowe.

LOCHS: Kk.: *Carlingwark, *Ken, Kindar, Moan (large black-headed gullery).

      Wg.: Lochinch Castle lochs (Black, White, Soulseat), Mochrum and Castle Lochs.

ESTUARIES: Kk.: Auchencairn Bay, Cree, Fleet Bay, Kirkcudbright Bay, Nith, Rough Firth.

      Wg.: Cree, Luce Sands, L. Ryan, *Wigtown Bay.

DUNES: Kk.: Preston Merse.

CLIFF SEA-BIRD COLONIES: Wg.: Mull of Galloway; Scar Rocks, Luce Bay.

MIGRATION WATCH POINTS: Kk.: Little Ross Lighthouse.

      Wg.: Burrow Head, Mull of Galloway.

Special Birds

Carrion/hooded crow: interbreeding zone.

Pied flycatcher: Kk.: a few pairs breed.

Heronries: Kk.: Dalskairth, Troqueer; Machermore, Newton Stewart.

Grey geese: numerous in winter; especially near Castle Douglas, Kk., where several species, including bean and lesser white-front, may be seen at once; Greenland white-fronts on L. Ken; feral greylags visit the Mochrum lochs.

Cormorant: Wg.: the breeding colony on the Castle Loch, Mochrum, is the largest inland one in Great Britain and is both the largest and the only inland one in Scotland.

Black guillemot: Wg.: nests in Portpatrick Harbour wall and near the lighthouse on the Mull of Galloway.

Reserves and Sanctuaries

Kirkconnell Flow (Nature Conservancy; P).

Silver Flowe (Nature Conservancy; NP).

Societies

Dumfries and Galloway Natural History Society.

Literature

" List of the birds of the Stewartry of Kirkcudbright," by A. B. Duncan, in the *Transactions* of the Dumfries and Galloway N.H.S., 1947.

Chapter on birds by Gavin Maxwell in *Glen Trool National Forest Park Guide* (1954).

INNER HEBRIDES

Habitats

CLIFF SEA-BIRD COLONIES: Canna, Islay, Sanday, Treshnish Isles (esp. Lunga and Dutchman's Cap).

Special Birds

Chough: breeds on Islay and Jura.

Heronries: Calgary, Mull; Coilessan, Mull; Inver, Jura; Kylerhea, Skye; Orbost, Skye; South Rona and Raasay; L. Spelve, Mull; Ulva.

Barnacle goose: regular in winter on Islay (esp. Gruinart Loch and Flats), Coll, Treshnish Isles and small isles off Skye.

Manx shearwater: breeds on Canna, Eigg, Lunga of the Treshnish Isles, high up on Rhum and on some islets off Skye.

Red-necked phalarope: breeds on Tiree.

Reserves and Sanctuaries

Rhum (Nature Conservancy; P away from L. Scresort area).

Literature

A Vertebrate Fauna of Argyll and the Inner Hebrides, by J. A. Harvie-Brown and T. E. Buckley (1892).

A Fauna of the North-West Highlands and Skye, by J. A. Harvie-Brown and H. A. Macpherson (1904).

The Birds of Iona and Mull, by H. D. Graham (1890).

Colonsay and Oronsay, by J. de V. Loder (1935).

There are more recent papers in the *Scottish Naturalist* on Canna (1939): Gigha (1950), Islay (1955), Raasay (1938), and Rhum (1957), and in *British Birds* on Tiree and Coll (1958).

I Went a' Shepherding, by Richard Perry (1944), is partly about Skye.

INVERNESS-SHIRE

Habitats

WOODLAND: Glenmore National Forest Park; Ancient pinewoods of *Abernethy, Dulnan, Glen Feshie, Glenmore and *Rothiemurchus on Speyside; Ancient pinewoods of Barisdale, Glengarry, Glen Loy, Glen Loyne, Glen Moriston, and L. Arkaig with Glen Mallie, west of the Great Glen; Ancient pinewoods of Strath Glass (Glens Affric, Cannich and Strathfarrar), and Guisachan with Cougie; Ancient pinewood of Glen Nevis.

MOORLAND AND MOUNTAIN: *Cairngorms, Gaick Forest, Monadhliath Mountains.

LOCHS: Alvie, Flemington, Garten, Insh, *Morlich, Pityoulish.

ESTUARIES: *Beauly Firth; Moray Firth, esp. from Langman Bay to Screeton.

Special Birds
See Highlands: Special Birds (p. 220).
Carrion/hooded crow: interbreeding zone in east of county.
Crested tit: woodlands in Strathspey and Strathnairn.
Osprey: a single well-guarded pair breeds near L. Garten.
Slavonian grebe: has bred for many years in the county.

Reserves and Sanctuaries
Cairngorms (Nature Conservancy; NP).
Loch Garten Bird Sanctuary (ospreys protected by RSPB).

Societies, etc.
Inverness Bird Watching Group

Literature
A Vertebrate Fauna of the Moray Basin, by J. A. Harvie-Brown and T. E. Buckley (1896), covers the east of the county.
A Fauna of the North-West Highlands and Skye, by J. A. Harvie-Brown and H. A. Macpherson (1904), covers the west of the county.
In the High Grampians, by Richard Perry (1948), deals with the Gaick-Glen Feshie-Cairngorms area.
The Cairngorm Hills of Scotland, by Seton Gordon.
Chapter on wild life by Seton Gordon in *Glen More National Forest Park Guide* (1960).
The Return of the Osprey, by P. E. Brown and G. Waterston (1962).

KINCARDINESHIRE (*see* Aberdeenshire and Kincardineshire)

KINROSS-SHIRE (*see* Fife and Kinross-shire)

KIRKCUDBRIGHTSHIRE (*see* Galloway)

LANARKSHIRE

Habitats
MARSHES: Possil Marsh.
LOCHS, RESERVOIRS: Carmunnock and Rogerton Res., East Kilbride; Crane Loch, Carnwath (black-headed gullery); Drumpellier Loch, Coatbridge; Rubbish dump pool and Bothwell Bridge area, Hamilton; Lenzie.

Special Birds
Heronry: Bothwell Bridge.

Reserves and Sanctuaries
Hamilton Low Parks (Hamilton Burgh).
Possil Marsh (Scottish Society for the Protection of Wild Birds; P).

Societies, etc.
The Andersonian Naturalists of Glasgow.
Scottish Ornithologists' Club, Glasgow Branch.

Literature
Glasgow and West of Scotland Bird Bulletin (now defunct).

LOTHIANS (East, Mid and West Lothian)

Habitats
MOORLAND: Lammermuir, Moorfoot and Pentland Hills.
LOCHS, RESERVOIRS: Mid.: Cobbinshaw Res. (black-headed gullery),
Cross Wood Res., *Duddingston, Dunsappie, *Edgelaw, *Gladhouse
Res., Glencorse Res., Harperigg Res., Lochend, *Rosebery Pool, St.
Margaret's Loch, Threipmuir Res.
W.: *Linlithgow Park.
ESTUARIES: Forth esp. (E.) *Aberlady Bay, *Tyninghame.
DUNES: E.: Gullane and Luffness Links.
CLIFF SEA-BIRD COLONIES: E.: *Bass Rock, Craigleith.

Special Birds
Hawfinch: E.: woods in E. Lothian are the only regular breeding haunt
in Scotland.
Heronry: E.: Tyninghame.
Night heron: Mid.: birds from a free-flying colony in the Edinburgh Zoo
wander about the district.
Gannetry: E.: Bass Rock.
Cormorant: large colony recently established on the Lamb.
Terneries: E.: Eyebroughty, Fidra.
Mid.: Inchmickery.
Gull roosts: Firth of Forth, Gladhouse Res.

Reserves and Sanctuaries
Aberlady Bay (East Lothian County Council; NP).
Duddingston Loch Bird Sanctuary, Edinburgh (Ministry of Works).
Eyebroughty, Fidra and the Lamb (E.) and Inchmickery (Mid.), islands
in the Firth of Forth (Royal Society for the Protection of Birds).

Societies, etc.
East Lothian Antiquarian and Field Naturalists' Society.

Midlothian Ornithologists' Club.
Scottish Centre for Ornithology and Bird Protection, Edinburgh (S.O.C.).
Scottish Ornithologists' Club, Edinburgh Branch.

Literature
A Vertebrate Fauna of Forth, by L. J. Rintoul and E. V. Baxter (1935), covers the bulk of the three counties, though most of the Lammermuirs and Moorfoots in Mid and East Lothian fall within the area of *A Fauna of the Tweed Area*, by A. H. Evans (1911).
The Birds of Midlothian, by J. K. Nash (1935).
The Birds of Aberlady Bay Nature Reserve, by F. D. Hamilton and K. S. Macgregor (1960).
" Check List of the Birds of Duddingston Loch," by D. R. Anderson and George Waterston (1961), a special issue of *Scottish Birds*.

MORAYSHIRE ⎱ *see* Banffshire, Morayshire and Nairnshire.
NAIRNSHIRE ⎰

ORKNEY

Habitats
MOORLAND: Eday, Hoy, Mainland, Rousay, Westray.
CLIFF SEA-BIRD COLONIES: Calf of Eday; Hoy; Marwick Head, Mainland; Row Head; Westray.

Special Birds
Long-eared owl: breeds on Mainland and one other island.
Short-eared owl: breeds on Mainland and one or two other islands.
Hen-harrier: as for short-eared owl.
Heronry: a small cliff heronry at Lyra Geo, Stromness.
Common scoter: breeds on one island.
Gannetry: Sule Stack.
Storm petrel: numerous breeding colonies.
Manx shearwater: breeds on Hoy.
Red-necked phalarope: breeds on one of the North Isles.
Sandwich tern: breeds on North Ronaldsay.
Great skua: breeds on Hoy and Papa Westray, now spreading to other islands.
Arctic skua: breeds on Papa Westray, and on the west side of Hoy, from Melsetter to the Summer Burn.

Societies, etc.
Orkney Field Club.

Literature
Bulletins of Orkney F.C.

A Vertebrate Fauna of the Orkney Islands, by J. A. Harvie-Brown and
T. E. Buckley (1891).

The Breeding birds of Orkney, paper by David Lack in *Ibis,* 1942-43.

See also G. T. Arthur on Orkney birds generally in *Bird Notes* (1950),
and Eric Duffey on Eynhallow in the *Scottish Naturalist* (1955).

OUTER HEBRIDES

Habitats

MARSHES: Balranald, near Hougary (N. Uist).

LOCHS: L. Bee, S. Uist (many non-breeding mute swans); L. Druidibeg,
S. Uist; L. Hallam, N. Uist.

ESTUARIES: Melbost Sands, Stornoway; Traighs Seilebost and Lusken-
tyre, S. Harris.

CLIFF SEA-BIRD COLONIES: *Flannan Islands; Haskeir, off N. Uist;
Mingulay; North Rona; *St. Kilda; Shiant Islands.

MIGRATION WATCH POINTS: Butt of Lewis, Flannan Is., St. Kilda.

Special Birds

St. Kilda wren: a greyer and more strongly barred race, confined to the
islands of the St. Kilda group.

Greylag goose: breeds on L. Druidibeg, S. Uist.

Barnacle goose: winters on machair and many smaller islands of Harris
and N. and S. Uist.

Gannetries: St. Kilda, Sula Sgeir.

Storm petrel: breeds on many islands.

Leach's petrel: breeds on the Flannans, N. Rona, St. Kilda and Sula Sgeir.

Manx shearwater: breeds on St. Kilda.

Red-necked phalarope: breeds from time to time between N. and S. Uist.

Arctic skua: breeds in Lewis and North Uist.

Iceland gull: regular in Stornoway Harbour in winter.

Reserves and Sanctuaries

Loch Druidibeg, South Uist (Nature Conservancy; P during breeding
season).

North Rona and Sula Sgeir (Nature Conservancy; NP).

St. Kilda (Nature Conservancy; NP).

Literature

A Vertebrate Fauna of the Outer Hebrides, by J. A. Harvie-Brown and
T. E. Buckley (1888).

St. Kilda Summer, by Kenneth Williamson and J. Morton Boyd (1960).

See also papers in *Bird Study* on the Flannans (1961), North Rona and
Sula Sgeir (1959), in the *Scottish Naturalist* on Haskeir (1955), and in
Scottish Birds on the Flannans (1959) and North Rona (1960).

PEEBLESSHIRE (Pb.), ROXBURGHSHIRE (Rx.) AND SELKIRKSHIRE (Sk.)

Habitats

WOODLAND: Rx.: The Border National Forest Park (Newcastleton and Wauchope Forests).

MOORLAND: Cheviots, Ettrick Forest.

LOCHS: Pb.: Portmore.

Rx.: Hoselaw; Junction Water, Kelso; Yetholm.

Sk.: Akermoor Loch (black-headed gullery); St. Mary's Loch.

Special Birds

Gull roost: Portmore Loch.

Societies

Kelso and District Ornithological Society.

Literature

A Fauna of the Tweed Area, by A. H. Evans (1911), covers most of the area except the south-western part of Roxburghshire.

Chapter on wild life by E. Blezard in *The Border National Forest Park Guide* (1958).

PERTHSHIRE

Habitats

WOODLAND: Queen Elizabeth Forest Park (the Trossachs); Ancient pinewoods, viz. Black Wood of Rannoch; Old Wood of Meggernie, Glen Lyon; Tyndrum; Glen Falloch.

MOORLAND AND MOUNTAIN: Ben Lawers, Ben Lui, Flanders Moss (enormous black-headed gullery), Forest of Atholl, Rannoch Moor.

LOCHS, RESERVOIRS: *Carsebreck, *Clunie, Dochart, Glenfarg Res., *Marlee, Lake of Menteith, Murthly Mill Dam (black-headed gullery), *Stormont.

ESTUARIES: Tay.

Special Birds

See Highlands: Special Birds (p. 220).

Carrion/hooded crow: interbreeding zone.

Whooper swan: regular in winter on L. Dochart.

Grey geese: Carsebreck, Strathallan.

Gull roost: Lake of Menteith.

Reserves and Sanctuaries

Ben Lawers (National Trust for Scotland).

Ben Lui (Nature Conservancy; NP).

Caenlochan (Nature Conservancy; P in late summer and autumn).
Rannoch Moor (Nature Conservancy; NP).

Societies, etc.
Garth Field Centre, Glen Lyon (Scottish Field Studies Association).
Perthshire Society of Natural Science.

Literature
A Fauna of the Tay Basin and Strathmore, by J. A. Harvie-Brown (1906),
  for the north and centre; *A Vertebrate Fauna of Forth*, by L. J. Rintoul
  and E. V. Baxter (1935), for the south.
Chapter on birds by C. E. Palmar in *Queen Elizabeth Forest Park Guide*
  (1954).

RENFREWSHIRE (*see* Dunbartonshire and Renfrewshire)

ROSS AND CROMARTY

Habitats
WOODLAND: Rassal Ashwood, near Kishorn; Northern group of ancient
  pinewoods, viz. Amat, Glen Einig, Rhidorroch, Strath Vaich; Western
  group of ancient pinewoods, viz. Achnashellach, Coulin, Loch Maree
  (esp. Coille na Glas Leitire), Shieldaig.
MOORLAND AND MOUNTAIN: Beinn Eighe (golden eagle), Ben Wyvis,
  Inverpolly (golden eagle).
LOCHS: Carron; Eye, near Tain; Maree.
ESTUARIES: Beauly and Moray Firths; Cromarty Firth, esp. Alness Bay
  and Bay of Nigg; *Dornoch Firth, esp. Skibo, Whiteness.

Special Birds
See Highlands; Special Birds (p. 220).
Greylag goose: a few pairs of wild birds breed in the Summer Isles and
  around Beinn Eighe, and of feral birds near L. Carron.

Reserves and Sanctuaries
Beinn Eighe (Nature Conservancy; NP).
Inverpolly (Nature Conservancy; P for part in late summer and autumn).
Rassal Ashwood (Nature Conservancy; NP).

Literature
A Fauna of the North-West Highlands and Skye, by J. A. Harvie-Brown
  and H. A. Macpherson (1904).
For historical interest, *A Hundred Years in the Highlands*, by Osgood
  Mackenzie (1921).

ROXBURGHSHIRE ⎫ *see* Peeblesshire, Roxburghshire and
SELKIRKSHIRE ⎭ Selkirkshire

SHETLAND

Habitats

WOODLAND: Kergord Plantations, Weisdale, Mainland.
LOCHS: Spiggie, S. Mainland (black-headed gullery).
ESTUARIES: Pool of Virkie, S. Mainland (best for waders).
CLIFF SEA-BIRD COLONIES: Fair Isle, Foula, Hermaness, *Noup of Noss, Sumburgh Head.
MIGRATION WATCH POINT: *Fair Isle.

Special Birds

Whooper swan: winters regularly, esp. at L. Spiggie, S. Mainland, and Uyeasound, Unst.
Common scoter: breeds in one district of Mainland.
Gannetries: Hermaness, Noss.
Storm petrel: many breeding colonies.
Manx shearwater: breeds on Fetlar and Foula.
Whimbrel: breeds on many of the larger islands.
Red-necked phalarope: breeds on Fetlar and Mainland.
Glaucous gull: regular winter visitor.
Iceland gull: frequent winter visitor.
Great and arctic skuas: common breeding birds.

Reserves and Sanctuaries

Haaf Gruney (Nature Conservancy; NP).
Hermaness (Nature Conservancy; NP).
Noss (Nature Conservancy; NP).

Societies, etc.

Fair Isle Bird Observatory (Fair Isle B.O. Trust).

Literature

Birds and Mammals of Shetland, by L. S. V. and U. M. Venables (1955).
Shetland Sanctuary, by Richard Perry (1948), is about Noss.

STIRLINGSHIRE (St.) AND CLACKMANNANSHIRE (Ck.)

Habitats

WOODLAND: St.: Queen Elizabeth Forest Park (Ben Lomond and L. Ard); Clairinsh and other islands in L. Lomond.
LOCHS, RESERVOIRS: Ck.: Gartmorn Dam.
St.: Carron Res., Craigmeddie Res., Lomond.
ESTUARIES: Forth, esp. Cambus and *Tullibody Inch, Kennett Pans (mouth of R. Devon) and Skinflats.

Special Birds

Carrion/hooded crow: St.: interbreeding zone.

Heronry: St.: Buchanan Castle.
Loch Lomond.

Reserves and Sanctuaries
Loch Lomond (Nature Conservancy).

Literature
A Vertebrate Fauna of Forth, by L. J. Rintoul and E. V. Baxter (1935).
Chapter on birds by C. E. Palmar in *Queen Elizabeth Forest Park Guide*
    (1954).

SUTHERLAND

Habitats
WOODLAND: Birchwoods in Strath Beag, L. Eriboll.
MOORLAND: Inchnadamph, Assynt; Invernaver, near Bettyhill (green-
    shank); Strathy Bog.
LOCHS: Brora, Laxford, Loyal.
ESTUARIES: Dornoch Firth, Kyle of Durness, Kyle of Tongue.
CLIFF SEA-BIRD COLONIES: Bulgach Is., *Clo Mor, L. Eriboll, *Handa.

Special Birds
See Highlands: Special Birds (p. 220).
Heronry: Eilean Ard, L. Laxford.
Greylag goose: a few pairs may still breed in the centre of the county,
    and a few remain from a feral flock near L. Brora.
Barnacle goose: winter flocks on islands of west coast, and on Island
    Roan in the Kyle of Tongue.

Reserves and Sanctuaries
Handa (Royal Society for the Protection of Birds).
Inchnadamph (Nature Conservancy; P in late summer and autumn).
Invernaver (Nature Conservancy; NP).
Strathy Bog (Nature Conservancy; NP)

Literature
A Vertebrate Fauna of Sutherland, Caithness and West Cromarty, by J. A.
    Harvie-Brown and T. E. Buckley (1887).
" The Clo Mor bird cliffs," by I. D. Pennie, in the *Scottish Naturalist*, 1951.
For historical interest, *A Sportsman's and Naturalist's Tour in Sutherland-
    shire*, by Charles St. John (1849).

WIGTOWNSHIRE (*see* Galloway)

Ireland

Societies
Irish Ornithologists' Club.
Irish Society for the Protection of Birds.

Literature
Irish Bird Report annually from I.O.C.
Bird notes also appear in the *Irish Naturalists' Journal*.
The Birds of Ireland, by P. G. Kennedy, R. F. Ruttledge and C. F. Scroope.
" The distribution and status of wild geese in Ireland," by R. F. Ruttledge
   and R. Hall-Watt, *Bird Study*, March 1958.

ULSTER

Counties Antrim (Am.), Armagh (Ah.), Cavan (Cv.), Donegal (Dg.),
   Down (Dw.), Fermanagh (Fm.), Londonderry (Ly.), Monaghan (Mg.),
   Tyrone (Ty.).

Habitats
MARSHES: Am.: Duncrue Street marsh, Belfast.
   Dw.: Downpatrick Marshes.
LOUGHS: *Neagh.
   Ah.: Beg, Castledillon.
   Fm.: *Erne, McNean.
   Ty.: Ballysaggart, Brantry, Eskragh.
ESTUARIES: Am.: Belfast Lough, Larne Lough.
   Dg.: Trawbreaga Bay, Carndonagh.
   Dw.: Carlingford Lough, *Strangford Lough.
   Ly.: Bann, L. Foyle.
CLIFF SEA-BIRD COLONIES: Am.: Carrick-a-Rede, the Gobbins,
   Rathlin Island, Sheep Island.
   Dg.: Horn Head (reputed the largest sea-bird colony in Ireland),
   Tormore.
MIGRATION WATCH POINTS: Copeland Is., Rathlin Is., Tory Is.

Special Birds
Garden warbler: breeds around Lower L. Erne, Fm.: also near Castle
   Hamilton, Gartanoul and Killykeen, Cv.
Golden eagle: a pair in Antrim is the only breeding pair in Ireland.
Heronries: Ah.: Castledillon, Drumbanagher.
   Cv.: Farnham.
   Dw.: Mourne Park, Quinton Castle.
   Ty.: Caledon, Parkanaur, Tullydoey.

Greylag goose: Dw.: Downpatrick Marshes, Strangford Lough.
  Ly.: L. Foyle.
White-fronted goose: Dw.: Downpatrick Marshes.
  Fm.: L. McNean.
Brent goose: Am.: Larne Lough.
  Dg.: Rossnowlagh; Trawbreaga Bay.
  Dw.: Strangford Lough.
Barnacle goose: Dg.: Aranmore and Inishduff areas; Sheep Island and
  nearby coast.
Eider: breeds coasts of Antrim and Donegal and one group of islands off
  Down.
Common scoter: breeds on one lough, Fermanagh.
Storm petrel: breeds on many Donegal islands, inc. Inishduff and
  Roaninish.
Slavonian grebe: regular in winter, in L. Swilly, Dg.
Red-throated diver: a pair or two have bred for many years in one district
  of Donegal.
Terneries: Am.: Maidens.
  Dg.: Illauncrone.
  Dw.: Copeland Is.; islands in Strangford Lough: Green Is., Carling-
  ford Lough.
Roseate tern: six colonies in Down.
Glaucous gull: regular in N.E. Ireland in winter.
Black guillemot: breeds in walls of Bangor Harbour and Ballywalter Pier,
  Down.

Societies, etc.
Armagh Field Naturalists' Society.
Belfast Natural History and Philosophical Society.
Copeland Bird Observatory, Down.
Limavady Naturalists' Field Club, Co. Londonderry.
Londonderry Naturalists' Field Club.
Rathlin Bird Observatory, Antrim.
Tory Island Bird Observatory, Donegal.
Ulster Society for the Protection of Birds.

Literature
Handbook of the Birds of Northern Ireland, by C. Douglas Deane (1954).
Birds of the Grey Wind, by Edward A. Armstrong (1940).
Paper on the birds of Rathlin Is., by L. N. Port, in *Irish Nat. J.*, 1959.

LEINSTER

Counties Carlow (Cw.), Dublin (Du.), Kildare (Kd.), Kilkenny (Ky.),
  Leix (Lx.), Longford (Lf.), Louth (Lh.), Meath (Mh.), Offaly (Of.),
  Westmeath (Wh.), Wexford (Wx.), Wicklow (Ww.).

Habitats

MARSHES: Du.: Booterstown.

Wx.: *North and South Slobs, Wexford.

LOUGHS, RESERVOIRS: Lf./Wh.: Ree.

Ww.: Broad Lough, Poulaphouca Res.

Wx.: Lady's Island Lake.

ESTUARIES: Du.: Baldoyle Bay, Dublin Bay, Rogerstown, *Swords (Malahide).

Lh.: Carlingford Lough.

Lh./Mh.: Boyne.

Wx.: Bannow Bay; the Cull, Duncormick; Tacumshin Lake; *Wexford Harbour.

DUNES: Du.: Malahide, *North Bull.

CLIFF SEA-BIRD COLONIES: Du.: Howth Head, Ireland's Eye, Lambay, Rockabill.

Wx.: Great Saltee.

MIGRATION WATCH POINTS: Wx.: *Gt. Saltee, Tuskar Rock (lighthouse).

Special Birds

Pied wagtail: roost in O'Connell Street, Dublin City.

Garden warbler: Lf./Wh.: L. Ree.

Of.: Shannon valley.

Blackcap: breeds regularly only in Leinster, especially in Ww., at Powerscourt, the Glen of the Downs and near Ashford.

Heronries: Du.: Newbridge, Donabate.

Lh.: Bellurgan Park.

Lx.: Portarlington, Woodbrook.

Of.: Charleville.

Ww.: Russborough.

Wx.: Ballycross House, Bridgetown; Barony of Forth, Tomhaggard.

Greylag goose: Ky.: Ballyragget.

Ww.: Broad Lough and the Murrough; Poulaphouca Res.

White-fronted goose: Lf.: Mouth of R. Inny, L. Ree.

Of.: Shannon valley.

Wh.: Shannon valley and between Loughs Sheelin and Ennell.

Wx.: North and South Slobs; Kilmore Quay.

Brent goose: Du.: Baldoyle Bay, Dublin Bay, Rogerstown and Malahide estuaries.

Wx.: Bannow Bay, Tacumshin Lake, Wexford Harbour.

Barnacle goose: Wx.: North Slob.

Gannetry: Great Saltee.

Terneries: Du.: Malahide, Rockabill.

Wx.: Lady's Island Lake, Tacumshin Lake.

Roseate tern: one colony each in Du. and Wx.

Black guillemot: breeds Bray and Wicklow Heads, Ww.

Reserves and Sanctuaries
North Bull Island, Co. Dublin.

Societies, etc.
Saltee Bird Observatory, Co. Wexford.

Literature
An Irish Sanctuary: birds of the North Bull, by P. G. Kennedy (1953).
Papers in *Irish Naturalists' Journal* on birds of Inner Dublin (1953) and
   the West Pier, Dun Laoghaire, Co. Dublin (1955).
In Praise of Birds, by C. E. Raven (1950), has a chapter on Ireland's Eye.

MUNSTER

Counties Clare (Ce.), Cork (Co.), Kerry (Kr.), Limerick (Lm.), Tipperary
   (Tp.), Waterford (Wf.).

Habitats
LOUGHS: Kr.: Akeagh Lough (wintering gadwall).
ESTUARIES: Tp.: Marfield Lake.
   Ce./Kr./Lm.: Shannon.
   Co.: Cork Harbour.
   Kr.: Tralee Bay.
   Wf.: *Back Strand, Tramore; Dungarvan Harbour.
CLIFF SEA-BIRD COLONIES: Ce.: Cliffs of Moher; Kilkee to Loop Head.
   Co.: Bull and Cow Rocks.
   Kr.: Blaskets, Skelligs, Tearaght.
MIGRATION WATCH POINTS: Cape Clear Island, Co. Cork.

Special Birds
Chough: common on coast.
Heronries: in a suburb of Cork City; Tullabeedy, Tp.
Greylag goose: Co.: Ballymacoda.
   Ce./Lm.: Mellon, Shannon estuary.
   Wf.: near Carrick-on-Suir.
White-fronted goose: Ce.: Ruan and Corofin areas.
   Kr.: Feale estuary.
   Tp.: Suir valley, Templemore to Camus.
Brent goose: Kr.: Tralee Bay and Castlemaine Harbour.
   Wf.: Back Strand, Tramore; Dungarvan Bay.
Barnacle goose: Ce.: Mutton Is., Mattle Is. and coast near Baltard.
Gannetries: Co.: Bull Rock.
   Kr.: Little Skellig.
Cormorant: tree-nesting colony on L. Bunny, near Gort, Clare.
Black-tailed godwit: wintering flocks, Cork Harbour and Shannon estuary.
Terneries: Bantry and Roaringwater Bays, Co. Cork.
Gull roost: Marfield Lake, Tp.

Kittiwake: Wf.: colony on ledges beneath the houses of Dunmore East.

Societies, etc.
Cape Clear Bird Observatory, Cape Clear Island, Co. Cork.

Literature
The Birds of County Cork, by R. J. Ussher (1894).
Papers on birds of the Blasket Islands in *Bird Study*, by S. M. D. Alexander (1954) and D. J. Munns (1956), and on birds of Great Skellig, by J. M. Harrop in *Irish Nat. J.*, 1959.

CONNAUGHT

Counties: Galway (Gl.), Leitrim (Lt.), Mayo (Mo.), Roscommon (Rs.), Sligo (Sg.).

Habitats
MARSHES: Rahasane, Gl., and many turloughs.
LOUGHS: Mo.: Carrowmore.
   Rs.: Ree.
   Sg.: Bunduff Lough, Mullaghmore.
CLIFF SEA-BIRD COLONIES: Gl.: Inishark and Inishmore.
   Mo.: Blackrock, *Bills of Achill, Clare Is., Stags of Broadhaven; north coast, esp. Downpatrick Head.
   Sg.: Aughris Head.

Special Birds
Chough: common on coast.
Garden warbler: L. Ree and Shannon valley, Rs.
Heronries: Gl.: Eyrecourt; Portumna Castle; L. Hibbert, Connemara.
   Mo.: Claggan Wood near Ballycroy.
   Sg.: Tanrego near Ballysodare.
White-fronted goose: Gl.: Carrowbrowne, Rahasane, Shannon valley, R. Suck north of Ballyforan, turloughs near Tuam.
   Mo.: islands in Clew Bay, Derrygraff Bog, R. Moy near Foxford, the Mullet.
   Rs.: Shannon valley.
   Sg.: Bunduff Lough.
Brent goose: Mo.: Achill Sound, Blacksod Bay, Broad Haven, Clew Bay.
   Sg.: Drumcliff and Sligo Bays.
Barnacle goose: Gl.: Davillaun Is., Inishbroom off Renvyle.
   Mo.: Inishgalloon off Achill Is., Caher Is., Clare Is., islands in Clew Bay, Kid Is. off Benwee Head, Inishkea off the Mullet (the largest known haunt).
   Sg.: Lissadell.
Cormorant: tree-nesting colony, L. Cutra, Gl.
Storm petrel: breeds on many islands, Mayo.

Red-necked phalarope: one small breeding colony, Mayo.

Ternery: Mutton Is., Gl.

Common gull: a widespread breeding bird in Mayo; L. Carrowmore has the largest breeding colony in Ireland.

Literature

A List of the Birds of the Counties of Galway and Mayo, by R. F. Ruttledge (1950).

Papers in *Irish Naturalists' Journal* on birds of Achill Is., Mo. (1942, 1951), Clare Is., Mo. (1945), and Inishmurray, Sg. (1956); and in *Bird Study* on Inishbofin and Inishark, Gl. (1957).

The Lesser Isles

ISLE OF MAN

Habitats

MARSHES: Ballaugh Curraghs and Tierby, Greeba Gap (long-eared owl, grasshopper warbler).

LAKES: Eairy and Kionslieu Dams, Mooragh Park.

CLIFF SEA-BIRD COLONIES: Chasms, Black Head, Spanish Head and Aldrick in south; Maughold Head in north.

MIGRATION WATCH POINTS: Calf of Man, Langness.

Special Birds

Hooded crow: breeds.

Chough: numerous in south.

Purple sandpiper: winters, Douglas and Port St. Mary.

Terneries: Point of Ayre to Rue Point.

Black guillemot: breeds near Peel.

Reserves and Sanctuaries

Calf of Man (Manx Museum and National Trust).

Spanish Head (do.).

Societies, etc.

Isle of Man Natural History and Antiquarian Society.

Manx Bird Club.

Literature

Annual bird reports in *The Peregrine* (Field Section of I.O.M.N.H.A.S.), also articles in *Journal of the Manx Museum*.

Bird-life in the Isle of Man, by H. W. Madoc (1934).

CHANNEL ISLES

The Channel Isles suffer from the political anomaly of being British islands off the coast of France by being neglected by both British and French bird watchers and ornithologists. Though they fall strictly outwith the purview of this book, a few brief notes follow on the more outstanding birds of the islands, which have many sea-birds breeding around their rocky cliffs and offshore islets.

Cirl bunting: breeds, Jersey.
Treecreeper: the species which breeds on Jersey and Guernsey is the Continental short-toed treecreeper (*Certhia brachydactyla*), which can only be separated in the field from our own *C. familiaris* by its voice.
Dartford warbler: breeds on Jersey.
Brent goose: the common wild goose of the Channel Isles.
Gannetries: on Ortac and Les Etacs off Alderney.
Storm petrel: breeds on Burhou and various small offshore islets.
Kentish plover: breeds locally.

Societies, etc.
Jersey Bird Observatory, St. Ouens (O.S. of S.J.).
Société Guernesiaise.
Société Jersiaise.

Literature
Annual Report published by Société Jersiaise.
Birds of the Channel Isles, by Roderick Dobson (1952).
A Record of the Birds of Guernsey, by H. le M. Brock (1950).

Some Addresses

Only societies and organisations with permanent addresses are listed below, for most local societies alter their addresses from time to time as their secretaries change. A postcard to the Council for Nature will bring you the current address of any of the local natural history societies, bird clubs or observatories or other bodies listed in Part Three, and of any journals not published by a society. Particulars of the bird observatories can also be had from the B.T.O., and of the county naturalists' trusts from the S.P.N.R.

Berkshire, Buckinghamshire and Oxfordshire Naturalists' Trust, 1 St. Giles, Oxford.

British Birds, 4 Little Essex Street, London, WC2R 3LF.

British Ornithologists' Union, c/o Zoological Society of London, Regent's Park, London, NW1 4RY.

British Ornithologists' Club, as for B.O.U.

British Trust for Ornithology, Beech Grove, Station Road, Tring, Herts.

Cambridgeshire and Isle of Ely Naturalists' Trust, 1 Brookside, Cambridge.

Council for Nature, Zoological Gardens, Regent's Park, London, N.W.1.

Edward Grey Institute for Field Ornithology, Zoology Department, South Parks Road, Oxford.

Fauna Preservation Society, c/o Zoological Society of London, Regent's Park, London, NW1 4RY.

Field Studies Council, 9 Devereux Court, Strand, London, W.C.2.

International Council for Bird Preservation (British Section), c/o British Museum (Natural History), Cromwell Road, London, S.W.7.

Irish Wildbird Conservancy, c/o Royal Irish Academy, 19 Dawson Street, Dublin.

London Natural History Society, c/o British Museum (Natural History), Cromwell Road, London, S.W.7.

National Trust, 42 Queen Anne's Gate, London, S.W.1.

National Trust for Scotland, 5 Charlotte Square, Edinburgh, 2.

Nature Conservancy, 19 Belgrave Square, London, S.W.1.

Natural History Society of Northumberland, Durham and Newcastle upon Tyne, The Hancock Museum, Barras Bridge, Newcastle upon Tyne, 2.

Norfolk Naturalists' Trust, 72 The Close, Norwich, NOR 16P.

Ornithological Field Station, Madingley, Cambridge.

Oxford Ornithological Society, c/o Edward Grey Institute.

Pheasant Trust, Great Witchingham, Norwich, Norfolk.

Royal Society for the Protection of Birds, The Lodge, Sandy, Beds. Scottish Office, 17 Regent Terrace, Edinburgh, EH7 5BN; Northern Ireland Office, 58 High Street, Newtownards, Co. Down.

Scottish Field Studies Association, 104 West George Street, Glasgow, C.2.

Scottish Ornithologists' Club, Scottish Centre for Ornithology, 21 Regent Terrace, Edinburgh, 7.

Scottish Wildlife Trust, 8 Dublin Street, Edinburgh, 1.

Society for the Promotion of Nature Reserves, The Manor House, Alford, Lincolnshire.

Sussex Naturalists' Trust, Woods Mill, Henfield.

Wildfowl Trust, The New Grounds, Slimbridge, Glos.

World Wildlife Fund, 7-8 Plumtree Court, London, E.C.4.

Yorkshire Naturalists' Trust, Clifford Chambers, 4 Clifford Street, York, YO1 1RD.

INDEX

INDEX

Italic figures refer to Plate numbers